DARK AGE ECONOMICS

Dark Age Economics

*The origins of towns and trade
A.D. 600–1000*

RICHARD HODGES

ST. MARTIN'S PRESS
NEW YORK

Contents

Preface   ix

Introduction   1

1. The Shadow of Pirenne   6

2. Trading Systems from Theodoric to Charlemagne   29

3. The Emporia   47

4. A Gazetteer of Emporia: in Ottar's Footsteps   66

5. Dark Age Argonauts and their Craft   87

6. The Objects of Trade   104

7. Subsistence Strategies   130

8. Systemic Change: the Ninth Century   151

9. Market Places and Principles   162

10. The Evolution of States   185

Notes   199

References   211

Index   224

For DEBBIE

Illustrations

1. Western Europe, *c.* 800   3
2. Relationship of the Frankish denier to the Arabic dinar   8
3. Three regional models   17
4. Distance-decay models   19
5. Long-distance trade in north-west Europe, *c.* 490–830   31
6. Histogram of coins from Dorestad   41
7. Monastery of Kiltiernan, Co. Galway (aerial view)   48
8. Section through a sunken hut at Löddeköpinge   51
9. Relief-band amphora   58
10. Tating ware jug   59
11. Model of a farmhouse found at Dorestad   61
12. Reconstruction of a Haithabu house   62
13. Comparison of emporia   64
14. Location of Ipswich   71
15. Extent of Middle Saxon Ipswich   72
16. Middle Rhenish imported pottery from Dorestad   76
17. Wine-barrel re-used as a well-lining from Dorestad   76
18. Location of Haithabu   79
19. Buildings and roads in Haithabu   80
20. Remains of a metalsmith's house at Helgö   83
21. Birka (aerial view)   84
22. Trade competition areas of the Frisians and Franks   93
23. The Utrecht ship   96
24. Changing technology in boat-building   99
25. The Bantry pillar stone   102
26. Diffusion of coinage   106
27. Organisation of coin production   107
28. Primary and secondary sceattas   113
29. Three early medieval kilns   119
30. The buddha from Helgö   121
31. Niedermendig lava quernstones   123
32. Distribution of Eifel mountain quernstones   125

33. Farm-unit in Roman-period Holland 133
34. Excavations at Chalton, Hampshire (aerial view) 134
35. Economy of the Irish rath 137
36. Faunal assemblage from Dorestad 143
37. Distribution of clasp buttons from Helgö 145
38. Ipswich ware vessels 146
39. Class 3 vessels from Hamwih 148
40. Estimated population of Anglo-Saxon England 164
41. Ranking of Late Saxon mints 167
42. Middle Saxon potting industry 169
43. Emporia and 'burgs' in northern Flanders 174
44. Schematic plan of Souburg 175
45. Coopers' workshops at Coppergate, York 184

Preface

The publication of this book marks a personal anniversary for me, since it comes ten years after I was privileged to go up to university to study archaeology and history. My teachers – among them Peter Addyman, Colin Platt, David Hinton, David Peacock, Barry Cunliffe and Colin Renfrew – offered me more than I could have expected, and the book is a culmination for me of that period of study. Colin Renfrew generously invited me to write it after the completion of my thesis which, through the kindness of the Southampton Archaeological Research Committee, had introduced me to the archaeology of the western European countries.

Flattered in this way, I set out to discover the difficulty of achieving what I was trained for. Needless to say, the results could hardly match the ambitions, but the book is an attempt to rework one of the most fascinating chapters of human history, helped by the new resources available after a decade or more of archaeology now – to quote Professor Sir Moses Finley – in flood-tide.

It benefits inevitably from the engineers of this flood-tide who are too numerous to mention here but are listed (at least) in my monograph on Carolingian and Anglo-Saxon pottery (Hodges 1980). I should like to express my thanks in particular to Agneta Lundström, who made my stay in Stockholm in 1977 a memorable one, and to Charlotte Blindheim, Professor W. van Es, Morgens Bencard, Hans J. Madsen, John Hurst and Alan Carter for sparing the time to discuss various critical matters. I also owe a debt to Professor George Dalton, with whom I have corresponded, and to Professors Grierson and Sawyer for valuable conversations which have kept me from straying too far from the point.

The mechanics of production have been made pleasantly easy by Dorothy Cruse, Jane Hall and Andrea Penny, who kindly typed my ms., and by Carol George who drew the figures before and after the arrival of her first child.

My colleagues at Sheffield have continually advanced my archaeological awareness and to them I am deeply grateful. I am especially obliged to Klavs Randsborg, who has provided me with the inspiration to continue with this project, and to Keith Wade, who has been an unending source of lively debate on many issues. I am very fortunate to have had criticism of the text from both Keith Wade and Professor van Es, who have saved me from many errors, though any that remain are my responsibility.

I should like to express my gratitude to Colin Haycraft and Deborah Blake of Duckworth for their valuable advice and patience as well as for some entertaining hours in the Old Piano Factory.

To my wife, Debbie, I remain in incalculable debt. She compiled the index, and has been the guiding spirit who has enabled me to transform my rough thoughts into a continuous text; to her, with the greatest pleasure, I dedicate the result.

March 1981   R.H.

Introduction

I hold it perniciously false to teach that all cultural forms are equally probable and that by mere force of will an inspired individual can at any moment alter the trajectory of an entire cultural system in a direction convenient to any philosophy. Convergent and parallel trajectories far outnumber divergent trajectories in cultural evolution. Most people are conformists. History repeats itself in countless acts of individual obedience to cultural rule and pattern, and individual wills seldom prevail in matters requiring alterations of deeply conditioned beliefs and practices.

Marvin Harris[1]

This book aims to meet an old challenge in new spirit. It begins by disputing the value of archaeology as a source for reconstructing the economy of Dark Age western Europe in the period 600–1000 A.D. Some claim that archaeology provides a new dimension to our understanding of the period, although this perspective is in fact derived from the synthetic framework, and the treatment of that framework, which are wholly the consequence of a new archaeological paradigm known informally as the 'New Archaeology'. The essence of this paradigm is embodied in Harris's thesis conveniently summarised by him in the quotation above. In this book, however, slightly at variance with Harris's beliefs, we shall ultimately attempt to examine the will of great men and their relationship to the cultural rule. There are two threads: the descriptive theme based on an economic model expounded in Chapter 1, and the analytical theme, seeking generalities to amplify and test the model.

The area of study is roughly the northern half of France, much of present-day western Germany and the Low Countries, which were to form the Merovingian kingdoms and the later Carolingian Empire. Britain and Ireland and the western Scandinavian countries, Denmark, Norway, and Sweden, are also included. However, I must stress that this is a stupendous challenge, if all the inter-disciplinary sources are to be examined, and must therefore make it clear that this book represents no more than a gleaning of sources familiar to the author, primarily in secondary form. I have not written a definitive or comprehensive work, but an essay in interpretation.

One serious problem is that the detail is complex and ranges across disciplines. The archaeologist, in particular, needs some simple historical structure from which to start. For the most part the details can be confined to footnotes, but a brief introduction will help to set the scene for our future discussions.[2]

In brief, we are aware of the continued inter-relationship between the provinces, which for four hundred years were part of the Roman empire, and the Mediterranean world. The migrations into and across Germany and France from the fourth to the sixth century, however, were destined to create a new socio-economic structure. As Tacitus showed in the first century A.D., the Germans maintained an entirely different form of society, one effectively determined by chiefdoms. The new settlers did attempt to integrate, not least because the rich web of Roman civilisation was the goal which they had almost certainly intended to achieve. Clovis, in the late fifth century, established a new civilisation, but its substance was slight. Successive Merovingian kings, who commanded regions of the continent, were internally divided; and under only a few leaders, notably Dagobert in the seventh century, did they even begin to emulate the socio-economic institutions they had sought to conquer. The transference from a Roman-dominated land-scape to a landscape in which Germans were integrated with native populations was effected with the aid of continued Mediterranean contact. The Roman empire survived in powerful form in the east, in Constantinople. Yet this Byzantine power, which under the great emperor Justinian was briefly to regain most of North Africa and Italy in the sixth century, was short-lived. The rise of the Arabic civilisation during the course of the seventh century presented a massive buffer to the ambitions of the later Byzantine dynasty, which itself was frequently subject to internal fission.

Byzantium, the inheritor of Rome's imperial ambitions, cannot be said to have disappeared; but it was a primary state on the far corner of the European world, and the subject, it appears, of pilgrimages rather than of fluid contact. It did, however, preserve the idea of imperialism, a notion which was almost certainly a strong influence, for example, on Charlemagne.

Carolingia emerged as a new polity, comprising those parts of the Merovingian empire which had been only loosely fastened together (Fig. 1). The structure had been slowly created by a series of powerful warrior-kings: Charles Martel, Pepin III and Charlemagne, who in the eighth century resisted the invasions of France by the Arabs and then began to extend their frontiers both to the north and to the south. When Charlemagne was crowned emperor in 800, he was emulating the achievements of the Romans, and he believed that he had restored western Europe to its proper course. But even before he died, in 814,

Figure 1 Map of western Europe *c.* A.D. 800, showing the extent of Carolingia.

there were political rifts which showed that his achievement was temporary. Louis, his son, maintained his power until about 830, but after that no single king was to control the empire. The remainder of the ninth century witnessed the fragmentation of the regions that had been bonded together, and only in the tenth century did the powerful states emerge which encompassed much of present-day West Germany and France. In the central decades of the tenth century the German state under the command of a new emperor, Otto the Great, reasserted a European command akin to Charlemagne's, but Otto's *Renovatio Imperii* was based on a vastly reorganised society and lasted longer.

Anglo-Saxon England developed from a patchwork of tribal units founded by migrants who crossed the North Sea between the fourth and early sixth century. They had vanquished a similar patchwork of sub-Roman units, whose most illustrious leader had been the legendary king Arthur. By 600 certain of the Anglo-Saxon kingdoms had begun to grow and were establishing the trade-links to Merovingia, as we shall see in Chapter 2. These were perhaps encouraged by St. Augustine's Christian

mission to England, which had arrived in 597 and by the early eighth
century had brought the entire community into the Christian orbit.
Bede has fortunately provided us with a detailed account of the seventh
and early eighth centuries which, with the later Anglo-Saxon Chronicle,
and the first laws and charters, documents the rise first of Kent and then
of East Anglia, Northumbria, Mercia and Wessex. By the eighth
century the nub of power in central England was in the Mercian
kingdom, where one powerful king, Aethelbald, in 757 left a great
ascendant territory to an equally aggressive chieftain, king Offa. Offa
ambitiously sought the grandeur which he knew that Charlemagne had
achieved, and aspired to connect his family through marriage to the
Carolingians. But Offa's achievement scarcely survived his death in 796,
though paradoxically he provided the institutional platform on which a
series of West Saxon kings, including Egbert, Aethelwulf and Alfred,
were to construct a nation. The West Saxons were the dynasty which
ultimately stemmed the incessant tide of Viking attacks that so
disrupted ninth-century England; and after 878, under king Alfred,
they were to reconquer the lands – the Danelaw – ceded to the Viking
migrants. Alfred's greatness was in part that he bequeathed a strong
territory to his son Edward the Elder, who with his own son Athelstan
forged the English nation. In 954, the Viking king Eric Bloodaxe
deserted York, thus leaving a nation in the control of the West Saxon
dynasty.

England during this period generated great wealth, and this was to be
the target of a second series of Viking raids which coloured the reign of
Ethelred the Unready in the late tenth century and the first two decades
of the eleventh.

By contrast, for much of this time the history of the North Sea littoral
and Scandinavia is obscure. The Frisian archipelago was quite different
topographically from what it is now. In the Roman period it had been
densely populated, as it was to be again during the early medieval
period as the mounded settlements of the period, the terps, indicate.[3]
The Merovingians annexed it in the seventh century, though they
consolidated their conquest only after 719, as we shall see in Chapter 5.
Much of its northern extent was then brought within the Carolingian
fold by Charlemagne, and this political dominance was reinforced by
English missionaries who had been active throughout the eighth century
to the north of the Rhine.[4]

Denmark, however, remained defiantly outside this world. Like
Frisia, it had experienced major migrations from the fourth to the sixth
century, and its depopulated communities had gradually adapted to a
restructured framework. When we first view Denmark it is through the
eyes of a ninth-century Frankish chronicler. The nation is loosely joined
together under the leadership of a king Godfred in part to counter the
imperial ambitions of Charlemagne. Godfred's rule was short-lived, and
his successors pursued a vicissitudinous policy of negotiation and raid

with Carolingia over the following half-century. This enabled the missions to penetrate the Baltic countries, and Ansgar's biographer, Rimbert, treats us to a brief account of his ninth-century travels from Denmark to central Sweden. In their footsteps passed Ottar, a Norwegian fur-trader, and Wulfstan, an Englishman, both of whom visited the court of king Alfred and told him of their adventures, which he recorded.

The history of the early tenth century is vague. A Swedish dynasty may have exerted some control over southern Jutland, as for a second time the Viking communities engaged in long-distance contact with Byzantium and Asia Minor. The end of this contact was to be the stimulus in part for Harald Bluetooth and Olaf Tryggvason in Denmark and Norway to instigate the formation of states. Harald's son Svein Forkbeard, with Olaf, also pirated silver from England to establish communities which, by the eleventh century, brought peace to a people traditionally infamous for their ravages of other countries.

Ireland was a country with a rich historical and archaeological heritage. The early acceptance of Christianity, though in a form that was consistent with an Iron Age culture, has thrown light on this isolated Celtic community. Its lists of kings are adequately documented, and its own fate at the hands of the Vikings during the ninth and tenth centuries is equally well established. Few great kings were to emerge before the later tenth century, and no polity was to persist before the Anglo-Normans invaded the island in 1169 and discovered traditions that dated back to the first millennium B.C. Yet Ireland underwent a cultural flowering in the seventh century, when its churchmen were the pride of Europe and monasteries were established on the continent and on rocky Scottish islands. Its art was civilised, but the civilisation soon proved abortive, as we shall see in Chapter 10.

This is the very barest outline of the European community through four hundred years – years which have largely determined the landscape we now see. The Dark Ages are traditionally the bleak period after a civilisation. But we can claim that there was no air of destitution in early medieval Europe, with the possible exception of the Merovingian period.[5] The collapse of the Roman civilisation may well be a classic systems collapse – a consequence of ecological, demographic and social stress[6] – yet the invading communities were destined to rebuild the ruins that were left. The immediate interest is that they undertook the reconstruction on their own terms, thus giving the medieval world a different cultural character from the Roman one. But they also conformed to processes which are embodied in trajectories found throughout history, throughout the world. Their achievement was a socio-economic structure that has persisted to this day.

Chapter 1

THE SHADOW OF PIRENNE

Great scholars, like other great men, cast long shadows, Pirenne held the world in thrall for half a century.

A. R. Bridbury[1]

The greatest and most awful scene in the history of man, according to Gibbon, was the decline and fall of the Roman Empire. Gibbon was fascinated by the slow and inexorable decay of the rich fabric that was for him the essence of civilisation. The barbarians, moreover, were unleashed to create a new Europe. One crucial element in this civilised world had been the markets which the imperial legions established in their new colonies. For whatever view we take of the pre-Roman urban institutions that existed in north-west Europe, we cannot deny that the ubiquitous market principle was a force planned by the Romans in their bid to articulate the Iron Age economies on a new scale. The markets were both sophisticated and highly vulnerable, and when the legions departed to Italy and the civilisation crumbled they met a predictable fate. The economy of post-Roman north-west Europe quite simply had to adapt to new socio-economic forces.

The decline of the Roman institutional fabric and the emergence of medieval society is a phenomenon that has long engaged the imagination of historians. Perhaps the first major treatise on the subject was by the Austrian professor Dopsch in the early years of this century. But it was the great Belgian historian Henri Pirenne who galvanised the interests of most medieval historians on the question. Pirenne's biographer asserts that as early as 1910 he was raising the issues that have made him famous, namely the nature of the imperial decline and the north's reconciliation to the cessation of contact with the Mediterranean world. Pirenne's thesis was as radical as the one propounded by his near-contemporary Bronislaw Malinowski in the field of economic anthropology (see below). In both areas of research the significance of economics in social contexts was being formally recognised for the first time.[2]

The essence of Pirenne's ideas was published in his Princeton lectures, *Medieval Cities*, and subsequently in a longer volume issued post-humously, fittingly entitled *Mohammed and Charlemagne*. Pirenne's great studies were concerned with the Merovingian and Carolingian empires and the economic trends that determined the half-millennium after the decay of Roman civilisation. Pirenne argued that the Roman economic institutions were largely maintained until the seventh century. It was the impact of Islam on the Mediterranean in the course of that century that destroyed north-west Europe's connections with the Mediterranean world. The Merovingian courts were cut off from their gold supplies in Africa and were compelled to accommodate a new economy – one which was primarily self-sufficient or natural, and in which the small part played by commerce was articulated by a modest silver currency. Pirenne believed that this world operated most successfully under the emperor Charlemagne in the last decades of the eighth and the first fourteen years of the ninth century. Yet Charlemagne's policies were cast in a mould determined by Mohammed. It was the ultimate wave of migrations from the north and east that proved to be the catalysts of change and that were instrumental in the emergence of a new urban society, the impact of which can only be compared perhaps with the industrial revolution nine hundred years later.

This thesis is one of the most celebrated in the annals of historiography, and its importance can be judged by the economic literature it has stimulated.[3] Fifty years later, it has been pointed out, historians are still arguing in Pirenne's terms.[4] One obvious reason is that the documentation central to his model is limited and, to some extent, ambivalent. Thus the same detail has been used to support, modify and attack the argument.

During the 1930s the debate took a new direction. Pirenne was interested in coins, as a result of his friendship with Prou, the doyen of Merovingian numismatics.[5] But it was Sture Bolin who first mobilised the massive amount of numismatic data to examine the questions posed by Pirenne and his critics. Bolin's thesis itself was not widely disseminated, but the papers he derived from it have been influential. Moreover besides advocating coins as a major source material, he drew attention to Scandinavia, beyond the boundaries of Carolingia, and to its extensive trade contacts established by the ninth century.[6]

The history of coinage is abundantly rich in source material – coins and coin-hoards by the thousand ... It may therefore appear that an examination of the hoards from Carolingian times will show fairly directly how close the connexions were between the Frankish and Arab worlds and whether trade within the Frankish Empire increased or declined ... by studying the composition of the coin-hoards found in western Europe and the radius of circulation of the coins, it would seem possible to determine the main lines of the development of internal trade.[7]

Bolin was concerned to demonstrate that 'one may reiterate Pirenne's paradox without Mohammed, no Charlemagne, but in disagreement, not in accord with his views'.[8] He showed how the design, the weight and the value of the Frankish *denarius* was dominated by the Islamic silver coinage of the period, and concluded that Carolingia followed, rather than shunned, Mohammed. Bolin's famous graph sought to prove his fine metrological point (Fig. 2), and he soon gained adherents from the

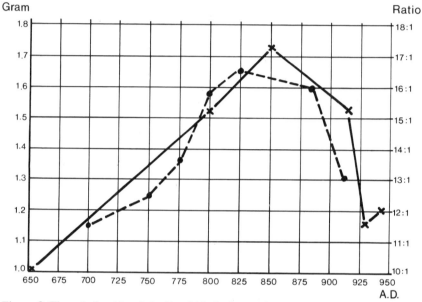

Figure 2 The relationship of the Frankish denier to the Arabic dinar. The changing weight of the denier is shown as a dotted line and that of the dinar as a solid line (after Bolin)

ranks of historians interested in the debate. Karl Morrison, however, an American numismatist, has taken a view almost diametrically opposed to Bolin's and one that supported Pirenne's critics also. 'Concerning the circulation of coin, there is no numismatic evidence of extensive contact with peoples outside the Carolingian empire; there is no support for theses which allege preponderent Arab influence on the Carolingian economy. On the other hand, the evidence clearly suggests free circulation of coin within the closed commercial structure of the empire . . .'[9] Morrison asserts that the coin alloy changes during the ninth century were determined not by the Arab revisions to their metrology but by internal civil wars within the Carolingian empire. Furthermore, while there are literally thousands of Arabic coins from Scandinavia very few have been found in Carolingia. (Morrison notes in this respect that the Carolingians tended to melt down foreign currency, but he fails to draw proper attention to this important fact in the context of his critique of Bolin. It is a significant flaw in his paper.)

Morrison's views on the circulation of coins within the empire have recently been elaborated by D. M. Metcalf in a series of papers. In particular, Metcalf sought to quantify the coins extant at any one time.[10] The attempt was laudable, but his method remains contentious. In essence, he calculated the number of coins that might theoretically be minted by each of the mint-dies recorded. The quantity per mint was arrived at by using a formula devised for English Elizabethan coinage: the estimation was based on the maximum use of each die.[11] The very considerable numbers of coins, running into many millions, both for Anglo-Saxon and for Carolingian coinage have been used by Metcalf to illustrate the prosperity of north-west Europe at this time. His papers have provoked a sharp response from Philip Grierson who, like Marc Bloch before him, was at pains to emphasise the social rather than the economic importance of coinage during the eighth and ninth centuries.[12] Grierson proposed much lower figures, which are briefly dicussed in Chapter 6. His study was part of his extensive work on the nature of trade and exchange in the Dark Ages. The celebrated paper delivered to the Royal Historical Society, 'Commerce in the Dark Ages: a critique of the evidence', is perhaps his most original contribution.[13] It effectively introduced the growing literature of economic anthropology to medieval history. In particular, Grierson was profoundly influenced by Marcel Mauss's *Essai sur le don*, published in 1925, and he was later to be much interested by Malinowski's *Argonauts of the Western Pacific* in which the first major account of the Kula ring appears.[14] Grierson's was an attempt to move attention away from the seemingly insuperable problems raised by Pirenne towards consideration of the character of exchange. He chose to emphasise the importance of gift-exchange in particular, diminishing the role of other mechanisms.

In the last ten years the main issues of the debate raised by Pirenne have seldom been examined. An area of common consent may have been formed. If such a consent exists in our history faculties, it is probably at variance with the views of Pirenne, Bolin and perhaps even Grierson. In fact it might be argued that most historians in recent years have avoided the issue where possible.[15] This attitude can hardly be applauded, for the sources available to the historian, commanding the 'mansion of history', are growing greater.

It was Grierson, somewhat of a revolutionary in his field, who wrote: 'It has been said that the spade cannot lie, but it owes this merit in part to the fact that it cannot speak.'[16] Such powerful condemnation of archaeology in the context of Dark Age trade – a most obscure historical problem, to paraphrase Sir Frank Stenton – is more than a little remarkable. Yet a dutiful silence was observed by archaeologists at the time. The silence needs to be briefly appraised, for it is symptomatic of the condition of medieval archaeology. Perhaps the youth of the discipline deterred its exponents from replying to Grierson; perhaps many of them believed the statement to be a harsh but realistic one. After the death of

Gordon Childe in 1957 British archaeology tended towards a state of theoretical apathy. Release from this condition, as we shall outline below, was not apparent until the late nineteen-sixties. Yet the formidable record of archaeological research into trade and urban origins in early medieval Europe was well established when Grierson delivered his paper in 1958. Such silence, it may be concluded, is witness to the role that medieval archaeologists believed their discipline must adopt – as the illegitimate offspring of Prehistory and History.

As Pirenne acknowledged, the impressive grave groups dating from the Viking period from Birka in central Sweden shed considerable light on Dark Age trade. H. Stolpe excavated these between 1871 and 1895, though it was not until 1940 that the finds were published by Arbman.[17] Indeed they were to find a central place in Arbman's great synthesis, *Schweden und das karolingische Reich*, published in 1937, which was much concerned with Baltic trade.[18] Yet by this time a number of excavations of the *emporia* referred to by the medieval monkish chroniclers were in progress, or had even been completed. Holwerda had undertaken extensive excavations at Dorestad soon after the First World War;[19] the results, quickly published, were impressive. So were the results of Jankuhn's first campaign at Haithabu, one of a series of settlements of this period excavated by the Germans in the 1930s, who were among the few to consider the archaeological evidence for urban origins and its significance for long-distance trade.[20] Blindheim has written that excavations at Skirringssal (Kaupang) in Norway, were seriously contemplated as early as this, so that some comparison might be made between a Norwegian and a Jutish site of the same period: sites allegedly visited by Ottar, the renowned ninth-century visitor to king Alfred's court. The excavations at Kaupang, however, were not begun until the 1950s, though the finds from the associated cemeteries, excavated in the nineteenth century, had by then been subjected to a preliminary examination.[21]

In England the enormous urban destruction caused by bombing during the Second World War provided an opportunity to explore hitherto impenetrable areas of our past. Besides the well-publicised excavations in the City of London, there were those in a slum suburb of Southampton. O. G. S. Crawford drew attention to the likelihood of an important Saxon predecessor of the medieval town in the area of St. Mary's, a district to the east of Southampton and on the banks of the River Itchen. Evidence of such a site had been found during the nineteenth century when brick-earth diggers, operating behind some of the houses, discovered Saxon coins.[22] Excavations from 1946 onwards revealed the rich pits which were dated to the eighth century and later and which illustrated considerable trading connections (see Chapter 4). Perhaps the real significance of this discovery is the slowness with which the data came to be integrated into the literature of the time. Only Gerald Dunning apparently was in command of this newly found data and its implications, and it was in the *Festschrift* for E. T. Leeds, *Dark Age Britain*, that he first discussed the trade routes of the later Saxon period.[23] His revision of this thesis for the Norwich symposium on Anglo-Saxon pottery in 1958 was an invaluable paper that laid the foundation for new data accumulated over the next decade.[24]

In fact the 1950s saw considerable advances in the field of Dark Age trade in archaeology, and not only in north-western Europe. In Russia excavations on a mighty scale were taking place at Novgorod to investigate the origins of the Rus. Excavations at Kaupang and Helgö were begun in the 1950s, and at Haithabu were soon to be resumed on an even larger scale. Cumulatively the archaeological evidence for trade was substantial when Grierson read his paper in 1958.

Since then much has happened. To quote Martin Biddle: 'In the second half of the 'sixties urban sites became a major field of British archaeological activity and a good deal of this effort has been directed to pre-Conquest problems.'[25] Indeed, as we shall discuss, this was a significant period for archaeology generally: one that witnessed a new theoretical paradigm. Yet few can deny the slightly sterile nature of the synthesis in medieval archaeology at this time – a point raised by Biddle in his recent appraisal of the Anglo-Saxon town.[26]

Medieval archaeology has been too much concerned with its role as an appendage to 'history' and too little with its role in archaeology. Like Classical archaeology it has been left stranded, most often merely illustrating *the facts*. Too much emphasis has been placed on artistic and architectural questions, and in certain cases there has been an exaggerated interest in topography. Moses Finley has summed up this mutually acceptable belief: 'It is self-evident that the potential contribution (of archaeology) to history is, in a rough way, inversely proportionate to the quantity of the available written sources.'[27] This in one sense is a truism. Yet archaeology and documentary history draw on very different sources, and it can justifiably be argued that archaeology has a more explicit role in well-documented contexts. This in no way diminishes its potential contribution, however, and could well serve to underline its importance.

The failure to understand this relationship has, of course, enlarged the gulf between the two areas of research, and as a result there is a distinct danger of medieval archaeology becoming an academic backwater as the humanities seek to be more scientific. In the reconstruction of past behaviour patterns, the fields of anthropology and geography have an enormous contribution to make to historical archaeology and vice versa. Yet there has been an intense shyness and a strong concern to uphold the good traditions based on observational values. A new historical paradigm is long overdue, and its creation may be accelerated by references to the theoretical concepts that archaeologists, anthropologists and geographers have been sharing.

Before discussing some of these theoretical concepts it is appropriate to emphasise briefly the evolution of archaeology's new paradigm. In the past decade the discipline has moved firmly away from its role as an illustrator of facts and has acquired an impressive body of theoretical literature. Indeed its concern to explain human processes by inter-disciplinary means has grown central to its pursuit.

Bruce Trigger has summarised this archaeological revolution as follows:

> Not long ago the theoretical literature in archaeology dealt mainly with excavation techniques and the processing of archaeological data. In recent years, the successful realisation of many of these empirical objectives, plus a rapidly increasing corpus of data, have motivated a younger generation . . . to investigate more carefully the problems that are involved in the explanation of the data and the study of prehistory in general. (They) are attempting (a) to investigate the theoretical structure of prehistoric archaeology, (b) to formulate a rigorous canon for the interpretation of archaeological data, (c) to pioneer new methods of analysis.[28]

The primary thrust of this 'new archaeology' has been the search 'for scientific achievement': a deep concern for explanation in man's past. David Clarke has termed this a 'loss of innocence', and it certainly coincides with a greater emphasis on the inter-disciplinary role of archaeology. The 1960s brought a revolution in scientific aids available to archaeologists in the field, while the 1970s were the era of the com-puter revolution, when an archaeologist could analyse his data more rigorously than was hitherto possible. These developments have pro-vided the means by which human laws and generalisations have been formulated, drawing on the similar fervour of activity in the fields of anthropology and geography, as well as of biology and cybernetics (cf. Marvin Harris's quotation at the beginning of the Preface).[29]

This 'new archaeology' has been forged in the highly competitive anthropology departments of the U.S.A., as well as in the Cambridge archaeology faculty in England. Lewis Binford has been the prophet of the American cause, to the effect that 'archaeology is anthropology or it is nothing' and that we should be 'thinking of our data in terms of total cultural systems'. 'As archaeologists, with the entire span of culture and history as our "laboratory", we cannot afford to keep our theoretical heads buried in the sand.'[30] In Cambridge it was David Clarke's great compendium *Analytical Archaeology*, designed to serve 'an undisciplined empirical discipline', that initiated a new paradigm. Like Binford's studies, it bridged the past and the future and was consequently soon outdated. In particular, Clarke's theoretical discussion of models based on entities has perhaps been overtaken by the American interest in processes of human behaviour. Now the two schools are fusing, as Anglo-American archaeologists are seeking to 'understand how one moves from ideas to facts or observations, and in turn, how one may then relate the empirical findings back to ideas in an evaluative manner'.[31]

The archaeological laboratory has also seen a revolution. Urban and rural redevelopment in western Europe, as well as in the U.S.A., have provided the impetus for field-work on an enormous and diverse scale. The growth in numbers both of archaeologists and of the projects in which they are involved has meant a rapid escalation of the literature. In north-west Europe this research has been at its greatest, of course, in the matter of urban origins and development. It is high time that the questions raised by Pirenne should be examined, not only in the light of this new information, but also in terms appropriate to a discipline that can no longer be accused of finding explanation impossible.

Let us now consider the models of trade and exchange that have been adopted by archaeologists in the past decade. After this we must examine briefly what is meant by urbanism, and finally we shall allude to the social implications of trade and urbanism, which will be the subject also of the final chapter.

Trade and exchange models

Trade and exchange have become one of the principal research areas in contemporary archaeology. The objects of trade are often found, and by the use of modern characterisation techniques their point of origin can be traced. Moreover quantitative methods developed by geographers and, to a lesser extent, by anthropologists permit generalisations about the distribution patterns of traded commodities. Trade also implies organisation, which necessarily regulates 'human activities both in terms of procurement (movement of goods including raw materials) and of social relations (human encounters with exchange of information and goods)'.[32] It can be argued that the degree of organisation may be understood in the light of the exchange pattern within that society.

Little discussion of primitive economics had taken place before Malinowski visited the Trobriand Islands during the First World War. In *Argonauts of the Western Pacific* he described the Kula Ring, a cyclical exchange network that operated in these islands, and discussed the economic, and to a lesser extent the social, implications of this famous system.[33] Soon after the publication of this case study came Marcel Mauss's *Essai sur le don*, in which this exchange mechanism was discussed in cross-cultural terms using data gleaned from ancient and medieval history as well as anthropology. The importance of these books lay in their successful propagation of the need for scientific examination of primitive economics, which had hitherto been the subject of 'bourgeois ethnocentrism'.[34]

Just as Pirenne has been attacked by fellow medieval historians, so the school initiated by Malinowski has come under fire from anthropologists. As a result two camps of economic anthropology have emerged. The camp directly influenced by, among others, Malinowski and Mauss,

known as the substantivists, firmly believes that modern economic
theory is inappropriate to the study of primitive exchange systems.
Consequently the substantivists have formulated a conceptual framework with its own terminology for use in these circumstances. The
opposing camp, known as the formalists, guided by the tenor of modern
economics, believe that the primitive economy is only a less complex
system and is thus as valuably analysed by the methods of contemporary
mirco-economics. They maintain that the substantivists have a
nineteenth-century impression of the noble savage, while the substantivists counter by pointing out the impossibility of reckoning supply and
demand curves when social values are so powerfully embedded in the
exchange system. The debate has real implications for archaeologists
and historians, who have largely followed the substantivists. In the
words of Marshall Sahlins, 'no ground for happy academic conclusion
that the answer lies somewhere in between' seems to exist.[35] The
substantivist case is most clearly illustrated by the work of Karl
Polanyi, the doyen of this thesis, by Marshall Sahlins whose *Stone Age
Economics* in particular has been of central importance in recent archaeological discussions of primitive exchange, and by George Dalton who has
furthered the anthropological analysis of exchange in complex societies.[36]
The work of these three scholars is the foundation stone of this book
though, as we shall see, more recent explicitly archaeological studies of
exchange networks are also important.

Polanyi wrote a series of seminal papers on the subject, the most
eminent of which was 'The economy as instituted process'. Here he
presented his substantive definitions of the terms economic, external
trade, money and markets. These he contrasted with the economy of
industrial contexts. In a famous statement he characterised the three
different means of moving cultural items: 'Reciprocity denotes movements between correlative points of symmetrical groupings: redistribution designates appropriational movements towards the centre and out
again: exchange refers to vice-versa movements taking place between
"hands" under a market system.'[37] This threefold typology has been
revised in subsequent decades, but it remains the core of substantivist
economics.

Marshall Sahlins has discussed the nature of reciprocity as the
distance between kin increases. In the sectors he has defined lies the
Domestic Mode of Production. In particular he terms the household
level of exchange/transfer as generalised reciprocity, the lineage and
village sectors as balanced reciprocity and the tribal/inter-tribal
exchange sectors as negative reciprocity.[38]

Neil Smelsner qualified Polanyi's definition of redistribution, inter-
posing what he termed a mobilisation economy between redistribution
and market exchange. This he believed was a system that utilised redistribution to further the ends of its elite only; in effect it is a stratified
redistributive system.[39] Recently Timothy Earle has reappraised the

concept of redistribution and defined a four-part typology which we have used in this book.[40] It is schematically defined as follows:

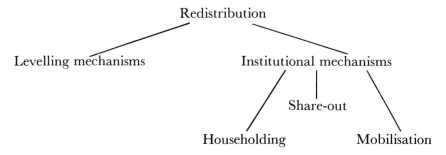

Earle argues that the levelling mechanisms, such as assemblies, potlatch, funerals and so on, counteract the accumulation of wealth by a central person; this contrasts with the other three parts of his typology. Householding, share-out and mobilisation are aspects of production and distribution within the group. Householding relates to the pooling of domestic produce and is the equivalent of Sahlin's domestic mode of production. Share-out is the allocation of goods from co-operative labour such as hunts. Mobilisation is the recruitment of goods and services for the benefit of an elite stratum. The development of chiefdom economies is therefore contingent upon their gaining some control over the levelling mechanisms and, through mobilisation, accumulating wealth.

George Dalton, with Bohannan, has elaborated Polanyi's brief references to primitive markets. In their edited volume *Markets in Africa*, Bohannan and Dalton establish the distinction between the institution of the market place and the principle of market exchange:

> The market place is a specific site where a group of buyers and a group of sellers meet. The market principle is the determination of prices by forces of supply and demand regardless of the site of the transactions.[41]

They then establish the existence of three societies in which the principle exists:

> (1) Societies which lack market places, and in which the market principle, if it appears, is but weakly represented;
> (2) societies with peripheral markets – that is, the institution of the market place is present but the market principle does not determine acquisition of subsistence or the allocation of land and labour resources;
> (3) societies dominated by the market principle and the price mechanism.

These studies have proved a powerful assessment of the problem.

During the 1960s there were many studies on the nature of markets. G. W. Skinner, for example, discerned a hierarchy of five orders of markets in China.[42] At the lowest level lies the minor or incipient standard market, a green vegetable market which specialises in 'the horizontal exchange of peasant produced goods' and handles virtually no imported items. Next comes the standard market, which is the starting-point for the upward flow of agricultural goods and the terminal point for the downward flow of imports. Next is the intermediate market – an institution that functions in between the standard and central market. The central market lies strategically on the transportation networks and possesses an important wholesaling function. Finally there is the regional market at the apex of the hierarchy, dominating the marketing of a vast area. At the same time geographers in Africa emphasised the significance of the periodic market, as well as the rings of week-day markets. Markets and fairs have been viewed as instrumental in establishing a hierarchical system of markets of the kind recognised by Skinner. B. W. Hodder has argued that the periodic markets in the Yoruba country of west Africa are effective for selling locally produced goods into the distributive network.[43] These function as green vegetable markets with the intention of concentrating both sellers and buyers, notably outside the house or palace of the first or most powerful ruler of a settlement. Only now are these periodic markets being replaced by daily ones, as market intensity increases.

Carol Smith, in an important recent study, has attempted to survey the regional character of these different modes of distribution.[44] She also tries to account for the fact that modes of production vary more than modes of social stratification. She argues that one should be able to predict the spatial distribution of the elite from the organisation and spatial extension of the distributional system. She therefore constructs a typology of different distribution systems which we have summarised in Fig. 3. Her spatial patterns can be summarised as follows:

(a) An extended network system where exchange is direct and wholly uncommercialised in usually independent tribal societies.

(b) A bounded system where exchange is direct and uncommercialised in feudal or chiefdom contexts, and where a few scarce resources exist.

(c) A solar central-place system where partially commercialised exchange operates through an administered market: usually in incipient states or empires where these centres are principally bureaucratic nodes.

(d) A dendritic central-place system in which there is a partially commercialised though monopolistic market which usually exists on the periphery of a modern economic system. In this there exists high stress because of limited internal specialisation.

(e/f) Interlocking central-place system, fully commercialised competitive market.

Several recent authors have drawn attention to these concepts in the early medieval period, and there can be little doubt that they have considerable value.[45] The dendritic central-place system, the solar central-place system and competitive markets are terms which abound in this book, for Smith's typology is an underlying framework for our interpretation.

Yet we have also been forced to modify some of her conclusions. The market forces in the dendritic and solar central-place systems are apparent with some qualification, as we shall demonstrate in Chapter 3. Furthermore, there is good ground for refining her colonial perspective of the dendritic central-place system, for this is clearly generated in circumstances where primary states are attempting to acquire scarce commodities from satellite areas. However, only the level of social organisation in both areas will determine whether traders from the satellite territory, as its monopolistic market and dendritic production-distribution system increases in scale, also travel to the primary one.

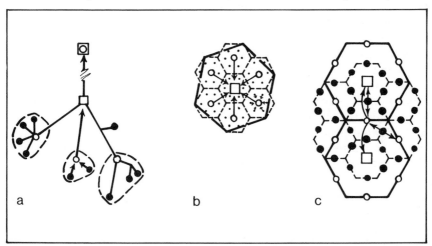

Figure 3 Three of the regional models proposed by Carol Smith: (a) a dendritic central-place model; (b) a solar central-place model; (c) an interlocking central-place system

All these are the descriptive models of distribution. The movement from one system to another has been largely determined as a case of gaining control over resources.[46] This, according to Hodder, appears to have occurred either as a response to the need for local exchange when the division of labour had attained a critical role in society, thus stimulating long-distance trade networks, or as markets arose directly as a consequence of long-distance trade.[47] The arguments are examined in Chapters 9 and 10.

These are models derived from economic anthropology and geography, and to a large extent their descriptive worth is limited in
prehistory. As a result archaeologists have been trying to develop means
of identifying the behavioural patterns which are the correlates of
reciprocity, redistribution and market exchange. To some extent this
has been achieved by isolating the character of the settlement pattern, or
by analysing the processing of energy or information required to
construct parts of the settlement pattern.[48] These kinds of model are of
critical value, but their limitations too are more than apparent when, for
example, monumental buildings do not even exist. Colin Renfrew has
therefore developed a most useful series of distance-decay models which
are intended to permit a greater understanding at least of the
organisational forces operating on the distribution of artifacts.[49]

In a recent paper he has termed this distance-decay property 'the law
of monotonic decrement'. 'In circumstances of uniform loss or
deposition and in the absence of highly organised directional (i.e.
preferential, non-homogeneous) exchange, the curve of frequency or
abundance of occurrence of an exchanged commodity against effective
distance from a localised source will be a monotonic decreasing one.'[50]
From this basis he has developed the following form (Fig. 4):

Down-the-line trade (Fig. 4.1) is the result of a large number of successive
exchanges of material from a source point: 'Individual sites do not in
general stand out as receiving unusually large quantities of material: this
argues against organised or preferential shipment. The simplest way of
visualising this transfer is to postulate a chain of villages, equally spaced.
Each village down the line would receive the obsidian through exchange
from its neighbour near the source, and pass on a given proportion, say
half or two thirds.'[51] Renfrew has also modelled this exchange network
mathematically, so that quantified data can ultimately be evaluated in
this respect.

When preferential nodes appear in a down-the-line network, however,
Renfrew identifies two major effects. First, the emergence of central
places ensures movement between only those sites, and thus these
cultural elements will pass on down the spatial hierarchy only in
reduced quantities. Secondly, there is a reduction of trade to lower-
order sites in the hierarchy: 'For whereas these were formerly sym-
metrically placed with respect to one another, this is no longer the case.
Those within the sphere of influence of a given central place are now
linked primarily through that place.'[52]

In what Renfrew has termed the *prestige chain network* (Fig. 4.2) nearly
all the goods received are ultimately sent on down the line, with the
result that the cultural element is only slightly less abundant at
considerable distances from the source. Renfrew considers it to
characterise ceremonial gift exchange of the kind Malinowski observed
in the Trobriand Islands. In effect, this network too operates between
central places or persons.

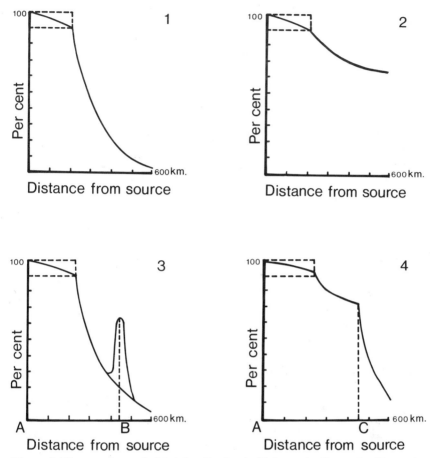

Figure 4 Distance-decay models (after Renfrew). (1) down-the-line trade; (2) prestige-chain trade; (3) directional trade (redistribution); (4) free-lance trade

Redistribution/directional trade is a modification of the hierarchically arranged down-the-line trade, where the existence of a central place or person serves to concentrate cultural elements (Fig. 4.3). *Middleman trading* (Fig. 4.4), however, affects the pattern more radically. 'Any middleman has an effective area of operation, outside of which he does not normally travel. Within this area, in the absence of any preferential service for central places, the fall-off of the commodity with distance from source will be much less rapid.'[53] Only at the boundary of his area of operation will the fall-off be extreme.

Renfrew himself has begun to revise these models,[54] but it can be stated with some confidence that their value has been considerable and a stimulating contribution to our understanding of trading systems.

Before considering further theoretical aspects which are fundamental to this book, it is worth repeating a statement recently made by R. McC.

Adams on the question of trade. Adams has grown slightly sceptical of
the archaeological conclusions drawn by some, and in response he
writes:[55]

> Trade and exchange are time-bound phenomena, the character of which
> is best understood when the standards of exchange value governing
> individual transactions can be related directly to those transactions . . . if
> trade is generally the dynamic, unstabilising force that the ethnographic
> record seems to suggest, wide fluctuations over short intervals are to be
> expected in the geographical range of trade, in the extent of local
> participation in trading networks, and in the selection of trading
> partners. Yet the archaeological record is characteristically an aggregative
> one, difficult to connect with short or precise time intervals.
>
> While the record of archaeological progress during recent years
> suggests that these difficulties will not prove as intractable as they might
> seem at present, at the very least it would appear that important
> conceptual advances in the study of trade are more likely to emerge and
> be adequately tested in the fields in which archaeological remains can be
> joined to a historical chronology and written economic records.

This is surely a rationale for this book. The tendency to aggregate
patterns can only be overcome by testing the appropriate archaeological
models against dated, historical horizons. Furthermore, there is the
danger that archaeology presents 'time-slices', and it is by comparing
one time-slice with the next that the trajectory a system takes is
determined. Fred Hamond has recently shown that alternative processes
and patterns can lead to identical outcomes. Indeed, simulation studies
are reinforcing Adams's viewpoint and are encouragement to generalise
from the archaeological data where there is tight chronological
control.[56]

Urbanism and medieval towns

Nucleated settlements, urban complexes or market-places are the nodes
in the exchange networks discussed above. The concept of urbanism has
been a central topic of discussion in this particular field of medieval
history as well as in general areas of archaeology, geography and
sociology. We shall approach the question from the two viewpoints
central to this book.

Maitland in 1897 answered his own rhetorical question about the
medieval borough, stating that it was a legally defined concept. In effect,
this repeated Aristotle's definition of the city-state. The view was upheld
by Pirenne, Rorig and Stephenson in their studies of aspects of west
European urbanism during the 1920s and 1930s. But when Vogel briefly
counterattacked, warning against this legalistic approach, we can see
the limited parameters within which these early twentieth-century
historians – even Pirenne – were working.[57] In their opinion, towns in

the early medieval period existed only in Carolingia; the absence of legalistic documentation argued against their existence in Anglo-Saxon England, Scandinavia or eastern Germany. This thesis must in part have stimulated the Nazi-propagated belief that it was the Germans who introduced the town as such to central and eastern Europe: German colonisation was seen as a prime mover in the formation of the Slavic states.[58] English historians may dismiss the prejudices of the Nazi dictatorship, but they were in fact harnessing scholarship of a significant kind to their inhuman cause. It may have been in part as a rejection of this approach that post-war historians like Ennen and Schlesinger have sought to define a town from a broader conceptual base, and thus no longer identify it as an isolated economic feature, but one that is regionally integrated. Hence Schlesinger, for example, has attempted to integrate the trading settlements, or *emporia*, into his analyses, rather than effectively dismissing them as did Pirenne, Rorig and Stephenson.[59]

This post-war approach has introduced the *Kritirienbündel*, or 'bundle of criteria', into the discussion.[60] Like Pausanias defining Panopeus, a city of the Phocians, we find M. W. Beresford defining a town as follows: 'Any place that passes one of the following tests: Had it a borough charter? Did it have burgages? Was it called *burgus* in the Assize Rolls, or was it separately taxed as a borough? Did it send members to any medieval Parliament?'[61] With this analytical method strongly paralleled by Childe's analysis in prehistory (see below), it is not surprising to find medieval archaeologists using the bundle of criteria. The influential discussion document *The Erosion of History*, published early in the 1970s, lists the criteria for a medieval town as follows:[62]

1. defences
2. a planned street-system
3. a market(s)
4. a mint
5. legal autonomy
6. a role as a central place
7. a relatively large and dense population
8. a diversified economic base
9. plots and houses of urban types
10. social differentiation
11. complex religious organisation
12. a judicial centre

The list illustrates the topographical features and institutions which archaeologists then believed it possible to identify with sound documentary work complemented by open-area excavations. Its limitations, however, are more than obvious now when such enormous research is simply not feasible.

The geographer's approach to urbanism is a highly scientific one concerned with complex issues. Wheatley's contribution to an archaeological seminar on the problem sums up his view of a protean issue:

It is impossible to do more than characterise the concept of urbanism as compounded of a series of sets of ideal-types social, political, economic and other institutions which have combined in different ways in different cultures at different times.[63]

Wheatley's pessimism may have been stimulated by previous attempts by archaeologists to qualify their terminology. Childe for one, in an important paper published in 1950, also considered the issue in terms of a bundle of criteria. The direct influence upon him was the nineteenth-century thinker Lewis Henry Morgan, rather than Pausanias, but the resulting attempt was much the same. Childe's criteria were:[64]

1. population
2. craft specialisation
3. central authority
4. monumental architecture
5. developed social stratification
6. writing
7. exact and predictive sciences
8. naturalistic art
9. residence rather than kinship-based communities

Childe's diagnostic criteria were, of course, features exhibited by the settlements that he had already designated as urban in the Near East. Furthermore, they were criteria that aptly fitted his then current Marxist perspective of social evolution – criteria which have been in part reintroduced by Jonathan Friedman and Michael Rowlands in an ambitious epigenetic appraisal of social systems and their evolution.[65] Renfrew has to some extent echoed Childe's criteria, although in a more simplified definition designed by Clyde Kluckholn: 'city dweller' and 'urban' loosely designate societies characterised by at least two of the following features:

1. towns upward of, say 5,000 inhabitants
2. a written language
3. monumental ceremonial centres

Renfrew adds:

> [This operational definition] embraces all those early cultures which are usually designated civilisations. And it excludes societies with only a single astonishing feature, like Stonehenge, or the temples of Malta, or indeed the Tartaria tablets of Romania.[66]

In an impressive study of settlement sizes, Renfrew then utilises this definition to establish the Minoan settlement hierarchy and the manner in which it functioned. Yet for reasons more than apparent this has limited value in western European pre- and proto-history before the late medieval period (with some imperial Roman exceptions). Indeed it is not so far removed from the legalistic view developed by historians such as Pirenne and others which has already been discussed, though of course Renfrew's definition has general applicability to what have been termed civilisations – the question he was then examining.

We might in fact agree that we cannot expect to find uniformity in urbanisation, owing to the different socio-cultural and environmental backgrounds of the human groups concerned. There is simply no case for this argument, for if we can discern the networks in which the nodes are present, as Carol Smith, for example, has done, we should equally be able to define the characteristics of the nodes. (Of course, it is a separate question whether we can identify these archaeologically.)

We must begin by asking precisely what is urbanism? Charles Redman answers as follows:

> Urbanism implies the characteristics that distinguish cities from simpler community forms; it also refers to the organisation of an entire urban society, which includes not only cities, but also towns and villages.[67]

This is a fair assessment of its commonplace meaning, though hardly a definition. Gideon Sjoberg, an urban sociologist, has formulated a definition in his book on the pre-industrial city:

> a community of substantial size and population density that shelters a variety of non-agricultural specialists, including a literate elite.[68]

The Polish urban archaeologist Witold Hensel has adopted a similar definition in his studies on Slavic towns, though he omits the necessity of a literate elite.[69] A more satisfactory definition would embrace elements of Redman's and Sjoberg's comments. An urban community is a settlement of some size and population which is markedly larger than communities concerned with subsistence alone; the majority of its inhabitants, moreover, are not engaged in full-time agrarian pursuits. Such a community should include the presence of more than one institution, so that a monastery or palace can only be termed urban if it is the focus of more people than merely monks or ministers and royalty. It is not possible to sustain proto-urbanism: a site is either urban or it is not.

In this book several types of urban communities are described and discussed: fairs, emporia, trading stations, monastic and royal communities which are the foci of periodic markets, and a hierarchy of market-places. To comprehend these particular types satisfactorily within our general framework we must first review three classes of urban community that have a global presence.

The port of trade is a phenomenon that resembles, superficially at least, several of these early medieval urban types. It was defined by Polanyi in his 1957 paper on exchange mechanisms cited above. In the words of two archaeologists recently: '[This] construct will remain a *deus ex machina*.'[70] Polanyi regarded the port of trade as 'often a neutrality device, a derivative of silent trade . . . and of the neutralised town'.[71] The site, in his view, offers security to the foreign trader, facilities of anchorage and debarkation, storage, and the benefit of judicial authority and agreement on the goods to be traded. Renfrew has stressed the neutrality element when examining the spatial implications of the port of trade[72] while Rathje and Sabloff have defined the port of trade as:[73]

1. being at a transition zone
2. being a small political unit
3. having a large population
4. being little concerned with retail distribution within the port's surrounding area.

In fact it has recently been argued that Polanyi was referring to a much wider range of sites than these very particular models. His essay on the port of trade includes examples drawn from early medieval Europe. The sites he discusses here may be broadly defined as:[74]

1. those where buyers are absent but sellers are resident.
2. those where buyers are resident, but which sellers visit for varying lengths of time.

This confusion suggests that the particular model correctly interpreted by Renfrew, Rathje and Sabloff is a rare occurrence, and that we should honour the goals Polanyi initiated by seeking a less ambiguous and more functional terminology.

One recent paper provides just such an alternative. K. G. Hirth has drawn attention to the gateway communities previously discussed by geographers.[75] He has tried to define them so that they can be utilised in prehistoric contexts. There is much here that is reminiscent of Polanyi's term, but it has greater clarity and is consequently a more functional concept. Hirth writes that 'as collection, preparation and movement of goods between regions became more complex, greater sophistication was required to divert economic activities. It was at this point that long-distance exchange began to figure prominently in the process of cultural evolution. The intensification of inter-regional exchange stimulated the emergence of new forms of socio-economic organisation. Trade specialists appeared and certain communities located along key trade routes prospered with increased inter-regional exchange.[76] 'These communities flourish at the passage points into and out of distinct natural or cultural regions . . . and link their regions to external trade routes.' He adds that they are 'structurally similar to dendritic market networks'.[77] He suggests that these communities functioned to satisfy demands for commodities through trade and were located to reduce transportation costs. Furthermore, they operate as commercial middlemen, concerned principally with wholesaling, in contrast to the retailing activities of a central-place system. Finally he examines the development and transmutation of these communities when competing places arise. At this juncture the gateway community declines to the level of its new competitors, though it will retain some control of its former hinterland and may evolve more complex forms of socio-political authority with which to combat increased economic competition.

This definition has much to offer, for the community distinguishes beyond doubt the emporia which are to figure prominently in this book. It also offers some guidance on how the competing markets of Europe arose, though of course it provides no explanation.

The third global institution, which has already been discussed in some detail, is the market-place. First, we should add, a port of trade and a gateway community are clearly often, though arguably not always, market-places. This book follows Bohannan and Dalton's definition, already cited, where the distinction between a society in which a market-place is peripheral and a society in which it is dominant is usefully emphasised. Secondly, it is apparent that certain gateway communities in north-west Europe functioned, in a period of transition, as monopolistic markets in a dendritic system, and *then* as solar central-place markets. Distinctions are not always easily made, but Table 1 may help to illuminate the relationship of the definitions.

Table 1

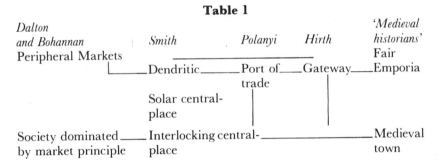

Dalton and Bohannan	*Smith*	*Polanyi*	*Hirth*	'*Medieval historians*'
Peripheral Markets				Fair
	Dendritic	Port of trade	Gateway	Emporia
	Solar central-place			
Society dominated by market principle	Interlocking central-place			Medieval town

We believe that these are pragmatic terms which can be used in conjunction with the network models that economic geographers and anthropologists have developed. In particular, there should be no bias attributable to the lack of documentation, as the settlement hierarchy or constellations of cultural material will prove the existence, and in all likelihood the character, of the nodes in the networks. Moreover we can fully concur with Sabloff and his colleagues when they say that 'trading centres are both sensitive indicators of change in economic and political structure and actual mechanisms of that change'.[78]

State formation

The formation of the state has received little attention in early medieval history. Political power has seldom been considered in spatial, social and economic terms. The early territories themselves are still badly defined, and the nature of kingship, while superlatively discussed as a philosophical concept, has seldom been exposed to the neo-evolutionary theses of social anthropologists. One rare exception at present is the attempt of

Aidan Southall, who compares the formation of the Alur state to that better documented for Saxon-Norman England.[79] A further attempt is that of Robert Carneiro, who uses Anglo-Saxon England as a fundamental state in an effort to measure cultural development in many different contexts, using Guttman's scalogram analysis.[80] Both analyses are essentially perceptive but peripheral to the goals of this book.

The discussion of this socio-political organisation is the subject, in part, of Chapter 10, so we shall leave the thrust of the current debate on state formation until then. There remains, however, to review briefly the contemporary models of social organisation.

Trigger, in a brief but lucid essay, has identified the various threads that have come to concern social archaeology in the last decade or so.[81] Darwinian evolutionists who proclaimed man's power to select and rationalise his human progression were largely refuted in a formidable reaction in the earlier part of this century. Childe, however, re-asserted the new evolutionary theses in a series of studies engendered in part by his Marxist conception of the past. He believed that major technological innovations were made only once and were then diffused from a common centre. Progress emanated from this point, though it was subject to environmental, socio-economic and spiritual parameters. Childe's model has been a central feature in British archaeology, but it has been generally refuted in America. There the school led by Leslie White and Julian Steward effectively denied the significant role to human actors; instead man was a dependent variable. White emphasised technology as an important variable, and Steward ecology. Both believed that there were developmental regularities which could be retrieved from the material record with which archaeologists work.

This American school has developed. Elman Service, notably, has proposed a unilinear sequence of human organisation, and Morton Fried (and latterly Friedman and Rowlands) have provided an alternative sequence.[82] Here it is only apposite to sketch the features of Service's and Fried's accounts as they affect this book.

Service has suggested a sequence that develops from band, tribe, chiefdom and state. It has been popular with archaeologists because of its simplicity. A chiefdom, in Service's view, comprises several groups (tribes) organised into a hierarchical social unit. There is variation in rank, but the hierarchy focuses on a single central person, the chief. There is usually some craft specialisation and perhaps some agricultural specialisation, and the economic mode of redistribution is a fundamental basis of the system (cf. Earle's analysis discussed earlier in this chapter). But there are regulating mechanisms that delineate the powers of the chief, and as a result his authority tends to be based on the presence of sumptuary rules. The state, by contrast, has a well-defined political organisation and, as we shall see in Chapter 10, the leadership is no longer fettered by regulations – or at least not in theory.

Fried's typology is less particular than Service's, but perhaps therefore not so generally valuable. Fried's lowest stage, egalitarian society, embraces Service's bands and to some degree simpler tribal organisations; next, ranked society embraces tribes and lesser chiefdoms.[83] Ranked societies have a hierarchy of status, and the transition to such a level usually occurs simultaneously with the shift from reciprocity to redistribution. Authority, however, is still focused on familial arrangements. The next level is a stratified society in which members have unimpeded access to the same fundamental resources, previously denied or restricted, and stratification facilitates increasingly complex divisions of labour. The state emerges from this last level almost unannounced and 'was hard at work concentrating its power on specific cases long before any reflective individual took the effort to isolate and identify the novelty'.[84]

In this book we have conformed loosely to Service's framework, though we are mostly interested in advanced chiefdoms, which tend to be cyclical and may best be defined as stratified societies. (Service's terminology certainly seems more appropriate to describe the kings and chiefs of early medieval Europe.) Therefore, to avoid confusion, I have resorted to the term 'cyclical chiefdoms', partly to emphasise their transient status, which is often conjoined with their honorary political status as overlords.

On the other hand we must consider how we are to recognise a chiefdom or the creation of the state in the archaeological record, even when the archaeology is reinforced by documentary sources. Several archaeologists have applied themselves to the question. They have demonstrated that in certain cases the evolution of political organisation can be identified, though the results often appear as a series of stages open to the kind of criticism discussed earlier in this chapter.

The nature of the ranking within the settlement pattern has been greatly emphasised, as well as the distribution of craft-specialists. Emphasis has also been put on the evidence of administrative materials, and the organisational correlates of distribution patterns (of goods) have been studied.[85] Models of these kinds are easier to test where stone buildings, including monumental structures, are to be found, so it is no coincidence that settlement analyses and studies of production-distribution patterns in prehistory have been focused on the so-called civilisations.

William Rathje has also proposed a cost-control model which aims to monitor the relative changes in quality and quantity of production.[86] The essence of this model is that a complex society will invest time and labour in the generation of prestige objects and monuments for social purposes. Once the state has been formed, however, there will be a shift towards mass production of standardised goods and monuments to generate wealth from all parts of the territory. There are obvious economic benefits from this policy, but Rathje also believes that the products will be a facet of the information processing necessary to unify the new entity. Standardisation, however, inevitably leads to simplification and a decline in quality as more goods are produced.

This book sets out to reveal the processes of urbanisation in north-west Europe after the decay of Roman civilisation. It is a well-worn track, but I have tried to avoid the footsteps of the travellers described at the beginning· of this chapter. In particular, emphasis is placed on the emergence, development and abandonment of the emporia, for these are the sites to which archaeologists have paid special attention and with which historians have been less concerned. Moreover by examining these from different viewpoints, we can discern the socio-economic processes which interest us.

Chapter 2 is an attempt to fit these emporia into the trading networks which have been, or can now be, identified. In effect, it is an attempt to present a history of the trade-routes until the ninth-century, when the system changed. Chapter 3 is an analysis of the nodes in the network, while Chapter 4 is a guide to certain of these sites. Chapter 5 examines the traders and their boats. Chapter 6 is concerned with traded commodities. The objects of trade included bullion, so this is a suitable place to deviate slightly and discuss the highly contentious question of currency. Chapter 7 attempts to balance the model by tentatively examining rural production and intra-regional exchange. To some extent it anticipates questions discussed in Chapters 8 and 9, since to make a valid point about subsistence systems we have to document their evolution. Chapter 8 offers a brief discussion of the events of the ninth century; the process of change from one urban phenomenon to another is examined with reference to systems thinking. Chapter 9 takes up this theme and examines the emergent competitive markets as well as the new web of trade-routes that occur as a result. Finally, Chapter 10 tries to document the processes of change, recapitulating to some extent the arguments variously used in the preceding chapters.

Chapter 2

TRADING SYSTEMS FROM THEODORIC TO CHARLEMAGNE

After the period during which the Mediterranean unity subsisted – from the fifth to the eighth century – the rupture of that unity had displaced the axis of the world.

Henri Pirenne[1]

The Roman world in the west contracted slowly but inexorably during the fifth and sixth centuries. By the time the Arabs had completed their conquest of north Africa late in the seventh century they were to look across at a Europe with a very different political configuration. The economics of these centuries in north-west Europe are particularly difficult to define. On the one hand, documentary evidence appears to show that the imperial institutions were maintained by the tide of migrants who had been lured westwards. On the other hand, the very contraction of the empire and the immense social reorganisation necessary to accommodate these large communities seems to argue against fluid continuity and the stable preservation of the Roman socio-economic system. Moreover, Tacitus' celebrated study of the Germans in the first century gives us a perspective, if a somewhat patronising one, on the invaders' very different economic institutions. In effect, these were institutions primarily focused on central persons, in contrast to the Roman economy which was based on central places. Archaeology is only just beginning to illuminate this, the darkest of all periods in the Dark Ages. In three areas it has proved effective.

First, the dendritic trade route northwards from the Rhine, the old Roman *limes*, seems to have come to a desultory end by the fifth century.[2] Its slow demise coincides with the major movements of north Germans and Jutes along the Frisian and Flemish coasts in the direction of England. However, these movements undoubtedly complicate any interpretation of trade routes. It must have been a period of upheaval; yet we should be careful not to dramatise the movement. Instead we should perhaps envisage the gradual abandonment of marginal landscapes such as those on which the villages of Wijster and Feddersen Wierde were founded.[3] It was a process that lasted several generations and included an element, perhaps, of budding-off of kin-related groups, rather in the manner of white settlers in more recent times.[4]

Secondly, the cemetery evidence from fifth- and sixth-century France (Merovingia) suggests that the late Roman economy was sustained in part to provide for the mortuary rite which was central to the Germanic social system. For example, there is clear evidence of regional trading of pottery in this connection by the sixth century.[5] The funerary rite also provided the motive for the continued production of some monumental art, and the localised trading of sarcophagi in Aquitaine is now excellently documented.[6] Yet evidence of a negative kind pointing to the marked contraction of the Roman-period towns to mere shadows of their former selves is powerful evidence indeed. In essence we seem to be witnessing the transition from a multi-regional, market-based economy to a society in which the market principle existed but may be termed *peripheral*, taking the form of periodic fairs (cf. the discussion of Bohannan and Dalton in Chapter 1). This transition must have been determined by the failure of the Germans to grasp the full significance of the market-place. However, while we may generalise in this fashion, the argument is still sadly light-weight. Outside the Rhineland archaeologists have not successfully assumed the charge imposed upon them by Pirenne and his critics.

Thirdly, the departure of the Romans from the British Isles had a considerable impact. The market-based system was clearly in decline in the last quarter of the fourth century. Rural production was run down and the decline of the villas was evident. By the early to mid-fifth century this system was effectively defunct, though as central places the towns – or some at least of them – were still partially occupied.[7] Beyond the Roman frontiers, trading systems extending to Ireland and Scotland quite obviously came to an end.[8] For a brief period the Irish and the Picts compensated by consistently raiding the now vulnerable sub-Roman communities. Southern and eastern England, by contrast, witnessed the gradual and perhaps organic emergence of new kingdoms dominated by north German immigrants. In response the sub-Roman British communities appear either to have fortified themselves in new territorial groups or simply to have integrated into the immigrant culture, which for a century or so maintained the settlement pattern of the late Roman period.[9] By the sixth century a network of isolated modules was being formed, and alliance-making factors may account for the individualistic movements of metalwork or pottery identified from this time. There is an impression, which is yet to be formally tested, of a localised economy, with artifacts being moved between kin-groups only.[10] The existence of primitive redistribution, however, is evident. Whether it was conditioned by the presence of long-distance trade systems to western Britain, on the one hand, and to southern and eastern England, on the other, is a questionable point. The evolution of

Anglo-Saxon hierarchies is a difficult issue; it is examined in the final chapter of this book.

This chapter examines the succession of west and north European trading systems from the later fifth to the ninth century. These are the settings for the sites and their components discussed in following chapters.

Mediterranean trade-routes northwards

Joachim Werner is the great student of long-distance trade in the migration period.[11] He and his colleagues have identified the systems extending northwards from the Mediterranean, as well as the movements around the North Sea and even into the western Baltic. The earliest trade route of consequence entering the new Germanic communities from the south may have been initiated late in the fifth century, when Clovis commanded much of north-west Europe, and during the reigns of Theodoric in Italy and Anastasius in Byzantium, who had gained some measure of control over southern European economic decay. Gold coins of Theodoric (493–526) have been found in cemeteries north of the Alps. These, however, may have come northwards with the Lombardic and Alammanic brooches which date from the first half of the sixth century. Lombardic coins of this half-century are found in the Rhine valley and, to a lesser extent, in northern France. This transalpine route clearly reached its zenith towards the end of the reign of Justinian (527–565), the eastern Emperor who briefly reconquered Ravenna. Coins of this period have been found in numbers along the same northerly corridor, which extended beyond the central Rhine to Frisia and thence either to southern and eastern England or to Scandinavia. Perhaps the most distinctive artifacts witnessing to this system are the Coptic bowls, 'tea-pots' and ladles which have been found in cemeteries and sites along the route.[12]

In essence Werner has distinguished a system which began in northern Italy and penetrated Switzerland, and also the upper Rhine in a peripheral way, and was clearly of most significance in the middle Rhineland and the Paris basin, where finds of this kind are aggregated. In these key areas lay the 'capitals' of the Neustrian and Austrasian kingdoms respectively. The scale of the 'commerce' was probably small, and the items taken northwards were apparently prestigious goods destined for emergent Merovingian courts and presumably representing alliance-making gifts or direct exchanges for the slaves, some of whom Pope Gregory was to notice in a Rome slave market. The scattered references to Jewish and Syrian traders, for example, operating in early Merovingian western Europe may indicate the mechanism by which these goods were moved from the Italian to Rhenish or Parisian foci.[13] Yet a powerful directional exchange system is not apparent since

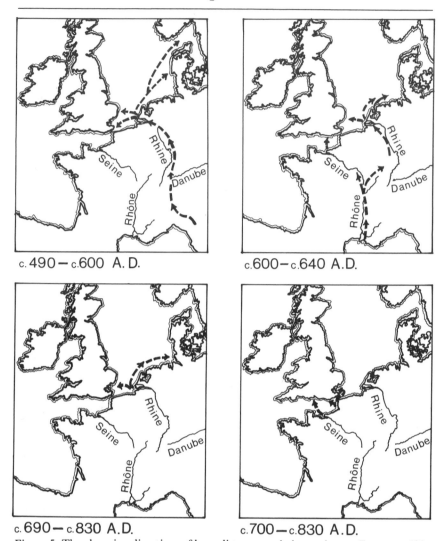

c.490 – c.600 A.D.

c.600 – c.640 A.D.

c.690 – c.830 A.D.

c.700 – c.830 A.D.

Figure 5 The changing directions of long-distance trade in north-west Europe, *c.*490–
830

concentrations of these artifacts have been recognised also, for example,
in Bavaria. In fact Renfrew's amended down-the-line exchange network
with central persons/places instead of a chain of villages may provide a
spatial expression of this trading system (see Chapter 1, Fig. 4.3).

The articulation of the separate systems, however, extending beyond
the Paris basin and the middle Rhineland at this time requires further
consideration. The Coptic bowl in the Sutton Hoo ship burial, Suffolk
(possibly an heirloom when buried) and the dozen or more cowrie shells
from Anglo-Saxon graves, originally from the Indian Ocean, are goods
that were perhaps brought by these two northerly arms of the
transalpine route. Procopius, writing in Byzantium in the second and

third quarters of the sixth century, had heard of farmers on the North Sea littoral who were ferrymen – the men who articulated this insubstantial trade route.[14] At Hérouvillette (Calvados) in Normandy, the grave of a mid-sixth-century chieftain who was probably a boat builder was recently found.[15] In addition to his tools there was a rich array of prestige objects, so he was probably a man of local rank, at least, and possibly one of the men known, indirectly, to Procopius.

At present, the period is still effectively prehistoric both in England and in Scandinavia. Yet individual finds contribute an added dimension when, for example, the North Sea pattern of Danish bracteates (probably Danish imitations of Byzantine gold goins) is considered. The many students of these ornate abstractions of coins dating to the sixth century have isolated their movement from Denmark to Frisia; to Kent, where more than a dozen have been found; to Normandy (two were found at Hérouvillette); and even to Herpes in Aquitaine.[16] Extrapolation from the later evidence suggests that this pattern may have been the result of gift exchange between courts, complicated by the contacts retained between the 'homelands' and migrants.

One further aspect of the later fifth- to sixth-century Mediterranean intrusion into north-west Europe is the system that bypassed the Merovingian courts by a sailing route round Iberia to late Celtic Britain and Ireland. Evidence of this trade route has become better and better documented since Professor O'Ríordáin published the Mediterranean amphorae from the royal site at Garranes near Cork in the 1940s.[17] The distribution of Class A ware (North African Red Slip) sigillata bowls and Class B ware amphorae extends from Somerset to Cornwall and includes several major sites in south Wales as well as major sites around southern and eastern Ireland.[18] This trade may have been sustaining a Roman system to the sub-Roman communities, bastions of Christianity, and to their Celtic allies who had also adopted Christianity by the late fifth century. Again, however, we must envisage a trading system bringing tablewares and wine and seeking slaves and possibly leather (a particular Irish speciality) in return. The concentration of finds at South Cadbury Castle (Somerset), Dinas Powys (Glamorgan), and Garranes (Co. Cork) illustrates the directional mode of this system aiming for central places and their persons. The important concentration of wares at the monastic settlement of Tintagel (Cornwall) points to the church's involvement in the system.[19] Further groups, however, from coastal sites like Topsham and Bantham (Devon) (see Chapter 4) point to the creation of administered 'nodes' for the handling of the trade. This presumably was a consequence of the system's growth in scale and the threat posed by the aliens to the native social structure (see Chapter 3).

The transalpine route and the sea route around Iberia seem to have declined in the last quarter of the sixth century. From this date Byzantine and Mediterranean artifacts are seldom found in north-west Europe until the tenth and eleventh centuries. The recession after

Justinian brought about by eastern conflicts may have been responsible for the contraction of the Byzantine interest in western Mediterranean and transalpine affairs. The world of late antiquity was entering its final phase of decay before the advent of the Arabs. But though it was in decay it still seems to have interacted with the north-west European communities. For this reason, perhaps, Provençe seems to have attained a significant role as intermediary between east and west as well as between north and south. The archaeology of this next phase is still vestigial, but the extensive studies of Merovingian gold coinage have provided some basis for reconstructing the next trade system.

The new network would appear to have issued northwards up the Rhône corridor as far as Burgundy, where it forked either towards Paris, capital of Neustria, or towards the middle Rhineland via Alsace or Trier, aiming for the Austrasians.[20] The identification of this system has been greatly facilitated by the widespread (decentralised) Merovingian mints which were constituted late in the sixth century. The products of these mints, and especially their context in coin-hoards, provide the fundamental source for reconstructing the trading system. Of course, there are obvious dangers in the interpretation of coin data, which are forcefully reviewed in Himley's homiletic discourse on numismatics and the Pirenne thesis.[21] A general synthesis, however, derived from the studies of Werner, Rigold and James, is now quite clear. Allied to this analysis, the scientific characterisation of the coin-alloys at various stages and at various mints for the Merovingian series has provided important complementary data illustrating the precise debasement of the coinage at a critical period.

The chronological range of the system extending northwards from Provençe can now be fairly accurately defined. The hoard from a grave (or collected graves) at St. Martin's, Canterbury, attests (the kingdom of) Kent's links with the French kingdoms as well as a Provençal 'connection' in about 580.[22] There was probably a down-the-line factor (Fig. 4.1) inherent in this movement northwards, so the coins may have been some years old by the time they were buried. The Escharen hoard, however, from the Rhine delta zone, dated *c.* 600, confirms the existence of the new system (Fig. 5). In this hoard there are several Provençal coins as well as a number of Burgundian, northern French and Rhenish issues. The Sutton Hoo hoard, dated *c.* 627, is an 'eccentric hoard', in which thirty-seven different Merovingian mints including Provençal issues are represented. The Wieuward hoard from Frisia near Staveren, deposited about the same time as Sutton Hoo, maintains the pattern represented by the Escharen hoard, while the Burgundian hoards from Chissey-en-Morvan (sometimes called 'Buis') and St. Aubin, dating from *c.* 631 and *c.* 640 respectively, contain significant numbers of Provençal minted coins. The latter hoard was buried close to the death of king Dagobert of Neustria in 639. He had proved a powerful king in his early reign, but latterly the debasement of gold in all the issues of the Merovingian mints may be evidence of growing economic stress partly invoked by decentralised minting. This step-wise descent in the gold component of the alloys first becomes evident in the 630s, and the debasement of the coins becomes more marked the further north the mint from Provençe. If it was caused by inflation due to the decentralised proliferation of mints exploiting a limited bullion, as J. P. C. Kent has recently suggested, we must ask why the bullion was limited and why the debasement increased against distance from Provençe.[23]

The answer seems to suggest that 'Provençe's' access to eastern gold was decreasing as the Mediterranean trade decayed. Recent excavations in Italy are beginning to confirm this hypothesis[24] – one in no way contigent upon the Arabs in the sense Pirenne suggested, but instead a consequence of the Byzantine military and economic failure. Such a sequence of events, however, would have threatened Provençe's role as intermediary between east and west, and between north and south, and we might therefore predict the demise of this system once debasement became serious. Inter-regional trade alone may, to some extent, have redressed the loss of the Mediterranean input into the system.

The next major hoard from north-west Europe is from Crondall, Hampshire, dated *c.* 650. Next in the sequence is the hoard from Bordeaux dating from the very last years of the seventh century.[25] From Crondall to Bordeaux there is a clear process of inter-regional (interterritorial) movement or contacts manifested in the hoards replacing the Provençal system. But before considering this regionalisation and the emergence of other trading systems created as a result, we must examine the impact of the Provençal system on its branches northwards to Britain, north Germany and Scandinavia.

Anglo-Saxon contact with the Parisian courts of Neustria, for example, would certainly account for the Provençal coins in the St. Martin's hoard from Canterbury. There is a firm historical foundation for these contacts, since Charibert I, who reigned at Paris from 561 to 567 gave his only daughter Bertha in marriage to Ethelbert of Kent. This was a significant political step, putting Kent positively within the Merovingian hegemony.[26] It also heralded the first Christian missions to England. In both cases extensive contacts substantiated by gifts were inevitable. This period embraces the first phase of Rigold's chronology of the gold coinage of Anglo-Saxon England (see Chapter 6).[27] It was a phase during which the transalpine route was at its zenith, along which may have come the cowrie shells and Alammanic coins found in England (see above). It is difficult to know whether the switch from the transalpine to the Provençal system late in the sixth century affected the Neustrian system to Kent. But towards the end of the sixth and during the first quarter of the seventh century (Rigold's Phase II), when the Provençal system was at its zenith, there is greater evidence of directional trade emanating from the Paris basin. In particular, a significant number of northern French pots dating roughly from this period have been identified in Kentish cemeteries; their distribution diffuses outwards from a Canterbury-Sarre focus.[28]

Several points can be made about the trade. First, the earliest coins attributed to Quentovic were minted at about this time, suggesting that this emporium (see Chapter 3) was founded near Étaples to administer the cross-Channel trade to Kent and south-east England. Secondly, the rich, extensive cemetery from Sarre on the Wantsum Channel, not far from Canterbury, implies a small but comparable site on the English side of the Channel.[29] It contains not only a significant number of rich, male burials but also several accompanied by scales with weights – the medieval index of a merchant. The existence of these sites suggests that the system was more regularly administered, and we may therefore infer its socio-political importance.

The localised distribution of, for example, imported pots illustrates the redistributive process within Kent, these being some reciprocal token, in return perhaps for the produce which the Kentish king traded (the commodities are discussed in Chapter 6).[30] The distribution of imports beyond Kent may demonstrate the alliance-making process in action, possibly in a bid to acquire slaves as well as other commodities. The imported pottery distribution, like the distribution of Merovingian gold coins in south-eastern England, illustrates empirically Renfrew's directional trade model, although this peak, some distance from the source, appears to be rather squat and almost flat on top (see the discussion in Chapter 1).

The political significance of the system will not have gone unrecognised by the other Anglo-Saxon kingdoms. In this case the Neustrians seem to have traded only with Kent, while the Rhenish system emanating from the Austrasian court seems to have traded principally with East Anglia. For obvious political purposes, the routes were probably exclusive to each kingdom. Two trade partners might be politically invidious.[31]

Like the Kentish system, the route extending to East Anglia was maintained from the sixth century. The southern European switch in Mediterranean origin was significant only insofar as a different range of artifacts were shipped across the North Sea. The emergence of Quentovic and possibly Sarre is paralleled by the foundation of a mint at Dorestad on the Merovingian border with Frisia early in the seventh century (see Chapter 4 for a description of this site); and, as we have inferred in Kent, so in Suffolk there is accumulating evidence of a trading site to control the inflow of goods at an administered location. Excavations at Ipswich have recently identified an early seventh-century settlement broadly contemporary in date with the reign of King Redwald, remembered in all probability at Sutton Hoo.[32] The debris left by the traders confirms their Rhenish origins and once more emphasises the two very different systems that divided somewhere in central France.

But this Rhenish system was probably more concerned with trade to Frisia and further north to the Baltic than with the house of the Wuffingas. The number of middle Rhenish pots (probably products of the Vorgebirge kilns) in the late sixth- and early seventh-century contexts in Frisia is an eloquent manifestation of this trade route.[33] The Vendel period glasses from central Sweden, products of the Rhineland glass houses, also seem to substantiate this already pervasive trading.[34] Bruce-Mitford in his Sutton Hoo studies has drawn attention to the widespread contacts maintained by the house of Redwald. In particular, the artistic connections with south Scandinavia seem clear. The flow of goods around the North Sea in the early seventh century illuminates the multi-dimensional character of this great ship burial, as well as those equally rich assemblages in the contemporary Vendel graves in central Sweden.[35]

There is, then, by 650 some indication that the trading systems stemming from the Rhineland and the Paris basin had begun to regularise exchange which, intermittently, had been in existence since about *c.* 500, during the reign of Theodoric. To what extent the trade was dependent on trade partners, between the Neustrian kings and Kentish king is not clear, but the founding of trading stations, at which traders might pause seasonally, indicates the gradual growth and emerging complexity of the networks.

One further network stretching northwards demands attention. It is probable, though by no means certain, that the demise of the Provençal system induced the Aquitainian court to look elsewhere to satisfy its economy. With this in mind, we note that there is tenuous evidence of long-distance trading networks reaching out to the Irish Sea province as well as southwards to Iberia.

The current excavations at the royal site of Clogher in Co. Tyrone (in Northern Ireland) confirm an earlier impression that the Class A and B wares which stemmed from the Mediterranean in the later fifth and sixth centuries are in no way connected with the Class E ware (Merovingian-style) pitchers, pots and bowls. A sequence in the ramparts at Clogher makes this chronological distinction clear. Class E ware seems to originate in western France, but so far it has been discovered only in the Irish Sea province.[36] The date of these vessels is difficult to establish, though typologically a seventh-century horizon seems most likely. The exclusive character of these finds in the Irish Sea province suggests a directional trade, perhaps parallel with those preferring the Anglo-Saxon courts. The discovery in England of Aquitainian gold coins in Rigold's Phases I and II before *c.* 627 (see Chapter 6), even though some were probably transmitted down-the-line, makes an early seventh-century horizon improbable for this Irish route, where no coins of this kind have been found. The near-absence of

Aquitainian coins from Rigold's later phases seems to confirm this otherwise tentative hypothesis, suggesting that Class E ware must therefore be later than *c.* 627. But the virtual absence of any gold coins from Ireland stands in stark contrast to Anglo-Saxon England until *c.* 650, when there is a drying up of gold bullion on the continent. Notably, during the middle of the century Aquitaine seems to have been establishing a positive independence from the other Merovingian courts which may have been made possible by the development of other contacts, such as with Ireland.

The discovery of a possible trading site at Dalkey Island, near Dublin, which was apparently fortified in the course of its participation in this trade, indicates an element of administration in a system that probably began irregularly.[37] There is slight documentary evidence, however, to show that the Irish monks, in the midst of a cultural efflorescence, participated in this trading, and indeed at this time they seem to have traded dogs and leather near Nantes. The evidence seems to show that the system operated in both directions, though on a most inconclusive scale.[38] Wine was probably the main commodity traded to the Celtic communities, while the Aquitainians were probably in search of slaves.

The Bordeaux hoard dating from about 700 points to some contacts with Iberia,[39] but here we must recall Himley's homily on the dangers of numismatic evidence and await further archaeological data. The hoard also contained a range of Loire and northern French coins and possibly indicates the inter-regional character of the trade which had begun to emerge in late seventh-century Gaul. This is even more apparent in the Plassac hoard buried about 735 at a time when the Arabs were actually penetrating western France.[40]

Before reviewing the major systems from the later seventh century, we must allude briefly to the reasons for the growth of the trading networks from the end of the sixth century.

The proliferating local mints in the Merovingian kingdoms, even in the absence of major market-places, provide an explanation for the growing importance and scale of long-distance trade. The stabilised political framework created, in effect, by Clovis late in the fifth century eventually gave rise to a hierarchical fragmentation. By the late sixth century, when most of the mints were founded, this fragmentation was more than evident. The result was increased local demand (probably at hierarchical level) for goods which consequently required labour to increase local production. It is scarcely surprising therefore that at this date slave labour figures prominently in the few documentary sources.[41] It therefore appears quite likely that Merovingian trade was developed with the surrounding, peripheral and socially less complex societies. At present, however, such generalisations have little substance. The emergence of the labour shortage, contingent upon increasing localised demand, needs widespread testing in local contexts, but it remains clear that despite the decline of the Mediterranean world the indigenous

wealth of the Merovingian kingdoms and the territories beyond possessed real economic potential. The reform of the debased gold coinage
in the 680s, which Pirenne interpreted as a sign of Merovingian poverty,
has now been seen to be an economic policy aimed at mobilising the
regional economies of north-west Europe. This reform confirms the end
of Byzantine (and earlier Roman) influence in the west and marks the
start of a period of maximisation irrespective of the Arabs. Charlemagne's empire was to be the ultimate justification of the policy.

The North Sea basin

A sketchy political framework for the long-distance trade systems
becomes clearer from about the middle of the seventh century. Long-
distance trade appears to be forged by kings or their emissaries, while the
role of freelance traders is often difficult to assess (see Chapter 5).[42]
During this period, of course, the Frisians are known to have been the
pre-eminent entrepreneurs of north-west Europe. Yet their position, as
we shall see, has come to be disputed.[43]

From the mid-seventh until the later eighth century the North Sea
basin was largely isolated from the Mediterranean world. During this
period two major trade-systems operated spasmodically; effectively they
emanated from the Neustrian kingdom, focused in the Paris basin, and
from the Austrasian court in the Rhineland. They seem to have persisted
even after these two great courts coalesced under the Carolingians from
Pepin III onwards. We have already noted the minor Atlantic network
stemming from the Aquitainian court (see above), which appears to
have persisted independently of the Neustrian (Parisian) and Rhenish
systems until the early eighth century. At this time the Arabs invaded
southern France and seem to have undermined the socio-political basis
of the system, which in turn left the Irish Sea provinces isolated for
several centuries on the fringe of Europe.

As we have seen, the origins of the Carolingian system emanating
from the Rhineland date back as far as the late fifth or early sixth
century. The Rhenish system had grown more substantial in its scale of
activity early in the seventh century, though its importance in the second
and third quarters of the century is still difficult to assess. There are, for
instance, miscellaneous mid-seventh-century gold coins from eastern
and southern England, and some of the imported wheel-made pots from
East Anglia and the east Midlands may be attributable to this period.[44]
Clearly the crucial switch from a gold to a silver standard by Pepin of
Herstal in the 680s was made to enlarge this overseas trade, as well as to
reassert firm control on minting and presumably the economy as a
whole. But at this date Dorestad, the emporium at the mouth of the
Rhine, recently had been repossessed by the Austrasians. (The Frisians
had captured it in about 650 and were minting their own coins, some of

which are referred to as Dronrijp type after a Frisian hoard which contained a large number of them.) The Merovingian coin reform, though not absolute at once (Rigold has identified gold tremisses spanning the initial silver sceatta series),[45] appears to be connected with Pepin's recapture of Dorestad after the death of the peaceable Aldgisl, the harbourer of St. Wilfred in 678–9, and the accession of Radbod, an apparently bellicose king.

The recent excavations at Dorestad have established that its first major phase is at the end of the seventh century, and so we may associate it with Pepin's economic strategy.[46] We may expect, however, that Frisian command of the trade emanating from here was maintained, since under this Merovingian hegemony runic sceattas were minted, as well as Frankish coins. Moreover the earliest silver coins issued by king Wihtred of Kent, perhaps in about 690, not only tried to maintain parity with the continental weights and values, but clearly imitated the Frisian rather than the Merovingian styles. This is further indicated perhaps by the apparent absence of planning in the formation of Dorestad, a feature which, as we shall see in Chapter 3, is in total contrast to the other large emporia of the period. Indeed the farming element within Dorestad suggests that farmer-traders under a Frankish administration controlled and operated the trade.

In about 714, however, king Radbod annexed Dorestad once more on behalf of the Frisians and maintained a vigorous stand against the Merovingians until he was eventually defeated by Charles Martel, and the territory was brought permanently within the late Merovingian hegemony in about 719.[47] The trade activity of this first major period is not enormous: there are some Frisian sceattas from southern England, including a hoard from Aston Rowant, Oxfordshire, and possibly a few pots from Ipswich which may be attributed to this date. A number of English sceattas has been found at Domburg, a small Frisian trading station (see Chapter 4). From the Frisian islands it is difficult to ascertain the exact date of the late Merovingian pots found in several terps, while the discovery of a Madelinus tremissis minted at Dorestad, from a grave-mound in north-west Jutland, scarcely adds much to our poor perspective on Frisian trade along the North Sea littoral.[48] Equally some of the Merovingian, Frisian and Kentish coins found in the assemblage of thirteen coins at Dankirke near Ribe in Jutland may have been brought here during this formative period of trade, though these probably came as an assemblage in the second decade of the eighth century, or even later.[49]

The war waged by Radbod against the Merovingians must have disrupted trade, especially if much of it had been ceded to Frisian entrepreneurs, as the disparate documentary sources would imply. It is no surprise, then, to see the second quarter of the eighth century as a relatively moderate phase in the Dorestad coin-histogram published recently by Jankuhn (Fig. 6).[50] Rhenish artifacts of the period

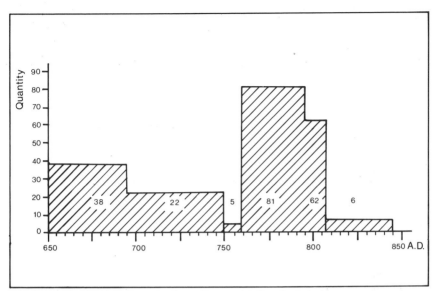

Figure 6 Histogram of the coins from Dorestad (after Jankuhn)

720–50, after the Merovingians had re-established control over the site, are only found in small numbers at Hamwih (Saxon Southampton) (see Chapter 4 for the quantity); some of the Ipswich vessels may date from this period also. The Dankirke collection, as stated above, includes a number of coins attributable to this period, including two Kentish sceattas (BMC 27 and 37) and at least two Frisian sceattas;[51] and from Haithabu, in a sunken-hut, there is a Wodan/monster sceatta of Frisian origin,[52] while from further north in Scandinavia there are a few Anglo-Saxon, Merovingian and Frisian objects possibly of this period. For example, from Kaupang there is an early Mayen ware vessel,[53] while from Helgö, the trading island in Lake Mälaren west of Stockholm, there is some metalwork and a Badorf-type pitcher.[54] There are very obvious problems, however, in asserting that some of these items were actually traded at this date, for the Viking-period hoards from Scandinavia illustrate the wide range (chronologically) of objects in use in western Europe in the first half of the ninth century. The occasional sceatta or brooch, for example, may easily have been taken along with a swag of ninth-century goods. In this respect pottery is perhaps the most objective indicator, being an item of limited intrinsic value and certainly not one the Vikings plundered for.

The low-level scale of trade in the third quarter of the eighth century also remains an enigma. This period spans the reign of Pepin III, when Austrasia and Neustria were united, and the early part of Charlemagne's reign. It was an auspicious phase politically. Pepin's reform of the coinage in the 750s may be a key to the enigma. Like the earlier Pepin's bold switch to a silver standard in the previous century, the reform was probably an attempt to centralise the issue of coinage. This implies that previously the regional economy was diffused and, in effect, concern with long-distance trade diminished.

We must now consider the major phase of Rhenish trade. The Dorestad coin-histogram (Fig. 6) clearly illustrates considerable activity towards the end of the eighth and during the first quarter of the ninth century.[55] The material evidence of this phase is impressive. For example, only twenty per cent of the Dorestad pottery is of native manufacture,[56] and the existence of at least two other Frisian trading-sites operating in conjunction with Dorestad is further evidence of the system's growth. This is the era of Charlemagne, and his European prowess clearly had an enormous impact on Carolingian trade. It may have been his treaty with the Danes, *c.* 782, which revitalised the Rhenish system northwards.

A period of intense international trade went hand in hand with Charlemagne's imperial ambitions, and by about 800 most of north Germany had been brought within the Carolingian orbit. As a result the new Danish king, Godfred, appears to have become alarmed. He broke the treaty with Charlemange in 808 by sacking a Saxon trading site called Reric, probably Alt-Lübeck.[57] (The Saxons had for some time been allied to the Carolingians.) Godfred brought the reluctant inhabitants of Reric to what the Frankish Annals describe as a new site in his territory. This was probably Haithabu, and the recent dendro-chronological dating of the earliest planned settlement on the shore of the Schlei points to Godfred as its architect.[58] Godfred, as the Annals tell us, was also the architect of the refurbished Danevirke, which was shown by recent excavations to have been an early eighth-century frontier rampart and ditch.[59] The new defences ran south of the emporium and emphasise the significance of long-distance trade in the war with Charlemagne. This enormous outlay is witness, beyond doubt, to the Arab trade which had begun to penetrate the Baltic from its Russian end and was to be of such importance to Scandinavian and, indeed, European history in the next two centuries.[60]

Godfred was soon assassinated, and some new treaty was made between the Danes and Charlemagne in his final years. As a result Reric was rebuilt and, it seems, fortified.[61] Of particular note are the considerable quantities of Rhenish artifacts from the early ninth-century levels at Haithabu and Ribe; these stand in stark contrast to the few such finds from the earlier south settlement at Haithabu.[62] The Carolingians, despite Godfred's bold stance, had effectively established a base on the Baltic.

Despite past claims by Erik Arup that the Frisians (on behalf of Carolingians) penetrated the lucrative commerce around the Baltic, however, the case remains insubstantial.[63] In contrast to the Haithabu and Ribe assemblages, there is very little Rhenish pottery from the Swedish and Norwegian emporia. There is a good deal of metalwork, but many of these pieces may well have been plundered, while in comparison with the Vendel-period glasses from Sweden there are remarkably few Viking-period glasses even from the thousand or more graves in the fields around the emporium of Birka.[64] Most of the glass from Kaupang, Paviken, Helgö, Birka and Wollin (on the Polish coast) survives in the form of sherds and includes fragments of Roman and migration-period vessels, which attest their wide-ranging origins. They were clearly acquired to make beads, which were strung together as prestige display gear of singular significance in the Viking and Slavic communities (see Chapter 6).[65] Charlemagne's drive to the Baltic, therefore, appears a little enigmatic (see Chapters 5 and 8).

Imported pottery from the Rhineland abounds not only in Dorestad but in Medemblik, to the north, on the route for Hamburg.[66] Similar vessels occur on the terp-sites on the North Sea littoral and have been found also in the small excavations at Emden, and in the merchants' *suburbium* beside the Hammaburg – Carolingian Hamburg. This Rhenish trade was also directed westwards via Domburg and en route for eastern England. In England, however, Rhenish artifacts are less frequent than those emanating from northern France, and together these distributions illuminate the competition that appears to have existed here in the trading of Carolingian luxuries.

What emerges is an economic efflorescence that happens to coincide not with Pepin's reform of the coinage, but with Charlemagne's in *c.* 793, when the silver content, and probably the intrinsic value of the denier, was increased. Was this international trading a response to strong centralisation of government, or was it the result of external forces which reinforced the hand of one of medieval Europe's most charismatic rulers? Godfred's destruction of Reric and the 'founding' of Haithabu leaves us in no doubt. The Arabic penetration of the isolated northern European communities was apparently as powerful then as it has been in the last decade. Charlemagne and Godfred, both directly and indirectly, seem to have been intent on partaking in the lively commerce.

The trade emanating from Neustria in the later seventh century, in contrast with the Rhenish/Frisian network, has received scant attention. Historically, the existence of the great fair at St. Denys outside Paris, founded in the seventh century and held early each October, provides some expression of the continued commerce encouraged by the late Merovingian court. The growth of Quentovic near Etaples is a further expression.[67] However, there has been a disappointing lack of archaeological data to substantiate this system. Moreover the location of Quentovic remains enigmatic. Only the excavations at Hamwih, Saxon Southampton, have to some extent redressed the balance.

The trade across the English Channel during the later sixth and early seventh century was directed at Kent. There is evidence to suggest that some goods were passed on to allied kingdoms, like Deira in the East Riding of Yorkshire.[68] A similar process may account for the rich assemblages found in several Isle of Wight cemeteries during the nineteenth century. The display objects span the transalpine phase and the early part of the Provençal phase. But equally they may have been brought directly to this small kingdom of Jutes (according to Bede)[69] from northern France. Whatever the truth, some early basis is provided for trading to the Hampshire basin, either indirectly (from the Kentish court) or directly.

The continuity of Neustrian trade-links with England in the third quarter of the seventh century has proved difficult to ascertain. The brief issue of Kentish gold coins tends at present to confuse the matter and suggests that imported gold had become scarce by the mid-seventh century.[70] However, king Wihtred's decision to follow the Merovingian switch to silver and his imitation of the Frisian sceattas point to some purposeful desire to maintain parity and thus commerce.[71] The restriction of the primary series of silver sceattas during the period *c.* 690–*c.* 725 to south-east England compels the conclusion that the earlier route was maintained, but until the trading site at Sarre or nearby Fordwich has been discovered we have little evidence with which to amplify the coin data.[72]

A new settlement was founded at about the beginning of the eighth century at Southampton, directly across the river Itchen from a less substantial settlement in the old Roman shore fort at Bitterne.[73] The extent of the first phase at Hamwih, Saxon Southampton, remains obscure, and it may have been fairly dispersed across the low-lying ground by the Itchen. It was evidently founded during the reign of king Ina (688–726), a warrior-king who forcefully consolidated the boundaries of Wessex and was the first in a series of eminent West Saxon leaders. The creation of Hamwih may well reflect the personal status he had acquired by the second decade of the eighth century.[74]

A recent chronological analysis of Hamwih has pointed tentatively to a minor primary phase when a few runic sceattas of the primary series were in circulation. This was followed by a major phase broadly correlating with the issue of the secondary sceattas; these date from *c.* 725–*c.* 750 and comprise debased silver coins minted in several places in southern, central and eastern England.[75] This was the period of Hamwih's zenith, and there is some likelihood that two types of secondary sceattas were minted in the settlement.[76] The phase is one of intense international activity, though among the many coins are notably a number of Mercian ones, which may be indicative of commercial interaction between the two kingdoms.[77] During the second quarter of the eighth century, however, Wessex had been drawn into the Mercian polity controlled by king Aethelbald. His hegemony included also London and Kent, and concentrations of secondary sceattas from both areas strongly point to his keen interest in cross-Channel trade.[78] The Hamwih activity, as well as these other concentrated coin-finds, suggest some formidable mobilisation of the Saxon economy in response to a late Merovingian commercial network extending from northern France.

A hiatus in the minting of sceattas in southern England, dating from the third quarter of the eighth century, has suggested a trading hiatus also. Moreover there is some temporal division between the second and third phases at Hamwih which seems to correspond to this phase.[79] Metcalf, the leading student of eighth-century coinage in England, has suggested some gross debasement of the sceattas between *c.* 725 and *c.* 750 leading to this cessation of trade.[80] Quite clearly this does not fit the model we have adopted in this book, for we have argued that the trade networks were controlled by the Merovingians from the sixth century. Moreover, as we shall discuss in Chapter 6, it fails to explain the next phase of heavier (Offan) coins with a high silver content. The collapse of the system rested on the collapse of the political framework on which it depended. The death of Aethelbald in 757, for example, may have been the cause; equally, an important factor may have been the death of Charles Martel.[81]

The explosion of Rhenish trade from the 780s was probably complemented by a re-emergence of the Neustrian system extending to Hamwih and other sites in southern England. The first series of Offan pennies were probably minted during the 770s by two Kentish kings bound to king Offa's growing polity. Their localised distribution reflects the extent of the primary series of sceattas a century earlier.[82] Similarly, the next phase of Offan pennies extended over an area as great as that covered by the secondary sceattas.[83] It was in this latter part of Offa's reign (757–796) that Hamwih once more came to life. The chronological breadth of this tertiary phase here is difficult to define. It may cover the last two decades of the eighth century and the first decades of the ninth century (see Chapter 8).[84] Its demise is a contentious matter, but it would appear to date from the beginning of the second quarter of the ninth century at the same time as Dorestad was in decline. As we shall see, it is significant that Hamwih's decline appears to coincide with the growth in West Saxon political prowess and the era of Egbert (Chapter 8).

This perspective of the Neustrian network is from the external point looking backwards. Moreover it is essentially based on the evidence from one extensively excavated site in conjunction with several numismatic analyses. Clearly there is an urgent need to test this framework with French data, while the discovery of Quentovic would be of critical value.

The Hamwih imported pottery, the Carolingian coin evidence and the documentary sources suggest that the system operated via three major emporia. These were Rouen (where excavations have found nothing), Amiens, which was accessible by river, and Quentovic. The catchment of these sites ranged from the southern Ardennes in the north to Normandy in the east. It is also likely that the old Roman roads linked Lorraine and possibly Alsace and Burgundy to these trading outlets on the Channel.[85] But more evidence is needed before this can be confirmed.

The ninth century witnessed the virtual demise of these two trading systems and the emergence of a vigorous regional trade, which is the subject of Chapter 9. First we must consider the components of these fifth- to ninth-century networks sketched here, beginning with their urban foci.

Chapter 3

THE EMPORIA

What eloquence could sufficiently extol the beauty of this church and the innumerable wonders of what we may call its city? For 'city' is the proper word to use, since [Kildare] earns the title because of the multitudes who live there; it is a great metropolitan city. Within its outskirts, whose limits were laid out by St. Brigid, no man need fear any mortal adversary or any gathering of enemies; it is the safest refuge among all the enclosed towns of the Irish.

Cogitosus, tr. L. de Paor[1]

Cogitosus, the eighth- or ninth-century biographer of St. Brigid, was in no doubt about the meaning of 'town' and 'city'. The monastic settlement of Kildare was a metropolis, in contrast to the other types of secular settlement such as farms, small nucleated 'villages' (see Chapter 7) and royal strongholds. Such sites were in all probability urban, for they were often royal centres as well as monasteries, and some provided the focus for fairs. Moreover within their encircling walls large populations seem to have been housed, though to what extent these artisans and farmers were working for the monks remains unclear. But was Kildare a town and were all monasteries towns? If we maintain that a town is either a market-place operating within what Carol Smith has termed an interlocking central-place system which is fully commercialised, clearly these were not towns. Liam de Paor, in discussing Irish towns, has arrived at the same conclusion; it is one that has several important implications.[2]

Many examples of these Irish 'cities' survive, enabling us to comprehend their scale without any difficulty (Fig. 7). Despite the great texts that emanated from them, and despite the prodigious descriptions of their huge size, we are not easily misled. Yet, when we consider the monasteries and royal settlements which were also foci of small artisan populations, as well as fairs, elsewhere in north-west Europe, a different issue appears to be raised. As these kinds of settlement were often in Roman centres, it is very complex. First there is the argument that these are not just monasteries, like for example

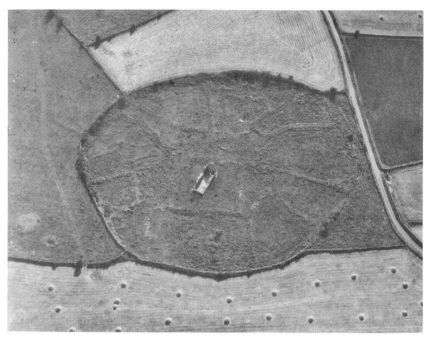

Figure 7 Aerial view of the monastery of Kiltiernan, Co. Galway, showing the internal divisions within the settlement (courtesy of Cambridge University collections)

Kildare, but cities maintaining the Roman tradition and therefore nodes in an interlocking central-place system. Secondly, the presence of an early medieval institution of this kind seems to indicate the continuity of the Roman market into early medieval times. These arguments are commonplace in the literature; their principal flaw is that the commercial system in which the Roman market-places operated simply does not exist in the period *c.* 500–*c.* 800. The industrial production and commercial transactions of these centres in towns like Tours, Trier, Cologne, Utrecht or Winchester was, in crude archaeological terms, scarcely more than that known from our Irish 'cities'.[3] Moreover archaeology has provided useful negative insights into these post-Roman centres. Towns like Tours, Trier, Cologne, Utrecht and Winchester contained many churches, rather like Clonmacnoise on the river Shannon, west of Kildare; but excavations have failed to reveal urban housing or, indeed, the artifactual data associated with regular marketing. The continued occupation of Roman centres by monastic communities in Anglo-Saxon England and Merovingia must not be misunderstood: these had become first and foremost the traditional seats of administrative power. In some of these walled old Roman centres, kings also maintained residences; yet again we must refer to our Irish model for a concrete perspective unembellished with the decayed trappings of Roman civilisation. And we must refer to the models presented in Chapter 1. Cologne, Paris and Winchester may have been urban, as we have argued that Kildare may have been. Yet they were not the foci of central-place markets and therefore not medieval towns as such until the ninth century at the earliest. It is a point that must be emphasised, and one which is central to this book.

Not all Irish monastic sites, we may suppose, were 'cities' even in the eyes of Cogitosus. Equally, not all monastic or royal centres maintained within the old Roman walls were urban. There was evidently a monastic settlement hierarchy just as there was a secular settlement hierarchy.

At the apex of the Anglo-Saxon settlement hierarchy were the residences of its peripatetic king. Sites like Yeavering, Northumberland, a *villa regalis* known as *Ad Gefrin* to its contemporaries, illustrates another feature of these institutional settlements. The excavator found not only the great halls befitting a royal centre, but a timber grandstand which, he calculated, held up to 300 persons.[4] The site shows that these institutional centres functioned as assembly points. The grandstand at Yeavering was probably constructed to accommodate a council debating the community's adoption of Christianity. Yet this spiritual or social aspect should not deter us from seeking some economic explanation for such gatherings. The social values of the kula ring, for example, concealed an important inter-island exchange network which was most unceremoniously enacted on the beaches while the great events were transacted with a flourish elsewhere.

In Carolingia, there is growing evidence to suggest that fairs were operated regularly at such institutional loci. There was clearly some demand for localised exchange. The celebrated October fair outside the gates of the Abbey of St. Denys, near Paris, is the best-known example.[5] However, a clause in the ninth-century *Capitulare de Villis vel Curtis Imperialibus* charges stewards on royal estates not to let workers dally at markets. It implies that some form of market was extant in Carolingia by this time. The pottery industries of the later Merovingian and Carolingian periods are also proof of some marketing of goods.[6] The scanty evidence points to *peripheral* marketing in which the institution operated intermittently and was far from firmly embedded in the fabric of society (see Chapter 1). Periodic markets outside royal palaces and fairs held close to abbeys may have been the mechanism of inter-regional and regional exchange, creating industrial specialisation such as pottery production on a limited scale. This was a partially commercialised system, and a major organisational step was required to enable this irregular exchange pattern to become fully commercial and thus influence every level of society. That is why, of course, when the change came it has seemed to many historians to have been a revolution, and indeed it was.

There were, then, urban communities in the period 500–800, but their scale was far more modest than anything we might term a 'city'. Their role as markets is difficult to determine from the sites themselves, where the trade was of an impermanent kind, but is most satisfactorily documented by the regional movements of artifacts. Such patterns must be more fully modelled so that the particular can be compared to an index.

The vestigial nature of these settlements – even of the Irish towns described by Cogitosus – has proved the nub of the problem for the early medieval archaeologist. One type of urban community from this period has been well-documented archaeologically and thus can be discussed in greater detail: the *emporia* – the sites which we briefly referred to in Chapter 1, in the context of Polanyi's definition of a port of trade and Hirth's of a gateway community. They are the nodes in the trading networks discussed in Chapter 2. We may define them as an expression of a territory's involvement in long-distance trade; they are always located at a junction most convenient to an international function. Moreover we may define them as primarily attributes of dendritic central-place systems. As long as these systems operated, their archaeologically most articulate manifestation is the emporia. When they failed to operate, some of the sites necessarily declined to a level consistent with the regional pattern of settlement, while some, as well-developed centres, appear to have been maintained as regional administrative centres. In the latter case, it is argued in Chapters 8 and 9, these sites were, for particular socio-political reasons, becoming the hubs of solar central-place systems as described by Carol Smith. In this chapter we are concerned only with the emporia that functioned in the trading systems described already, though an attempt is made in the next section to emphasise also the difference between an emporium operating in two different networks.

A typology

There are many contemporary references to emporia in north-west Europe. It is far from certain that the monkish writers were themselves clear about the term, but broadly it might be claimed that they were describing nodes in long-distance trade networks. Of course, they were slow to accommodate their terminology to socio-economic changes. Thus, as we have suggested above, the term emporium was used to describe sites that related to regional systems other than a dendritic one, especially if that site was experiencing only a functional transmutation.

Three types of site can be distinguished; the first two figure integrally in long-distance trade systems, while the third marks the transition to a solar central-place system. (All the sites mentioned in this section are described in detail in the next chapter, where references to specific topographic, chronological and economic points will also be found.)

A. The earliest and most vestigial of gateway communities are the fairs which were held on boundaries, mostly in fact on the coast. Foreign traders probably visited these for short periods annually or perhaps seasonally. They remain a rather enigmatic phenomenon, though perhaps we can find some functional similarity in the Icelandic medieval fairs.[7] The archaeological evidence for sites of this kind is slowly accumulating. The small-scale trading at Bantham (Devon) and Dalkey Island (Co. Dublin) may represent fairs of this type. The enigmatic sixth- to seventh-century trading settlement of Dorestad may have existed alongside a Merovingian villa in the environs of the later emporium. The excavations at Löddeköpinge in southern Sweden have revealed a very impermanent first phase with numerous sunken-huts of a rural character filled with alternate layers of wind-blown sand and occupation debris (Fig. 8). This may well prove to be the site of an annual fair. The excavator, moreover, has drawn attention to the clustering of the huts and speculates whether they might be the dwellings of boat-crews. He seeks a parallel at Haithabu, where the eighth-century phase comprises several similarly discrete clusters of structures, though here the sunken-huts are of a type which can be termed urban only insofar as they are not structures commonly found on rural sites (see below).

B. The second class of gateway community represents a major

Figure 8 Section through a sunken hut at Löddeköpinge, Sweden, showing the alternating bands of sand and occupation levels (courtesy of Dr. T. Ohlsson)

attempt to maximise this hitherto periodic long-distance trade. This class is distinguished by planned streets and dwellings which overlay the earlier clusters of structures. Ohlsson has identified this at Löddekö-pinge; it has been shown to occur at Haithabu, and recent excavations at Hamwih have shown that it occurred during the second quarter of the eighth century. At this juncture these settlements were housing not only increased alien traders but also a considerable native work force to provide for the mercantile community. Such centralised planning involving a large number of native artisans must have had considerable socio-economic implications.

C. When the trading rationale for the maximisation to type B declined, the emporium could either be abandoned or it could continue to function within a regional economy. The latter framework pre-supposes the emergence of some local diversification and the controlled encouragement of that diversification which was a result of the regional impact of the type B emporium. In that case, the site maintained its native work force and its ('partially commercialised') production level. (The shift to a 'fully commercialised' system was contingent upon the inception of a state-like control; see Chapter 10.) There would be few imports as a result of this economic strategy, though as its character changed and it became the seat of government, aliens would journey to it irrespective of trade-networks. If, as a regional central-place, it be-came politically significant, its defence would also be of much concern.

This model describes many of the Viking-period emporia in Scan-dinavia and Ireland. They began as trading-stations, but assumed an administrative function in the periods of fluctuating long-distance trade. The fortification of Haithabu and Birka, for example, at relatively late dates may be explained by this model (see Chapter 4). Certainly the paucity of traded material from Aarhus in the tenth century may be explained in part by its formation as a response to a new economic framework; the same may also be true of tenth-century Dublin.[8]

The early medieval emporia can be further defined as we have discussed in Chapter 1. There are the sites that functioned, in effect, as entrepôts on the coastlines of the primary (Merovingia/Carolingia) component of the long-distance trading systems and those that operated in the secondary components. In the primary entrepôts virtually only sellers were present, as they prepared to set off for their voyages to the emporia they served, where not only other sellers but as many buyers were also present.[9]

Location and control

All the emporia were placed on or near territorial boundaries, and all those we have discussed in this and the next chapter were located near or on coastlines. Many probably grew up from coastal fairs (type A), but none of the inter-regional fairs placed beside inland institutions appear to have grown to the scale of these coastal sites. (Inter-regional fairs are discussed again in Chapter 7 with reference to specific examples.)

In fact most of the emporia were located in sheltered places where the early medieval boats with their shallow draughts might be easily beached. The Carolingian sites, for example, were all some distance from the English Channel or the North Sea, with the possible exception of Domburg which was on an island. Hamwih, Sarre and Ipswich, as well as London, lay beyond their respective estuaries, where a smaller river met a principal one. Ribe in Denmark lay behind extensive coastal marshes on a small river; Haithabu is superbly sheltered in an inlet of the Schlei a short distance from the Baltic. Kaupang in Norway lay by a fjord; Löddeköpinge and Västergarn lay near the sea, while Helgö and Birka are islands in Lake Mälaren, which in effect is an inland seat that divides Sweden as well as giving access to the Baltic in the east.

Were the locations of these sites determined by their sheltered position and the ease with which boats might be beached at them? Or had these very sites already been chosen for precisely these reasons by courts for their own, previously limited, trading? We shall probably never be certain: it is a chicken-and-egg problem.

This coastal location, however, is a function of the socio-political reason for the trade. Dalton has cogently described the commercial rationale:

> . . . long-distance trade under aboriginal conditions was usually very different from modern commercial international trade. It was not a reflection of cost differentials; rather, goods were sought abroad that were not obtainable at home. It was not a continuous activity, but consisted rather of sporadic expeditions. It was typically confined to relatively few goods and there was no monetary standard linking together the different domestic systems of the traders . . . Usually each side traded for other goods or for treasure that was not ordinary commercial money. Except for specialist trading peoples like the Phoenicians and the Hausa, trade was rarely basic to livelihood. To import, not to export, was the prime impetus.[10]

As we have seen in the last chapter, the motive for the long-distance trade systems was the acquisition of prestige-goods, scarcities and, on occasions, slave labour, none of which was available in, for example, Carolingia. As we shall see in Chapter 6, it seems well established that the commerce was confined to few goods. The sporadic nature of the trading systems has also been alluded to. For political reasons, at least, the systems appear to have flourished and declined according to the trade-partnership extant between the leaders of the territories involved, though these partnerships may have operated within a wider political and economic framework.

Kings and chiefs, then, were instrumental in the trading-systems, which appear to have developed to a formal level from the directional trade between courts. Why this should have happened is not altogether clear, but it may be that the native king considered the alien traders a potential threat to his socio-political role. The traders might intercede between the king and his kinsmen, selling them goods that were vital to him[11] – goods that he issued as social transfers either to maintain some kinship relationship or as some tributary receipt for the very commodities that he passed on to the aliens. The shift of commercial activity from a court location to a coastal/frontier location suggests that a more continuous activity was in motion. It also suggests that the agents of the system had changed from alien court emissaries to alien traders from courts. Some regular (rather than irregular) arrangement was now envisaged. This to some extent is the emphasis of the letters exchanged between Charlemagne and Offa, late in the eighth century, though by then the trading system appears to have grown to some size and complexity.[12]

Peter Sawyer has written a perceptive essay on the interaction of kings and merchants in the early medieval period.[13] He demonstrates their strong association from the paucity of documentary sources. 'The king's direct interest', he writes, 'in men "who came across frontiers" is made clear in another late seventh-century law, from Wessex, in which it is declared that the king should receive a large part of the wergeld (the blood-price) of any stranger.' The laws of king Ina of Wessex issued early in the eighth century illustrate the disadvantages, legally, that an alien might experience once inland.[14] Here was a clear disincentive, and one republished in king Alfred's laws late in the ninth century. On many occasions the positive attempts to contain the activities of traders to a defined frontier location is made clear. One poetic example recalled in the thirteenth-century *Laxdaela Saga* occurs when Olaf, son of an Irish slave-princess, returns with Vikings to visit his unsuspecting grandfather. His companion, Orn, says: 'I don't think we have landed at a good place, for this is far from the harbours and market-towns where foreigners are supposed to have safe-conduct; and here we are, left high and dry like sticklebacks on a beach. I think I'm right in saying that under an Irish law they can confiscate all our goods, for they claim everything as flotsam even when the sea has ebbed less from a ship than it has here.'[15] And, just as they predicted, trouble ensued, though ultimately all was happily concluded when Olaf and his grandfather were made to recognise one another. Finally, we should allude to another West Saxon incident. 'This responsibility of the king's agents for merchants,' writes Sawyer, 'provides the background for Aethelweald's account of the first Viking attack on Wessex: when Beaduheard, the king's *exactor*, heard that three ships had arrived he quickly rode "to the

port, thinking they were merchants rather than enemies, and commanding them imperiously he ordered them to be sent to the royal vill, but he
and his companions were straightaway killed by them." '[16]

The historical evidence for royal control of long-distance trade either
directly or through agents is widely confirmed in the early medieval
period. The king of Wessex appears to have possessed a *villa regalis* at
Hamwih; one existed either in or near Ipswich; Bede tells us that the
king of Kent held property in London late in the seventh century. The
Carolingians had agents in Quentovic and Dorestad, while king
Godfred's remarkable creation of the settlement at Haithabu has
already been reviewed (see Chapter 2). Blindheim has alluded to the
king of Vestfold's control (? and local residence) at Kaupang; and the
kings of Uppland quite clearly kept a firm surveillance on the commerce
at Birka.[17] Proving, or indeed confirming, this archaeologically is
difficult. A structural hierarchy within the settlement has to be
established, or some evidence found of major organisational control.
The *hochburg* at Haithabu and the comparable site at Birka may
provide evidence in the former category,[18] while the marked organisation
of streets, for example, is a sign of royal or chiefly authority.

The incidence and distribution of coinage, as well as their mint-
marks, provides a powerful indicator of centralised control over long-
distance trade at this period. Equally, the fluctuations in mint control
during the late Merovingian and Carolingian periods provide one
possible explanation perhaps for the similar fluctuations in the trade-
systems. Decentralised or uncontrolled minting clearly undermined
royal authority, as Charlemagne's reforms to counter it tend to
demonstrate. It was this authority that was unquestionably the motor
for the long-distance trade.

From an early date the church was almost as economically motivated
as the secular hierarchy. The constant raids by Vikings on major
monasteries illustrate the immense wealth that had been collected by
the early to mid-ninth century.[19] The location of Europe's greatest fair
at the gates of the Abbey of St. Denys illustrates their mercantile
interests. So does the mercantile gathering that grew outside the
bishop's palace at Verdun, as eunuchs were taken south to the slave
markets of Spain during the mid-ninth century.[20] Similarly, we may
point to the bishop of Utrecht's property in Dorestad and Medemblik,
as well as the prominent role of the missions in Haithabu and Ribe.[21]
And missions were forging a new path to the Baltic, in company with
merchants.

It is easy to over-emphasise this aspect of Christianity, since most of
the sources were written by monks. Yet, just as Christianity divided the
social functions of kingship, so it split the economic role (see Chapter 10).
The archaeology of early medieval monastic sites in the British Isles has
demonstrated their industrial significance beyond all doubt. Workshops
have been found in recent excavations at Jarrow and glass kilns at Burgh

Castle and Glastonbury.[22] Kilns were also found at the Irish monastery of Nendrum, and slag from settlements as remote as Skellig Michael (Co. Kerry) in the Atlantic illustrate the concern with metal-production for agrarian tools as well as jewellery.[23] These industrial activities illuminate Cogitosus' urban perspective of the Irish monastic community cited above. Kathleen Hughes has further confirmed it by asserting that the *Hisperica Famina* (an Early Christian text) is a kind of tract on the monastic economy.[24]

Finally, the church was occasionally permitted to issue coins in Middle Saxon England. C. E. Blunt has shown that one group of the Offan pennies minted late in the eighth century were probably issued by Iaenberht, archbishop of Canterbury (the first of a series of pennies issued by Saxon archbishops of Canterbury).[25] The economic power of the church is here illustrated; for Offa, in fact, was known to have been on bad terms with this archbishop. Other late Merovingian, Carolingian and Saxon examples exist to amplify this one, thus effectively dismissing any claim that the coins were minted merely for social purposes like the payment of Peter's Pence to Rome. Clearly there was a significant economic motive.

Archaeology

In the case of types A and B, the archaeology should be highly distinctive. Since traders were in residence for periods ranging from a week to whole seasons (or even years), the artifactual evidence should be dominated by traded materials, as well as by materials that the traders might bring with them in anticipation of a long stay. There should also be a detectable pattern of artifacts used as media of exchange lost in the process of trading. We must also examine the native aspect of such a settlement. Once the community grew to any size, food would have to be brought to the settlement in a well-organised fashion.[26] The native artisans would also be required to construct dwellings and store-houses and to provide basic necessities such as nails, wood-working equipment and perhaps clothing. We must also examine the demographic side of the emporia: was it just boat crews that were visiting, or is there evidence of farmer-traders bringing their families.[27]

In the most vestigial type of emporium, the type A, imported artifacts were relatively few by comparison with those found in the type B emporium. Haithabu provides a suitable illustration: the eighth-century 'south settlement' produced virtually no imported pottery, while the planned settlement created by king Godfred abounds in imported ceramics.[28] Imports are also scarce at Löddeköpinge and at Helgö in the early phases. By contrast, there is no marked lack of imports in the vestigial primary phases at Hamwih and Ipswich. There are two points to be reviewed here. First, we must consider whether those settlements lacking imports, like the 'south settlement' in Haithabu, were not emporia at all, but merely coastal villages which were developed at a later date. Certainly, the only case for eighth-century Haithabu is its location and the urban, as opposed to rural, pit-houses which were excavated there.[29] Secondly, the presence or absence of imports will be conditioned by such factors as length of stay, the nature of local artifacts and the intrinsic value of the artifacts themselves.

The same factors will, of course, condition the presence or absence of imports in the larger type B settlements. Here, however, the semi-permanent nature of the community may well result in the limited and irregular trading of artifacts to native craftsmen, which will create a spatially more extensive spread of imports across the settlement. Increased trade should also mean increased breakage and loss of imported goods. It seems most likely, however, that the imported artifacts which dominate the emporia assemblages were once equipment brought by the traders for their own use.[30] We need only reflect on the imperial attitude to trading-stations in the recent past to find cultural values most forcefully represented. These are literally the last outposts of imperialism. Of course, this will depend on the nature of the native equipment, as well as on the room available in the traders' boats. Pottery is a useful index in this instance. Probably only certain types were traded (though these may have been used by the traders themselves); and there is a limit to a pot's lifespan, so it would seldom, we assume, have been subject to down-the-line processes. Roman ship-wrecks have provided examples of the pottery used by traders of wine (in amphorae), while the Mayen pots from an eighth- or early ninth-century wreck in the Rhine provide an illustration from the early medieval period.[31] (Mayen pots are seldom found on settlement sites other than emporia beyond the catchment area of the Mayen industry itself, located near Coblenz in the middle Rhineland.) A Rouen-type cooking-pot was one of the few finds from the early tenth-century Graveney boat (see Chapter 5); this type is frequently found in Hamwih at an earlier date.[32]

How can we distinguish the traders' pottery from traded pottery? Much depends, of course, on the range of wares from which it was drawn. If the industry was a highly centralised one, as was the case from the eighth and ninth centuries in the Rhineland, a distinction may be difficult to make. But if the traders were drawing on a number of smaller kiln-centres, or on domestic industries, their wares will probably be more varied. The nature of this variability warrants further statistical research. At Hamwih and Ipswich, for example, there is a marked variability in the imports, many of which come from northern France, where many small kilns (regionally spaced) were presumably supplying courts and monasteries as well as the emporia and toll-stations.[33] The traders were evidently bringing their own cooking-pots and wine-pitchers so that their cuisine could be effectively made without using the crude native, Middle Saxon, wares. In these two assemblages virtually no pot is matched by another, so great is the variability. By contrast, the traders who were operating in Dorestad, Ribe and Haithabu, for example, were supplied by the centralised Badorf-type kilns located in the Vorgebirge hills in the middle Rhineland (Fig. 22). These kilns mass-produced wares in limited forms, so the variability tends also to be limited.[34]

Some pottery that was traded as a commodity can be readily identified, but this is not always the case. The relief-band amphorae made in the Vorgebirge kilns are an obvious distinctive type that held

Figure 9 Relief-band amphora: 53 cm high, 40 cm at its broadest (courtesy of the Rheinisches Landesmuseum, Bonn)

wine – one of the luxury trades (Fig. 9). We must assume that their incidence in the emporia was infrequent, and that those found were the few broken in transit or traded to native artisans operating within the settlement. But there has been a long-standing European tradition of trading pottery accoutrements with wine. This presumably heightened the ritualistic aspect of the consumption of this luxury commodity. Black- and red-figure ware vessels are classic first-millennium B.C. examples of the trade, while there are many later medieval examples. In the later medieval period, however, the distribution of these types of pottery coincides with mercantile communities, and we may suspect that the traders themselves liked to possess certain fine wares as well as more utilitarian forms. This is well illustrated by the distribution of Tating ware during the period with which we are concerned.

Figure 10 Tating ware jug from Birka, Sweden (grave 551) (courtesy Statens Historiska Museum, Stockholm)

Tating ware is a distinctive Carolingian pitcher-type, typologically unique, which was decorated as a rule with tinfoil applied in cross and lozenge shapes (Fig. 10). It was undoubtedly the finest pottery available in north-west Europe in the period between *c.* 770 and *c.* 825.[35] The cross motif and its initial discovery in pagan graves in Sweden led to the suggestion that it was used by the missionaries active around Birka early in the ninth centuy. This ware has been found on sites as far away as

Russia and England, however (Fig. 10). Its most frequent context is in emporia: at Dorestad, Hamwih, Ribe, Haithabu, Kaupang and Birka. Moreover imitations have also been found at these sites. The obvious conclusion seems to be that this widely traded ware was made at a centre in the Rhineland probably operating under monastic patronage and was traded as a fine, prestige ware that possessed Christian implications. Hence it may have been prized by traders, missionaries and pagans alike as, in a sense, a primitive valuable (cf. p. 108).

Tating ware is one most obvious traded type because it has occurred in all classes of settlement including the emporia. Another pottery type, the Class 14 black ware, frequently found at Hamwih, has also been found on a wide range of settlement sites. Again, we can deduce that the traders retained some of these for their own use.[36]

Clearly the statistical data on variability and quantities of pottery will prove valuable when we model the underlying regularities inherent in long-distance trade. Moreover the pattern of finds from within the settlements will also prove interesting, and will illuminate the extent to which traders were exchanging imports with artisans in the settlement.

The theoretical implications of coinage and the nature of early medieval currency are discussed in some detail in Chapter 6. In brief, where coinage exists we should assume its loss to be consistent with the frequency of trading activity. This, however, will be conditioned by the intrinsic value of the coins themselves. First, we should only expect low-value coins to be lost; stored bullion, if lost, we should expect to discover in monastic or royal contexts rather than in the traders' zone in an emporium. Secondly, with so many weight changes during the early medieval period, we must be most sceptical in comparing coins of one period with those of another. For example, the intensity of activity at Hamwih in the period *c.* 725–750 is similar to that during the period *c.* 790–825. But more than five times as many sceattas from the first period have been found compared with pennies dating from the later period. Such a comparison has enormous implications in any interpretation of the large numbers of coins from Dorestad, for example (Fig. 6).[37]

The topography of these early medieval type B urban settlements is becoming clearer as a result of open-area excavations. Streets laid out on a grid-plan have been found at Haithabu and Hamwih (in contrast to this is the less well-planned design of Dorestad, which we have yet fully to explain). In these sites, the tenemental divisions seem to indicate the existence of the property divisions sometimes alluded to in surviving charters. At many of these sites the building programme appears to have been transacted over areas unusually large by later medieval standards, and much space was allocated, for example, to the ninth-century (?) merchants in Haithabu. The widespread digging of pits in Hamwih and Ipswich for clay extraction or rubbish disposal perhaps suggests that only a low premium was placed on land; the settlement might always be

Figure 11 Model of a farmhouse found in the excavations at Dorestad (courtesy of R.O.B., Amersfoort)

expanded.[38] But our present understanding of this early urban topography is far from clear. For example, in several of the emporia there is a confused pattern of artisans' buildings. Workshops dominate the jetty area at Kaupang, while a smith's house and furnace have recently been identified near the shore in Hamwih. It remains to be seen whether artisan and traders' quarters actually existed, or whether there was a more fluid arrangement.[39]

The urban structures, where they exist, vary considerably. The Dorestad complex has been extensively revealed; Professor van Es claims that many of the structures are small farms that have parallels on rural sites (Fig. 11). Only the wharf-front buildings stand out as urban in the sense that they do not conform to the rural pattern. These have been found packed into the restricted water-front space. The Haithabu architecture is also well-preserved. Essentially two types of building have been excavated: sunken-huts and small timber halls (Fig. 12). The sunken-huts with corner fireplaces are more substantial than the Jutish *grubenhäuser*, which at this time were generally outhouses or workshops; the small partitioned halls, by contrast, are very different structurally and much smaller than the long-halls frequently depicted in the epic poetry and well known from village excavations. These Haithabu houses, in fact mark the start of a tradition of urban buildings quite distinct from rural ones.[40] The small sub-rectangular cottages from Kaupang, Norway, cannot be fitted into the Viking-period vernacular architecture; nor can the dry-stone walled buildings from Helgö (Fig. 20) which had sunken-hut outhouses, but this is principally because there

have been too few excavations on domestic sites in these areas. At
Löddeköpinge the sunken-huts have been subjected to rigorous analysis
by Ohlsson, who concludes that these are probably dwellings – and, we
might add, of a type often paralleled in Scania and, to the west,
in Denmark.[41] The Anglo-Saxon houses in Hamwih and Ipswich are
barely known. Philip Holdsworth has recently published a boat-shaped
structure from Hamwih and looks for its origins 'in trade links with the
Low Countries and the Rhine mouth'.[42] This is perhaps a little doubtful
and it remains to be seen whether a distinctive urban architecture
developed here as in Haithabu in response to central planning
requirements.

Finally, on the subject of houses, Foote and Wilson remind us that
many of the ships' crews may have slept in their boats, while traders may
have erected tents or shacks in an encampment around the permanent
nuclei of the emporia.[43] This is evidently a conclusion based on later
descriptions of such settlements, but it urges us to be wary of the data. In
particular, if correct, it suggests that the artisans in the settlements
possessed a great deal of imported equipment. Only excavations round
the edges of the emporia will satisfactorily test the hypothesis.

Chapter 7 reviews the industrial production in the emporia within its
regional rather than international dimension, in an attempt to model
the supply of food to the urban community. Clearly industrial
production and food-production are two aspects of these sites which are

Figure 12 Reconstruction of a Haithabu house at Moesgard, Denmark (courtesy of the
Forhistorisk Museum, Moesgard)

particularly well-documented, and each forms a significant step in the evolution of a market-based society.

The analysis of the skeletal data from most of these sites is still in progress, so only provisional remarks can be made on the nature of the urban populations. Stolpe excavated more than a thousand graves at Birka – just over half the cemeteries that lie around the site. Of these some 130 are accompanied by one or more weights of a kind used by merchants on their balances, suggesting that one-tenth of the sample may have been traders of one kind or another.[44] (Only three graves contained balances.) We must remember, however, that the site was used over some two hundred years by persons with a life-expectancy of 30–40 years. The fluctuating pattern of occupation makes the calculation of a resident population somewhat speculative.

Several thousand graves are also known at Haithabu – possibly as many as 5,000. Klavs Randsborg has calculated that this represents a population of about a thousand, a number eight to ten times larger than the rural and royal settlements examined in Denmark.[45] Herbert Jankuhn's excavations of one cemetery at Haithabu revealed 41 men, 23 women and 16 children.[46] The number of women in the settlement seems to have been restricted, though families were evidently present.

Three small cemeteries and a number of isolated inhumations have been found in Hamwih, as well as a large cemetery containing 76 persons of whom all but five were adults. Similar large cemeteries have been found in Dorestad, where more than sixteen hundred bodies have been excavated. Furthermore, extensive cemeteries containing many hundreds of graves have been found recently at Löddeköpinge.

Three points emerge from the preliminary data. First, by early medieval standards these were truly urban communities. Secondly, the native element in the cemeteries examined to date, though difficult to interpret, seems very high, and aliens and merchants seem relatively few. Thirdly, the grave goods from Haithabu and Kaupang, as well as those from Helgö and Birka, emphasise the wealth pertaining to the merchants whose last journey was to these emporia. Their grave-goods alone begin to illuminate the nature of the commodities traded in these urban communities.

Ultimately the populations of these emporia will prove useful indices for their comparison. The present means – comparison of the extent of settlement – is notoriously difficult. Fig. 13, however, is a summary attempt at such a comparison to enable some very crude perspective of scale to appear. It shows, for example, that the English emporia are far larger than those better known from Scandinavia. Hamwih and Ipswich are in the order of 50 to 100 ha respectively, while Haithabu and Birka are within defences enclosing 24 and $11\frac{1}{2}$ ha respectively. The comparison also emphasises the difference in scale between type A and type B. Compared with sites in the order of 12 to 100 ha, in the case of the type B emporia, Dalkey Island is no more than $\frac{1}{2}$ ha; the eighth-century

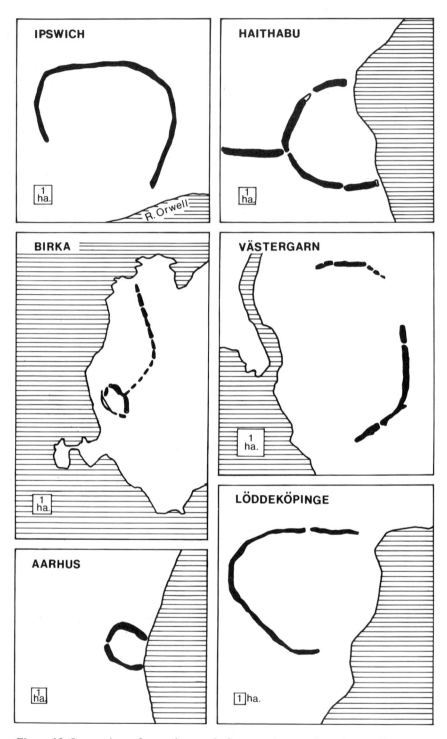

Figure 13 Comparison of several emporia from northern and north-west Europe

occupation at Haithabu is hardly any larger, while the first phase of Löddeköpinge is only about 2–3 ha.

Evolution

We have seen that the emporia were an expression of administered long-distance trade, which in the case of the examples beyond Carolingia was also an expression of imperial needs. The rationale to import rather than export, the converse of our modern long-distance trading system, was the underlying motive of this early medieval commerce. We have outlined how these communities were encouraged by royal patronage once the scale of court-directed commerce had crossed a certain threshold and was, we believe, a threat to the socio-political system if not legally confined to some neutral location. The irregular exchange networks initially operating at nodes that were little more than fair-grounds has been discussed in this and the previous chapter. The creation of the type B emporia, with their planned character, marks a major socio-political action best modelled by the sudden flip-over point in a catastrophe-theory model, such is the speed with which it appears to occur.[47] The development was evidently aimed at maximising the hitherto irregular trade, but it meant that the artisans supplying the settlement's needs were now party to the commerce itself. Moreover such a move inevitably undermined the previously centralised regional exchange systems. The implications for kingship were considerable; it had to adapt itself to a new socio-economic environment. Clearly the Anglo-Saxon kings succeeded in this, while arguably the Scandinavians were less successful.

Chapter 4

A GAZETTEER OF EMPORIA: IN OTTAR'S FOOTSTEPS

And from Sciringes-heal, he [Othere] said that he sailed in five days to that port which is called Aet-Haethum [Haithabu] which is between the Wends, and Saxons, and Angles, and belongs to Denmark.
Introduction to King Alfred's translation of Orosius[1]

This chapter presents a brief survey of the emporia discussed in the last chapter. It is, however, an archaeological survey, and as such it is limited to those sites where artifacts have been found corroborating documentary sources, or where either field-surveys or excavations have established the presence of the settlement. Its scope is also limited in two other respects. First, only sites concerned with the trade-routes discussed in Chaper 2 are considered here. These comprise Irish, French, British, Low Countries, west German and Scandinavian sites. The Slavic sites and the settlements on the great trade-route through eastern Europe to Byzantium or the Caspian Sea have not been included. These sites, including Szcecin and Wollin in Poland, Grobin and Alt-Ladoga in Russia, belong to the Russian route southwards. Secondly, the sites described here are those that operated from the sixth to the ninth century. It will be apparent that certain sites only developed during the course of the ninth century and were most active in the decades after 900. Their inclusion is perhaps slightly arbitrary, but as they are often referred to in other chapters they seem to deserve some description here. But most emphasis is placed on the description of sites which functioned as nodes in dendritic central-place systems; if settlements functioned primarily in a solar central-place system, marketing urban-based products, they are not relevant to the discussion. Therefore some of the entries will appear cursory, even though extensive excavations may have been carried out.

The aim is simply to provide a guide to the extensive literature, and thus to amplify the largely abstract discussions which have focused on these sites. Moreover it may be viewed as a contemporary tourist's guide in the manner of Ottar, the Norwegian who visited king Alfred's court, or Al-Tartushi who passed through north-west Europe in the mid-tenth century (and was most happy at the prospect of returning to civilised Cordoba).[2]

Dalkey Island

Dalkey Island has been associated with the dun of *Setga* in the tenth-century poem *Lebor Gabala* (the Book of Conquests). It lies just off the coast of Co. Dublin, to one side of the Irish Channel. Excavations in the 1950s were concerned with the promontory fort enclosing the quarter of a hectare that lies on a northern tip of the small island.[3]

This promontory was an important Bronze Age site, which had been abandoned and was not reoccupied until either the later fifth or the sixth century. The excavations revealed a midden from this period which contained imported Bii and Biii amphora sherds as well as imported glass and a range of bronze pins. It dates the occupation to the phase of Mediterranean trade which took a course around the Iberian peninsula to the sub-Roman and Celtic communities (see Chapter 2). The next phase includes another midden, as well as the fortification of the promontory itself. The excavator dated these two phases by the presence of E-ware, the (?) Aquitainian imported pottery. As we have seen in Chapter 2, this probably dates from the seventh century.

Who exactly controlled Dalkey Island is not clear, but we must bear in mind its strategic situation near the mouth of the Liffey, as well as the important route that lead from near Dublin to the west coast.

Bantham, Devon

A scatter of imported pottery has been found on Bantham Head, a low promontory near the mouth of the river Avon. The site lies nearly 10 km west of Kingsbridge and was found late in the ninteenth century. B-ware amphorae of the late fifth or the sixth century – a double-edged comb, whetstones, spindle wharfs and a spearhead – were collected. This was evidently a vestigial kind of settlement, perhaps rather like those of similar date at Topsham near the mouth of the river Exe and at Luce Sands in Gallowayshire.[4]

Hamwih, Saxon Southampton

Hamwih occupies the low ground by the side of the river Itchen. It is located to the east of the modern and medieval town, which lies at the end of a gravel spine that runs down the Southampton peninsula. The Middle Saxon settlement seems to have been formed by a lagoon that developed behind a sand spit at the mouth of the Itchen. The site lies almost opposite the Roman fort at Bitterne, where sub-Roman occupation is attested and where a few Early to Middle Saxon artifacts as well as a Christian cemetery have been found.[5]

Hamwih was first noticed in the nineteenth century when brick-earth diggers revealed Saxon pits containing numerous coins. O. G. S. Crawford drew attention to the likelihood of a historical site here and encouraged the first excavations after the Second World War. The 1946–50 excavations established the wealth of Saxon and Carolingian material in trenches some distance from the river. The size and extent of the site, however, was firmly illustrated by the excavations that began in the late '60s and are still in progress. These show it to have been 40 or more hectares in area and to have stretched from the shore-line to the slopes of the gravel spine in the area known as Kingsland. Open-area excavations have revealed parts of a planned street-system with gravel roads running in an easterly direction towards the Itchen. The streets all appear to have been re-metalled at least once, though pits cut into them suggest that they fell into disuse as the settlement contracted, presumably in the ninth century. Tenement divisions have also been identified, many of which enclose plots full of pits. Some of these pits have been shown to have remained in use for many years. Several post-built structures have been found, including an alleged boat-shaped house; also a barrel-lined well, the most elaborate of its kind. At least four cemeteries have been located; in the largest of these is a timber structure, possibly a church. Furthermore, the present church of St. Mary's, situated in the centre of the Saxon settlement, may be Saxon in origin.

The imported pottery attests extensive northern French contacts, while there are also groups of imported glass-ware, metalwork and bonework. The faunal studies have already demonstrated a preponderance of aged sheep of an abnormally large kind in the assemblages from the pits, while an important aspect of the diet was the Solent marine resources, with large numbers of eels and oysters, for example. Local industries in the heart of the settlement are shown by vestigial evidence to have included potting and metalworking; a bone-comb maker also lived in the settlement at one time. Glass sherds suggest the existence of glass bead-making, but this is far from certain.

The numerous sceattas and few pennies indicate an eighth- and ninth-century settlement which was perhaps abandoned in favour of the more defensible promontory. Recent attempts to refine this chronology have advocated a decline in the second quarter of the ninth century (see Chapter 8 for a review of the evidence). Further interest in the site has also been generated recently by the debate about the site's name. Hamwih seems to have been the seldom-used Carolingian name for the settlement, while the West Saxons referred to it and the royal site, located either here or on an adjacent part of the peninsula, as Hamton. Strictly speaking the latter name should prevail, but the terminological debate has arisen because of the familiarity of Hamwih in the literature; hence it is used throughout this book. This place-name discussion has confirmed the more interesting documentary references to the site which include a mention of St. Willibald embarking for the continent, as well as Viking attacks. The most interesting documentary insight, however, is that the settlement had lent its name to the shire by 755, indicating its bureaucratic as well as mercantile function in Wessex.

Sarre, Kent

Sarre lies to the north-west of Canterbury across the now dried-up Wantsum Channel on the Isle of Thanet. There is some evidence to suggest that this was the emporium serving Kent, at least from the sixth to the eighth century. An extensive and exceptionally rich cemetery of sixth- to seventh-century date was found here. John Brent excavated nearly three hundred graves during the nineteenth century,[6] the majority of which were of males. These inhumations were accompanied by fine pieces of jewellery, imported pottery, Merovingian and Byzantine tremisses. Brent also pointed to the existence of two remissions of toll granted by Kentish kings to certain boats coming to Sarre in the eighth century. Sarre was maintained as a minor ferry-crossing point until as late as the Elizabethan era, for Leland visited it then.

Sarre, like Southampton, would have been a very sheltered beaching point. Like Southampton, it had double tides, and also access to the heart of the kingdom of Kent along the river Stow. But until the gently undulating fields around the modern hamlet are archaeologically examined we shall remain uncertain of its significance. Fordwich, which is mentioned also in the toll remission of 726 by Eadbert of Kent, may have functioned as the emporium, being barely 5 km from Canterbury on the river Stow. Equally, the old Roman forts at Reculver and Richborough at either end of the Wantsum Channel have notably produced a large number of Middle Saxon coins; and these sites cannot be ruled out as emporia, though each is known to have been a monastic centre. Finally, this network of sites was almost certainly superseded by Sandwich to the south of Richborough as the Wantsum Channel silted up. Exactly when this occurred is not known.

London

Early medieval London remains an enigma. Bede records that it was the 'trading centre for many nations' in 604; he also mentions the sale of Imma, a slave, to a Frisian merchant in London in 679. Bede refers to royal and ecclesiastical property here, while the bishop of Worcester in the early eighth century is permitted tax-exemption on his trading within the emporium.[7] Archaeology in fact has gone some way towards contradicting this picture. Extensive post-war excavations by Professor Grimes found virtually no evidence of Middle Saxon occupation within the Roman city. Similarly, more recent campaigns by the Department of Urban Archaeology of the London Museum have failed to find pre-ninth-century data.

At the time of writing, the accumulated evidence points to a series of 'farms' along the banks of the Thames. These have been found at the Savoy Hotel, at the back of the Treasury in Westminster and at Battersea. Further down the Thames sites have been discovered at Staines as well as the royal mill at Old Windsor. At each of these sites a few imported sherds have been found, as well as Ipswich-type ware, attesting contact with northern France and coastal contact with East Anglia.

Besides the documentary evidence, the existence of a major mint here has long been discussed, producing coins from the late seventh century onwards.

The recent excavations at New Fresh Wharf and elsewhere within the City indicate major reoccupation of this area during the ninth century. The excavators favour an early-to-mid-ninth-century date, though only the dendrochronological evidence from the wharf structure will confirm it.

Ipswich

Ipswich lies at the confluence of the river Orwell and the tributary river Gipping, commanding a great estuary that opens out into the North Sea (Fig. 14). This was an important route in later prehistory and during the Roman period, as a wealth of imported finds from the Gipping valley attests. Moreover the settlement is situated about 20 km west of Sutton Hoo, the burial ground, it is believed, of the Wuffingas of East Anglia.

Because of continued occupation on this low-lying terrain, excavations have been very restricted. An early date for the site was first suggested by the extensive early seventh-century cemetery found by Mrs. Layard in Hadleigh Road, 4 km to the west of the modern centre (Fig. 14). This is a rich example of a major cemetery of the period, though the early-twentieth-century excavation has limited the full interpretation of the burial ground in the light of the recent excavations.[8]

The first Middle Saxon occupation was established by West's excavations in Cox Lane during the 1950s. These proved the existence of an active settlement probably with a pottery industry, and with trade connections across the North Sea. The full potential of the settlement was not fully appreciated, however, until the present programme of research by Wade from 1974 onwards, when the extent and dating of the emporium were established. During the 1960s there was a reluctance to

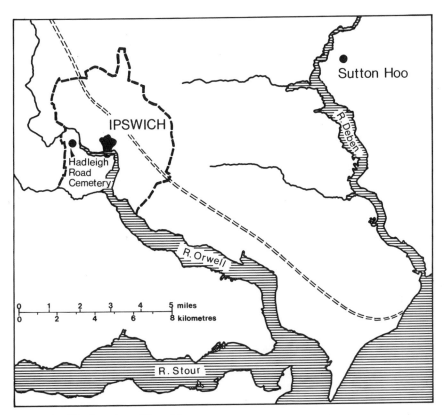

Figure 14 The location of Ipswich

undertake further work here, perhaps as a result of the absence of contemporary references to the site as well as the scarcity of Middle Saxon coinage that might have been minted here.

Small-scale excavations have demonstrated that there was a nucleus located here from the end of the sixth or the early seventh century onwards. As we have seen, this may belie fluctuations in the historic record, though from the imported ceramic evidence it can be suggested that Ipswich experienced a trading 'peak' in the early seventh century and at the end of the eighth or in the early ninth century (Fig. 15). Kiln debris and the vestigial remains of kilns were found in the Cox Lane area and document 'a specialist industry of some magnitude'. The range of Ipswich ware, the product of this industry, and its East Anglian distribution alone confirm it as a unique artifact in Middle Saxon England (Fig. 38). It blends a few continental styles into an Early Saxon local tradition but, unlike other Middle Saxon pottery, it was made with some proficiency. The extent of the pottery within modern Ipswich clearly indicates the extensive occupation of this low-lying ground. If the

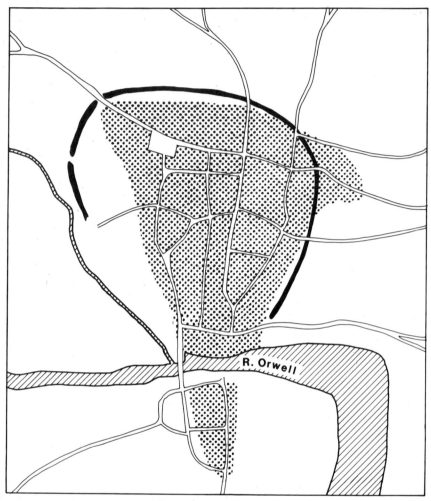

Figure 15 The extent of Middle Saxon Ipswich and the outline of the later defences

spread reflects human occupation, Ipswich was a major emporium in Anglo-Saxon England, covering as much as 100 ha.

Besides imported pottery, much of which is derived from the Rhenish area, there is a small but fine collection of glass-ware probably made in the Rhineland also, and a few imported pieces of metalwork and bonework. Boat rivets have been found in some numbers.

The scarcity of coins from the site is most problematical. Present studies of East Anglian coinage point to the minor minting of East Anglian sceattas and pennies, but no series of any note seems to exist. It is interesting that two of the four sceatta-finds to date have occurred near the 'thing-place' to the north of the commercial area. Wade has speculated that the royal settlement controlling the emporium may have been located hereabouts.

Norwich

In the past the Middle Saxon settlement at Norwich has been described as a trading-site and, with Ipswich, as a major trade outlet in East Anglia.[9] But thanks to the judiciously designed research-programme of the Norwich Survey it is now possible to comment satisfactorily on the previously disparate evidence.

Using place-name evidence preserved in the (rich) later documentary history of the town, and linking that to the spread of Middle Saxon Ipswich ware, we discover the existence of several small settlements. Needham, set back from the river Wensum on a slight bluff, is the best documented of these. Norwich lies in the bend of the river where the later cathedral was built; there are also two smaller communities at Westwik and probably across the river at Coslany.

A settlement area of some 20 ha by 900 A.D. has been postulated by the recent research, though this has yet to be established by archaeology. Quite clearly, however, there is no comparison with Ipswich. The location of Needham, the main focus of settlement, is strange if it was an emporium, while the comparative dearth of imported material from the period is eloquent enough when reviewed in connection with Ipswich.

A recent historical appraisal has suggested that it was a royal settlement. This idea is substantiated to some extent by the Late Saxon and post-Conquest documentary evidence. Such an institutional function might explain the complex of settlements, as well as the few imported finds.

York

Alcuin, the eighth-century expatriate of York (and friend of Charlemagne), writes of York as an *emporium terrae commune marisque*.[10] He refers to a Frisian group in the settlement; and Frisians are mentioned again in Altfrid's Life of St. Liudger, composed before 849. Furthermore, numerous late eighth- and ninth-century coins have been found in a zone around the minster. One, it has been argued, is a Dorestad issue, and a recent note has suggested the discovery of a York-minted coin in Dorestad.

Yet, in spite of this evidence, it still remains doubtful that York was either an emporium in the sense described in this book, or, indeed, a settlement of any permanent scale before the mid-ninth century. Many excavations have sought seventh- to ninth-century layers and yet none have been found so far. At some stage we have to accept the power of this kind of negative evidence.

Domburg

Domburg was located on the sand dunes of Walcheren, an island in the mouth of the Scheldt.[11] All traces of the settlement had been removed by the twentieth century, though some planning of the surviving features was undertaken in the nineteenth century. A fine collection of metalwork and bonework has been studied and published, while coins including English sceattas are known from here. This unstratified collection suggests a rich trading settlement, ranging in date probably from the seventh to the ninth century.

Westenschouwen

This is a dune-site on the island of Schouwen in Zeeland, similar to the well-known Domburg settlement.[12] Finds were collected at various times during the first half of this century. Their variety and range suggest that, like Domburg, it may have been a small emporium dating from the eighth or ninth century. Capelle's recent monograph on the site illustrates Rhenish wares, bone-combs and a rich array of metalwork, including keys.

Dorestad

The site of Dorestad was first recognised during the nineteenth century when L. D. F. Janssen published a paper on graves from the neighbourhood of Wijk bij Duurstede. Just after the First World War J. H. Holwerda undertook an important series of excavations which revealed just how rich the site was in terms of wooden structures and artifacts. The opportunity to examine a greater part of this settlement arose when major redevelopment of the present village was planned. In a campaign lasting nearly ten years almost 50 ha have been excavated, demonstrating that the emporium extended over an area well in excess of 40 ha.[13]

Dorestad lies at the confluence of the rivers Lek and Rhine, at a point where central Holland once became a series of islands and waterways. It was well-placed, being at the junction of routes to the north, the west and the heart of Europe, then in the middle Rhineland. It may also have been located on the old boundary between the Austrasian kingdom and Frisia, though this is not yet proved. Field-work has revealed extensive Roman-period native settlement in the area, some of which continued into the Carolingian period. But it seems probable that the principal focus of settlement from the Roman period until the tenth century, at least, was a fort, perhaps part of the Roman *limes*, lying on the south bank of the Rhine.

The recent excavations suggest that the settlement at Wijk bij Duurstede dates from the last quarter of the seventh century (perhaps the 680s, when Pepin is recorded to have reconquered this area) and was inhabited until the ninth century.

Such extensive excavations have made it possible to identify the topography of the site. Along the ever-shifting bank of the Rhine was an expanse of timber walk-ways, constructed on piles, at the end of which were jetties. These developed in the course of the settlement's life, extending almost a hundred metres out from the first row of buildings. The micro-differences in construction of the walk-ways has suggested that each was built by its own user, presumably the merchants who inhabited the simple rectangular structures nearest the shore.

In the centre of the nucleus, rather different structures have been found. These comprise farms of a typical Frisian kind with byre and accommodation incorporated within buildings about 8 m wide and between 22 and 30 m long (Fig. 11). These buildings are each set within the characteristic fenced enclosures and accompanied by wells and sometimes granaries (cf. Fig. 11). Thirty to forty of these have been shown to exist in no apparently designed order. In their midst is the finer of the two cemeteries so far identified. This is enclosed by a fence, and the graves surround a rectangular building, a stone well and another timber structure which may be a bell-tower. It is evidence, at least, of a Christian element of some size within the settlement, but of what date remains to be seen.

The vast quantities of finds are dominated by middle Rhineland imports (Fig. 16). Some 80 per cent of the pottery assemblage is attributed to production centres in the Vorgebirge (hills near Cologne) and Mayen area, while the remainder, all hand-made, is local in origin. Casks made of silver fir and oak, re-used as wells, must have brought wine from the region of Mainz (Fig. 17). Niedermendig lava querns from the Eifel mountains were fashioned here; stone mortars from the Ardennes (the Meuse valley) have also been found. Glass-ware, possibly from the Cologne and Trier regions, is well-known, and there is an exceptional range of metalwork, from a gold ingot to the great Christian brooch. The brooch is dated to the second half of the eighth century; Professor van Es has attributed it to a workshop somewhere in the Swiss-Burgundian-Alamannic area. A superb coin series has also been found, including a number issued in Charlemagne's reign with twelve-oared boats depicted on their obverse.

The faunal assemblage has shown that pigs and cattle were the principal animals consumed by the inhabitants, though fresh-water and sea-water fish (some from northern Frisia) have been retrieved in

Figure 16 A range of Middle Rhenish imported pottery from Dorestad (courtesy of R.O.B., Amersfoort)

Figure 17 Section through a wine-barrel re-used as a well-lining in Dorestad (courtesy of R.O.B., Amersfoort)

substantial quantities. Evidence of cloth-making, metalwork, jewellery, bone-working, ship-building, basket- and wood-working all contribute to our understanding of what are the best-excavated emporia considered in this book.

Medemblik

Medemblik (ancient *Medemelacha*) is still a town, tucked inside the Zuyder Zee and looking across towards Staveren, the site of a Carolingian monastery which flourished in the later medieval period.[14] Limited recent excavations in Medemblik have shown that it was probably built at the junction of several waterways which have since silted up. The two main areas examined have located Merovingian-period pottery, as well as an intensive later eighth- to ninth-century phase. Little structural evidence, however, has yet come to light.

A few pits, a substantial bank and an oven were found in the Schuitenvoerderslaan excavations, but no houses. (The excavator has pondered the existence of turf houses here on the evidence of the post-holes.) The finds include a range of locally made Frisian cooking-pots, as well as a substantial assemblage of imported Rhenish pottery.

It seems more than probable that Medemblik was located on the northerly route once taken from Dorestad. The historical summary published so far points to an imperial (late Merovingian/Carolingian) interest in the settlement from the eighth century. Pepin III appears to have granted the bishop of Utrecht one tenth of all property in the diocese, including Medemblik, in 753.

Emden

Emden was perhaps a small stop-over place on the northerly journey. The Carolingian settlement grew close to, or even on top of, an earlier Frisian village. The ninth-century settlement was sampled in the 1950s and an area about 250 m long by no more than 50 m broad was found to have been occupied. This nucleus was expanded in the later tenth or eleventh centuries.[15]

Hamburg

Hamburg was an important port-of-call on the journey northwards and the scene of a Danish attack in 845 which was vividly described by Rimbert in the *Vita Anskarii*. Early medieval Hamburg was investigated by Reinhard Schindler between 1947 and 1959. During that time about 3,000 m², approximately 2 per cent, of the early medieval town was examined. The excavations were focused in two localities: the former cathedral precinct and the southern parts of the old town by the river. Schindler identified the Carolingian *Hammaburg*, the fortification enclosing the ninth-century nucleus which was attacked in 845. This rectangular fortification is roughly 100 m by little more than 100 m, and gives a useful impression of the scale of these early medieval monastic communities. The *suburbium* also mentioned by Rimbert was confined to an area about 150 m by 100 m to the west of the *Hammaburg*. The excavation trenches were really too limited to give any impression of the topography.[16]

Haithabu

Haithabu, or Hedeby (in Danish), lies on the shore of Haddeby Noor, a lake at the head of the river Schlei which opens into the Baltic Sea. Its location was strategic, for the Schlei is navigable for much of its length, and with a land crossing of 17 km to the river Treene it would have been possible to reach the North Sea.[17] Moreover, placed at the base of Jutland, it was of course a focus of routes from north Germany and Denmark, as well as the Baltic coastline in the direction of Poland (Fig. 18).

The low-lying ground is now dominated by the massive rampart that encloses some 24 ha and is linked to the series of earthworks which dissect the peninsula known as the Danevirke (Fig. 18). The settlement area was overlooked by the *hochburg*, which was deserted by the later Viking period when this hillock became a burial ground. The Frankish Royal Annals attribute its origin to the year 808, when king Godfred of the Danes attacked the Slavic town of *Reric*, allied to Charlemagne, and forcibly transferred its merchants to Sliestorp – (?) Haithabu. Haithabu was visited during the ninth century by Ansgar, who founded a church here. Ottar, the visitor to king Alfred's court, visited Haithabu on his Scandinavian voyages; so did the Saxon Wulfstan. The Cordoba writer and traveller Al-Tartushi was unimpressed, and his description smacks of an aesthete visiting barbarians. The settlement was possibly under Swedish control, probably of king Sigtrygg, son of Gnupa, in the early tenth century. The Swedes were allegedly ousted by Henry I of Germany in 934, but by 1049 it was once more in Danish hands, for in that year Harald Haldrada sacked the town.

The first major excavations took place just before the last war and have proved to be of considerable importance. Since then there have been several other campaigns, not only on the interior, but on extramural areas of occupation. Surveys of the surrounding area have revealed the density of Viking-period monuments, including an especially fine series of rune stones. Under-water surveys have discovered a boat, as well as a rich array of loot lost by the jetties and rubbish thrown into the Schlei.

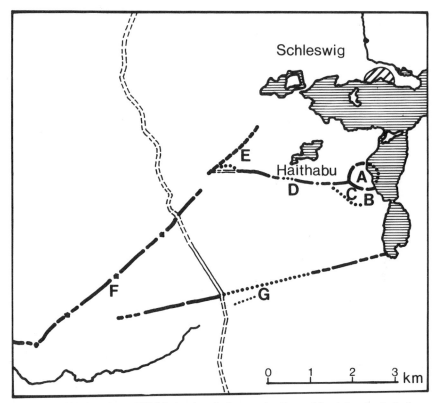

Figure 18 The location of Haithabu in relation to the Danevirke (after Jankuhn)

Several small settlements were probably founded here in the eighth century; these were probably nucleated by Godfred in 808 or thereabouts and probably fortified a century or so later. Excavations have distinguished a series of roads leading down to the lake and have satisfactorily discovered a range of dwellings for each phase (Fig. 12). A culvert carrying a stream ran down the centre of the settlement (Fig. 19).

Substantial quantities of imported Rhenish pottery have been found here, as well as of Slavic ware. Soapstone vessels from Vestfold have also been found; Niedermendig lava querns appear to have been finished here from the rough-outs exported from the Rhineland. There is abundant evidence of metalworking – of jewellery as well as utilitarian items – and some suggestion of glass-working. A mint was created here about 825, issuing coins in the first place that were copies of the contemporary Dorestad issues, bearing a boat on one side.

Clearly when all the vast amount of artifactual and structural evidence from the excavations has been articulated within a chronological framework, it will prove of enormous importance, as this emporium linked the North Sea basin to the Baltic Sea basin.

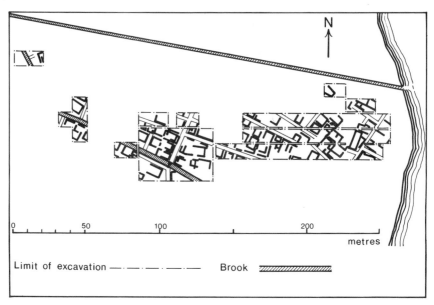

Figure 19 Schematic plan of the buildings and roads within Haithabu (after Schietzel)

Ribe

Ribe is situated just south of Esbjerg on the Jutish peninsula, looking directly out towards the North Sea.[18] It is just inland, now some 10 km from the sea on the river Ribe, separated by marshes from the low-lying west coast. The ninth-century missionary Ansgar moved here from Haithabu, where he founded a church in 826 before making his perilous crossing to Birka. From 948, in fact, it was the seat of a bishopric, and the town has developed more or less continuously, ecclesiastical and mercantile functions being important to its growth.

The presence of the modern town built over the earlier one has naturally restricted the excavations. The sample areas investigated so far, however, show that there was a small Viking-period nucleus on the northern bank of the river. (This perhaps was shifted in the tenth or eleventh centuries to the south bank, around the cathedral located there.)

A number of plank- and post-built structures as well as several sunken-huts have been found. The artifacts assembled to date (1979) include 18 sceattas, several of which are Frisian, a small but significant collection of Rhenish imported pottery, including Badorf-type tableware, Relief-band amphorae, Mayen ware and Tating ware. Evidence of glass-bead production has been found, as well as a range of metalworking, including fine jewellery.

As yet a mid- to late eighth-century date seems appropriate for the earliest occupation. Of interest to the later Viking period is the apparent absence of a rampart, though further investigation may alter this conclusion.

Kaupang

The excavations at Kaupang in south-east Norway, overlooking Viks fjord, were primarily designed to test whether the Viking-period farms 'really do lie on the site of that "port" which Alfred's Orosius calls *Sciringes heal*'.[19] Alfred's informant was a merchant farmer called Ottar, from northern Norway, who had travelled extensively in the Baltic. The debate about the location of Skiringssal is an old one. It was first raised when Nicolaysen excavated the cemetery at the nearby farm of Lamøya in the nineteenth century. But it was not until the 1950s that the trading site was found.

Kaupang (as it has become known) is located on a narrow strip of land along the side of the Kaupang creek. A complex of six house-plans, all in a poor state of preservation, was discovered with cobbled paths or roads leading to stone piers. Two of these houses (nos. II and III) were workshops. So far, however, only about 14,000 m² of an estimated 400,000 m² has been uncovered, though it is doubted whether this entire area was in fact built on.

The finds range in date from the later eighth to early tenth century and include Arabic, Frankish, Anglo-Saxon and Haithabu-minted coins. A few Rhenish vessels and some Frisian hand-made cooking-pots, as well as a substantial number of Slavic pots, have been found. There is evidence of soapstone processing (drawing upon the raw material from southern Vestfold), of glass-bead production and of metalworking. Moulds for the lead weights used in merchants' scales have been found, and so has a lead ingot. Boat rivets indicate some boat-repairing.

Whether it is the site Ottar visited will probably remain in question, but it is undoubtedly a fine example of a Viking-period emporium.

Löddeköpinge

An extensive site survey was initiated in and around the commune of Löddeköpinge early in the 1970s.[20] The village lies 12 km west of Lund on the northern bank of the river Lödde, about 3.5 km from the coast. Here an important Viking-period settlement, Vikshögsvären, and its cemetery have been excavated.

The settlement comprises 54 sunken-huts cut into the natural sand on the ridge overlooking the Lödde. The excavator has also described a bank and ditch, which may have enclosed the settlement, rather like those at Haithabu, Västergarn and Birka. Randsborg, however, believes that it was a fence rather than a wall, which would explain its now vestigial character. If it did enclose the settlement, Vikshögsvären was very large indeed, for more than 25 ha would have been enclosed. The huts have a special character, having filled in with 'alternating layers of floor material and drift sand', and it has been postulated that this is evidence of seasonal occupation (Fig. 8). The comparative lack of rubbish-pits seems to confirm this suggestion, while the excavator has pointed to the marked clusters of huts. These, it has been speculated, may reflect 'ships' crews or groups of merchants with common interests!

Finds include large numbers of Slavic pots, glass beads, a range of metalwork and stone implements, including a honestone with a graffito on it, and one coin probably minted in Haithabu early in the ninth century.

This ninth- to tenth-century settlement will obviously prove to be of great interest as more of it is discovered. Its size, combined with its vestigial character, are already striking features.

Västergarn and Paviken

On the west coast of the island of Gotland lies the great enclosure of Västergarn. The similarity of this great earthwork to the defences at Haithabu and Birka has long been noted, though no excavations have yet established what lies within the interior. Just to the north of it, however, recent trial excavations have located a major site on low-lying ground by the Idån Channel which connects the inlet of Vikmyr to the inlet known as Paviken and thence to the sea.[21]

A field-survey using phosphate analysis indicated the extent of the settlement, while trial excavations gave some insight into its character. Plentiful industrial activity was suggested, including glass-bead production, metalworking and boat-repairing. The range of material suggests an emporium that was to some extent a stop-over point on the route from central Sweden to Russia, as well as a sheltered point for the Gotland community to foster its own mercantile community. (Gotland throughout the early medieval period, and especially during the Viking Age, was exceptionally wealthy, the massive hoards of gold and silver being an undeniable index of its prosperity.)

The fortifications at Birka and Haithabu date from the later tenth century, and it is equally conceivable that Västergarn's granite bank overlaid with earth was raised at this time. Paviken appears to date from the later ninth and tenth centuries: whether there was a shift of settlement during the tenth century, or some nucleation as at Haithabu, remains to be tested.

Helgö

Helgö is an island about 3 km long and 1 km wide, at its widest, close to the northern shore and in the eastern channel of Lake Mälaren in central Sweden.[22] The 'Iron Age' fort commanding the precipitous eastern end of the island has long been known, but it was not until the 1950s that the later site was discovered. The chance find of a Coptic ladle, of a type traded during the later fifth and the sixth century to northern Europe (see Chapter 2) led to a sustained campaign of excavations.

The excavations have identified a series of discrete structures at the eastern end of the island. Several of these comprise structures with dry-

Figure 20 Remains of a metalsmith's house at Helgö, Sweden (courtesy of the Statens Historiska Museum, Stockholm)

stone wall foundations probably for timber halls, set on small terraces where sunken-huts (probably outhouses) have also been found (Fig. 20). Some of the sunken-huts also contain ovens, which has suggested that they were temporary homes, at least, like those from Haithabu. The burial ground lies in what is now woodland on slightly flatter ground at the western end of the island, some distance away from the main industrial settlement.

The main discovery has been the smithies, producing a range of elegant metalwork. The excavation of a major collection of moulds has permitted a total reappraisal of the late Vendel and Viking jewellery of Sweden. By 1972, 227 mould fragments for headplates for relief brooches, 338 for footplates, 526 for clasp buttons and 315 for dress pins had been found. Furthermore, thousands of mould fragments for other jewel types, dress mounts and sword pommels have been tentatively identified. Debris from these workshops also includes gold and silver in hacked form; weights and scales for measuring out the metals and hundreds of crucibles have also been discovered. The jeweller's craft and its accompanying trade is being evaluated and documented.

Other finds from the excavations span the sixth to the ninth century; they present some interpretative problems since the next island is Birka and the grave-field there was quite clearly started late in the eighth century. A hoard of fifth- to sixth-century coins may represent the first phase. The Coptic ladle and a Badorf-type vessel suggest a seventh-century date; a fine Irish crozier of the eighth-century may be attributed to the Viking raids which were initiated late in the eighth

Figure 21 Aerial view of Birka with the fortified hilltop in the foreground (courtesy of the Statens Historiska Museum, Stockholm)

century; to this period can also be attributed the Tating ware vessels and possibly the magnificent north Indian, seventh-century buddha (Fig. 30) which symbolises the opening up of the Viking road to the east. Other industrial activities include glass-making, probably to produce beads.

So far the organisational aspects of this site remain an enigma, particularly frustrating in the light of its important industrial component.

Birka

Birka is the celebrated settlement on a small island to the west of Helgö in Lake Mälaren.[23] The island is about 3.5 km long, though some of it may have been submerged in the Viking period, and the settlement lay at the north-eastern end (Fig. 21). The 'black earth' would appear to indicate the principal occupation area enclosed within a great rampart some 2 m high and located below a hillfort. Burial grounds surround the settlement and cover some 9 ha.

The first excavations here were made by Joseph Hadorph (1630–1693), royal custodian of antiquities. In 1826 Alexander Seton, a mining engineer, opened the first graves. Between 1871 and 1895 Hjalmar Stolpe excavated about 1,100 of the approximately 2,000 graves, producing exemplary illustrations of each. These include cremations, as well as richly furnished inhumations. The graves have been dated by the Arabic, Frankish and few Anglo-Saxon coins in them and range from the later eighth to the last half of the tenth century. The dead were buried with a great variety of jewellery, and also with Frankish and Slavic pots, a few glasses and an exceptional number of vestments, which have survived in fragmentary form, including Chinese silks and gold-threaded garments. 130 of the graves contained one or more weights of the kind used by merchants, while only three contained the scales as well. These must be the *negociatores* to whom Rimbert refers in his life of Ansgar, the ninth-century missionary, who visited Birka in 829, when he was greeted by king Bjorn and by Hergeir, the town captain, and again 852 when Ansgar was accompanied by his later biographer.

Excavations within the 'black earth' area have been very limited. This part faced a gently sloping beach, and remains of timber piles have been reported, suggesting that piers and perhaps moorings for larger boats were located here. A small lagoon also exists to the east of the settlement, and there has been some speculation that it may be partly man-made. Ambrosiani's recent excavations have forcefully demonstrated the artifactual wealth of the 'black earth' area. In some 120 m he has reported 18 coins, 100 combs, 500 bronze fragments, 250 glass fragments and 10,000 potsherds, including many more examples of the various types found in the cemetery.

The settlement was evidently a thriving international centre when Ansgar visited it, but the large numbers of bone skates suggest that its function may have been as a regional winter market held when Lake Mälaren was iced up. The rampart, with conspicuous gaps in it, was built over a grave containing a coin of 925, and is generally considered to have been constructed late in the settlement's history, enclosing about 11.5 ha. At its height, it is believed to have had a population of between 700 and 1,000, but by the eleventh century Adam of Bremen tells us that it was deserted. By this date, 1060 or so, the main focus was around the royal residence of Sigtuna on the northern shore of the lake.

Chapter 5

DARK AGE ARGONAUTS AND THEIR CRAFT

There is little evidence of direct trade between England and Gaul in this period, and that Charlemagne regarded its suspension as an effective act of hostility towards Offa is remarkable.

F. M. Stenton[1]

In view of our discussion of long-distance trade in the previous chapters, we might surmise from these remarks of Sir Frank Stenton's on Middle Saxon trade that the argonauts of the North Sea are obscured from us. To some extent this is true historically. Yet there are a number of disparate references to traders on which we can draw, and we must necessarily mobilise the archaeology to present postulates that may be tested. The distribution of artifacts that were traded, as well as the debris of traders, permits the first steps in this direction. Then we must focus more clearly on their function and calculate their numbers by reference to the settlement and cemetery archaeology, as well as the boats.

Traders and trade competition

The most prominent traders in north-west Europe were the Frisians. During the period from the seventh to the ninth centuries the documentary sources indicate their presence in most countries.[2] As we have seen in Chapter 2, the Frisians appear to have controlled the trade emanating from the Austrasian court in the Middle Rhineland. This may have begun as early as the late fifth century when the first groups of Theodoric coins arrived in northern Europe, but a much more likely date for the formation of their role in this trade is late in the sixth or early in the seventh century. The 'founding' of Ipswich in Suffolk might imply some more regularised trade, though its real character remains enigmatic in view of the present late seventh-century dating of the excavated settlement at Dorestad. The wealth of Vendel-period artifacts from Sweden, however, many of which were Rhenish products, substantiates the importance of this Merovingian trade-route, while the prolific number of Rhenish pots in Dutch cemeteries – such, for example, as that at Rhenen[3] – illustrate either the indigenous wealth of the Frisian farmers or their early interaction in this trading system as trader-farmers.

The role of the Frisians after about 650 – after the closure of many of these cemeteries – remains surprisingly unclear. Their alleged annexation of Dorestad at about this time – an earlier site as yet undiscovered – suggests that it had been previously under Merovingian control. For about thirty years the Frisians were permitted to retain autonomy of this key site, probably as a result of a treaty arrangement between king Aldgisl and the Austrasian court. Aldgisl welcomed St. Wilfred when he wintered at Dorestad in 678–9 and seems to have resisted the intriguing Ebroin, the Austrasian mayor of the palace, who requested that Wilfred be surrendered to him for aiding his rivals. It was soon after Aldgisl died and was replaced by the warlike Radbod that Pepin II reconquered this area, including Dorestad.[4] And if the dendrochronology of the excavated site is interpreted successfully, Pepin ordered the creation of a new emporium. Pepin also reformed the coinage about this time, which led to a similar reform of the Frisian coinage, which in turn influenced the style of the new Kentish sceattas (see Chapter 6 for further details). This currency relationship implies that each region or territory was sufficiently involved in trade with the others to warrant this reformation of the extant coins.

The agrarian nucleus of the (new) Dorestad is one of its striking components. We must wait to see whether the archetypal Frisian rural houses of this settlement were part of the late seventh-century foundation. If they were, we may assume with confidence the continued role of trader-farmers in the commercial activities emanating from the Rhine, though under Merovingian hegemony. In 716, king Radbod of the Frisians, who had been checked by Pepin in 689, overran Dorestad as Charles Martel usurped the Merovingian throne and a period of political strife ensued. The Frisian king lived only until 719, and in that year Charles re-established Merovingian control over Dorestad. From this date the Merovingians and their successors, the Carolingians, initiated the annexation of Frisia – a plan that was enacted in company with English missionaries lead by Willibrord.[5]

Numerous references to Frisian traders span the period from the later seventh to the ninth century. Bede refers to a Frisian in London in 679, while Alcuin in a letter mentions the expulsion of the Frisian colony from York in the 780s.[6] Alcuin names one Black Hrocbert, a trader in Dorestad, and refers to the trade-link between Dorestad and England.[7] Frisian merchants were permitted to visit the October fair at St. Denys near Paris from the middle of the eighth century. Frisians had founded a *scola* at Rome in 779. Moreover, Frisians were active in Germany: they were at Xanten, Duisburg, Mainz and Worms. In Mainz, they were engaged in the trading of spices and silks.[8] A celebrated Frisian called Ibbo was the commercial agent for the monastic community of St. Maximin at Trier, while Ermoldus Nigellus, living in Strasbourg early in the ninth century writes as follows:

Utile consilium Frisonibus atque Marinis,
Vendere vina fuit et meliora vehi.[9]

It is useful to sell wine to the Frisians and to maritime nations, and to import better products.

The *Vita Anskarii*, written by the ninth-century biographer Rimbert about the celebrated missionary, implies that Frisians were active in the Baltic. Moreover two eleventh-century rune stones from Sigtuna, a market on the northern shore of Lake Mälaren, contain references to a guild of Frisians there.[10] The existence of this guild, however, is debatable, since the men commemorated in the stones were undoubtedly local Swedes, and it is thought possible that they were maintaining a corporation of traders first introduced by Frisians at Birka. The historical authenticity of both references is oblique, and while Erik Arup has made much of the Frisian connection, Ansel Christensen has more recently contended the issue. Archaeology must be the arbiter.

We have first to fix the archaeological identity of the Frisians, which is not altogether easy. The material evidence from Dorestad provides the most useful data. Here nearly 80 per cent of the pottery is imported from the middle Rhineland; it comes either from the Badorf-type centres in the Vorgebirge (Fig. 16) or from the Mayen centres in the Eifel mountains.[11] This pottery was, as we have seen in Chapter 3, either broken in transit or used by the traders – or both. We may suggest that its distribution beyond Dorestad will to some degree be an index of Frisian activity – *if*, of course, the Frisians actually controlled Dorestad. In Chapter 2 the pattern of trade has already been outlined, so we may here simply summarise the evidence to suggest:

1. Modest seventh- to eighth-century trade to eastern England, along the North Sea littoral and possibly to eastern Jutland, via Dorestad, Domburg, Westenschouwen and Medemblik.

2. A major, brief phase in the late eighth and early ninth century to eastern England, along the North Sea littoral (Frisia) and to Jutland, largely concentrated via Dorestad and thence outwards to Medemblik and Haithabu/Ribe.

Frisian presence, beyond Jutland, as we have already noted in Chapter 2, seems to be minimal, though the concentrations of Carolingian goods at Haithabu remain beyond doubt. Christensen's point seems vindicated. Moreover Frisian presence to the west was not so imposing as was once imagined.[12]

The ship on certain of the Carolingian coins from Dorestad appears to endorse the nautical prowess of the Frisians. It was a motif, incidentally, imitated by the first moneyers of Haithabu early in the ninth century.[13] Yet, less familiar, though symbolically as important, are the ship motifs on certain primary sceattas from south-east England, and the Louis the Pious issues from Quentovic in northern France.[14] If the Frisians really did control the Rhenish sea-way, once in the North Sea they faced competition.

Frankish and Saxon traders are scarcely as prominent in the chronicles and letters that survive from this period. The exchange of letters between Charlemagne and Offa, however, demonstrates the existence of traders visiting each others' territory.[15] The *praeceptum negotiatorum* of Louis the Pious is a rare indication of the privileges accorded to Frankish traders by the ninth century.[16] It grants protection and 'diverse privilèges à des personnages qualifiés fidèles *nostri et negotiatores*'.[17] It would appear to suggest that *negotiatores* were established members of many courts and monasteries. Thus, just as we discover the Frisian at the monastery of St. Maximin, so we may expect the great monasteries like those at St. Denys and Verdun, for example, to have maintained traders. These agents, like those from the minor courts, were generally subject to the tolls imposed by the imperial government that administered the trading communities like Dorestad and Quentovic. (In fact the granting of immunity from these tolls has permitted some insight into the nature of the commerce at these coastal centres.)[18] The imperial toll-masters at Quentovic were evidently men of some stature, since Abbot Gervold acted as intermediary in the diplomatic estrangement between Offa and Charlemagne.[19]

English merchants were also attached to certain monasteries, as the immunity from toll granted to the bishop of Worcester, trading in London in 716/717, would seem to imply.[20] English merchants were, in fact, present at the St. Denys fair almost a century before the first reference to the Frisians; they had also established themselves in Rome about fifty years before the Frisians.[21] Did Ceolfrid, Bede's abbot, embark from the Humber in 716 in an Anglo-Saxon boat? Wilfred travelled to Dorestad in 679–80: was it on a Saxon boat? Willibald in 721 embarked on his continental journey at Hamwih. The most explicit reference to these cross-Channel traders emanating from England is in Charlemagne's letter to Offa. There Charlemagne charges the Saxon traders with attempting to pass themselves off as pilgrims in order to avoid the tolls. If true, it is a telling indictment of the scale of Anglo-Saxon commerce.[22]

Jewish traders, often referred to in the sixth century in Gaul, once more attract attention during the ninth century as they become involved in the slave-trade in Spain. The Jews promoted the route that began in the Rhineland and passed through Verdun on its way to Cordoba, along which passed Slavic eunuchs.[23] Their role in this inhuman trade was fiercely condemned by the more virtuous clerics of the time. Indeed, Agobard, bishop of Lyons, reproached Louis the Pious in a pamphlet entitled *De insolentia Judaeorum*.[24] Syrians too had been prominent in the Merovingian period, but it is as likely that they represent no more than the individual traveller-trader, like those Arabs who journeyed north in the tenth century and later. For specific reasons discussed in Chapter 8, the ninth century witnessed a notably cosmopolitan spectrum of commercial agents in north-west Europe. Hence, for example, there is an allusion in the *Vita Anskarii* to northmen from Birka and Haithabu trading in Dorestad.[25]

If we use the artifacts as an index, the Frisians appear to have been less prominent in the seventh- to ninth-century long-distance trade than has often been assumed. In Middle Saxon England, Rhenish wares, the type-material associated with them, are restricted to south-east England, though even there these are commonly found with other wares that we have associated with traders emanating from northern France.[26] This zone is similar to that in which late seventh-century sceattas, clearly influenced by Frisian motifs, are also found. These sceattas have sustained the traditional view of the role of the Frisians in North Sea trade, but their design, which has cultural ramifications, should in no way be confused with their 'commercial' use. Similarly, the importance of the Frisians in the Baltic has been questioned. The thrust of these arguments, however, depends on any interpretation of Dorestad, as already outlined above.

Compared tó this simple equation, documenting the Frankish activity of the period is rather more difficult. This could be predicted, since the middlemen were, we believe, individual agents for various institutions. There should be much less homogeneity involved in the artifactual evidence of either traded debris or the debris of traders. Of course, in the case of pottery, this will be partly determined by the nature of the production centres at the time, but the historical model can none the less be tested.

Hamwih and Ipswich provide an interesting body of data with which to test the model. Hamwih has a great range of pottery, much of it imported. The local wares are very limited in their typological variability, and crudely made (Fig. 39). The imports are particularly varied, with a minimum sample of 270 vessels, scarcely including any forms that repeat one another. The fabric variability is equally marked, with more than thirty different classes, though several classes may have been produced in the same centre.[27] The variability in contrast to the Dorestad imported assemblage may indicate the presence of equally varied merchants, rather than smashed cargoes. The limited range and crudeness of the local Middle Saxon wares may have induced Carolingian traders, destined to spend some time within the settlement, to bring their own pottery in which they could cook and serve their food in a culturally acceptable manner. Not all the pottery will have been brought for this reason; the finer vessels, and in particular the elegant black-ware pitchers, may have been broken in transit (see Chapter 3). These vessels, unlike the majority of the classes, are widely disseminated around southern and eastern England.

The nature of the evidence is rather different from that for the Frisian/Rhenish system, but it appears to satisfy the historical model presented above. Whereas the Rhenish imports constitute no more than three per cent of the pottery from Hamwih, they constitute more than fifty per cent of the much smaller sample of vessels from Ipswich.[28] The imported pottery from Middle Saxon sites, however, is predominantly Frankish in origin. It points to the presence of court or monastic agents in the emporia in both eastern and southern England. The distribution of the imports, moreover, indicates the greater quantitative bulk of these Frankish wares. In effect, the trading zones can be tentatively delimited.

Fig. 22 illustrates these zones on the basis of the distribution of pottery. In future the coinage and glass, as well as utilitarian items like hones and querns, should be included to test the validity of the model.

The idea of trade competition has received attention in the archaeo-logical literature recently. Richard Bradley has made some general comments which it is useful to repeat. Trade competition, he writes, should have the effect that the field of any particular traded item may be restricted by the presence of a competing business in the same area. On the other hand, in a region where there were no 'intervening oppor-tunities' of this type, we should see the uninhibited extension of this field. In practical terms its effect should be this: that a trader avoids an area where he must share his business with a competitor and instead extends his operations where he can secure a monopoly. The distributions of the traded items will almost appear to repel one another.[29] Bradley's comments appear to be directed without reference to the various exchange and distribution types discussed in Chapter 1; yet these remarks have been shown to have validity in pre-market, as well as in market, contexts. In particular, Ian Hodder has used a gravity model derived from Reilly's studies of competing business to predict the point of interaction lying between two known distributors.[30] Renfrew has also explored the value of the gravity model to illustrate the trade competition extant in the western Mediterranean using obsidian as his data.[31] This Neolithic problem is to some extent analogous to that in the North Sea under consideration here. Whether it is really possible to calculate the interaction zones as accurately as Hodder and Renfrew have suggested is, at present, debatable. Their data, as in this early medieval context, are surely too crude and the samples too disparate.

The incidence of some competition is historically interesting. Several points need to be made. First, as we have seen in Chapter 2, the cross-Channel route emanating from courts around and in the Paris basin and

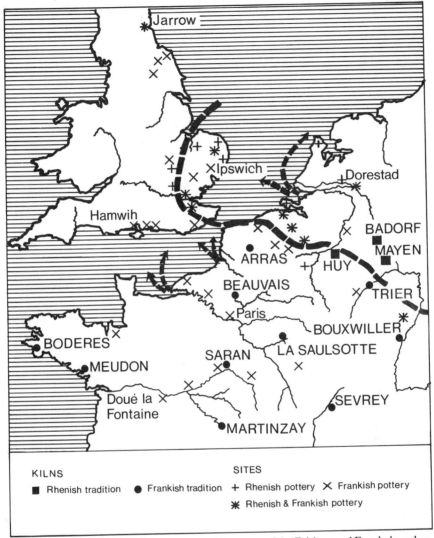

KILNS

■ Rhenish tradition ● Frankish tradition

SITES

+ Rhenish pottery ✕ Frankish pottery

✱ Rhenish & Frankish pottery

Figure 22 Map showing the trade competition areas of the Frisians and Franks based on the products of Carolingian pottery kilns

directed through sites like Quentovic, appear to have flourished at times when the Frisian activity was relatively less intense. Only at the end of the eighth century, during Charlemagne's reign, and possibly during the early and late seventh century, does there appear to be real competition. We should note, however, that if Hamwih and Ipswich are truly indicative of the scale of this trade, in the late eighth century the 'commerce' focused on southern England was far greater than that to the smaller northern emporia (see Chapter 3).

We should also note that 'every trader need not have taken the most efficient course to achieve a full market'. And, for example, there are not only a few Rhenish pots from Hamwih, but also a Frisian-type comb.[32] Herein may lie the historical dimension of the Frisians, as well as of other ethnically distinctive traders. Were the monkish chroniclers not more likely to record the unusual traveller than the familiar one? Moreover, as the ninth-century Anglo-Saxon author of the gnomic verses in the Exeter Book undoubtedly appreciated, the Frisians were romantic figures, as all lone wanderers tend to be:

A dear welcome guest (is one)
To his Frisian wife when ship comes to rest;
Back are come her husband and his vessel,
Her own provider, and she invites him in,
Washes his sea-stained garment and gives him fresh clothes;
She grants him on land what his love requires.[33]

Early medieval shipping

The most complex machine in the early medieval world was probably the sailing vessel.[34] Nautical archaeology sheds some light on the superlative craftsmanship of builders like the chief in the cemetery at Hérouvillete.[35] The early medieval period is, of course, rich in boat-finds. Over 400 boat-burials are now known; these include Sutton Hoo, Vendel, Valsgärde, Tune, Oseberg, Gokstad and Ladby. Yet the sample is not a useful one, especially when we review the evidence for trading ships; and we are able to contribute little to our perspective of trading, though the potential is considerable. As a result our remarks are limited to some tentative points which only further boat-finds will illuminate.

The Roman shipping fleet was evidently enormous and particularly well-organised: Roman-period harbours and wharfs, as well as boat-houses and repair yards, are now well-known from north-west Europe and the Mediterranean. Indeed the Empire functioned on the principle that 'it cost less to bring a cargo of grain from one end of the Mediterranean to another (by boat) than to carry it another seventy-five miles inland'.[36] Boats brought 175,200 tons of Egyptian grain to Constantinople as late as the sixth century; boats were, therefore, an integral part of the imperial commercialised marketing system. These ranged in size from 100 to 500 tons, though it is alleged that grain barges – leviathans – with a capacity of up to 1,200 tons existed.[37]

A bland but telling contrast can be made between the late Roman (Byzantine) vessels and those of early medieval northern Europe. Recent excavations off Yassi Ada (south-west Turkey) have revealed a seventh-century, 40-ton vessel;[38] its date must be similar to Sutton Hoo

1, the burial-ship of an East Anglian chieftain. The Yassi Ada vessel had a deep draught. It was about 19 m long, and spacious enough to include a galley in the stern, in which there was a tiled fire-box. This was apparently a wealthy merchantman with room for a cargo of 900 amphorae; Sutton Hoo, by contrast, was a great open rowing boat, almost 27 m long, with scarcely any room except for its rowers.

Sutton Hoo is a fair representative of the surviving seventh-century boats from north-west Europe at this date. Like the other boats of the period it was a clinker-built vessel (the lower edge of each plank overlapping slightly the upper edge of the plank below and rivetted to it at frequent intervals by iron clench-nails, clenched on the inside over an iron washer known as a rove). The Sutton Hoo ship had a keel-plank rather than a keel, which means that it could not have supported a heavy mast and sail; it also had a steering oar. Probably forty oarsmen were needed to propel it through the water.[39] Its structure is evolved from the Nydam boat, a pine vessel, deposited in a Danish bog in about 400, and we assume a Teutonic tradition of ship-building.

Table 2[40]

	Length	Beam (at widest)
Sutton Hoo	27 m	4.25
Gokstad	24 m	6.25
Oseberg	21 m	5.10
Ladby	20.6 m	2.9

The principal development in the period from 600 to 900 in ship-building was the design of a structure that was both strong and yet might be propelled by a sail as well as oarsmen. The Kvalsund boat found 150 miles north of Bergen and dating from around 700 is broader-hulled than the one at Sutton Hoo and has an incipient keel that might have supported a mast. This boat was 18 m long and needed 20 oarsmen. The evolution of the classic Viking ship had taken place by the next century, as is shown by the superbly crafted Gokstad and Oseberg ships. The Oseberg boat had, in fact, suffered a cracked mast-partner, which had been repaired before it was used as a funerary vessel. Both boats are very broad in comparison to beam (see Table 2), and both have developed keels. The Ladby boat, the very essence of a fighting long-ship, also had a keel, but as Table 2 shows its ratio of length to beam was clearly designed with speed in mind. Despite its slim figure, recent experiments with a replica have shown it to be capable of carrying horses as well as a full complement of oarsmen.[41]

These so-called long-boats – chieftains' boats, for the most part – have attracted a great deal of attention. In interpreting the migrations these rowing boats give some clue to the numbers involved, and the replicas have provided insight into the speed with which they might travel, as well as their durability (see below).

In contrast, rather little is known about the other types of vessels. In the tradition of the evolving keel there is the Bårset boat, possibly a *byroingr* in contemporary terms, which was found near Kvalsund. It was only 13 m long and needed 18 oarsmen. This eighth-century vessel can be compared with the Rong boat, also from this region, which dates from the ninth century and was 13½ m long and fitted out for 16 oarsmen. We must imagine that these were coastal ferries which were presumably used occasionally for trading. But, only the Åskekarr ship dating from the mid-ninth century is beyond doubt a mercantile vessel. This has a well-developed keel, but was only 16 m long. It may have been boats of this kind that inspired the Löddeköpinge (whetstone) graffito of a boat with its mast, and possibly furled sails and hooded steersman. The graffito vessel also apparently has a deep draught. It is rather unlike those depicted on the Gotland picture stones, as well as on the Haithabu coins, which have rows of shields and were presumably fighting ships.[42]

Figure 23 The Utrecht ship (courtesy of the Centraal Museum, Utrecht)

The examples cited so far illustrate a developing tradition of boat-building which was largely perfected for purposes of long-distance raiding, as well as coastal travelling, by the ninth century. There is, however, a second and indeed older, tradition of boat-building that seems to have been of some significance at the time.

The second tradition is best illustrated by the well-preserved Utrecht ship (Fig. 23).[43] This is a vessel of the so-called Celtic tradition which comprises either skin-made boats stretched over a wooden frame, or boats that were of the same design, but in timber. The Utrecht ship is of the latter kind. It was discovered in December 1930 by a gang of navvies digging a canal in northern Utrecht. The vessel probably dates from the eighth century and is 17.8 m long and nearly 4 m in the beam. It is clinker-built but has a keel-plate like the Sutton Hoo ship, for example. The steering gear was missing, but a hole in the eleventh floor-plank, fairly well forward, suggests that it may have had a mast for a light sail, though no evidence of a central mast has survived. The boat is curved in profile and rounded at either end, rather in the manner of 'a hollowed-out banana'.[44] As a result of its form and its forward mast, it has always been assumed to have been a river-boat and, in effect, an early medieval successor to the well-known Roman Rhine barges which have been found in much the same part of Holland. Yet there seems a good case for suggesting that the Utrecht ship was the kind of vessel that was plying along the North Sea littoral and also across to Britain. First, the Carolingian coins issued at Quentovic and Dorestad illustrating ships depict curved boats of this kind, generally propelled by over twenty oarsmen. Such sketchy accuracy might well be in doubt, were it not for the Haithabu coins, which are usually thought to have imitated these Carolingian issues. These early ninth-century Danish coins show boats with distinctive keel-lines; these are boats that were not curved. The Haithabu mint-master was clearly making a distinction of which we should take note.[45] Secondly, the sea-worthiness of boats is beyond doubt, as the extensive trips of the Irish monks in skin-curraghs indicate.[46] Some of these curraghs had small sails which drew the vessels along at a good pace (see below). Moreover a recent reconstruction of a curragh and its use in the Atlantic has demonstrated that these vessels ride the waves rather than cut through them. This particular reconstruction was used to cross the Atlantic.[47] Thirdly, the Parker Chronicle, when it notes Alfred's building of a navy, tells us that West Saxons were designing their ships differently from those either of the Danes or of the Frisians.[48] The case for the Utrecht ship as a typical sea-going vessel is a tenuous, but nonetheless critical, one. We may justifiably conclude that it is a rare example of a merchant-ship.

This book is directed essentially towards the different economic systems operating before and after the ninth century. Therefore we must attempt to test this economic threshold in maritime terms. The emergence of a commercialised marketing system should bring with it the kind of organised maritime system which we alluded to in the Roman period. Evidence is clearly being accumulated. The construction of a wharf at London during the ninth or early tenth century has recently been revealed.[49] Boats were to be docked rather than beached. The location of Southampton may have been determined by boats with deeper draughts, which could not negotiate the shallow Itchen but might dock at the end of the peninsula.[50] The abandonment of Quentovic early in the tenth century and its replacement by Wissant further north, but on the coast, suggests that the cross-Channel ships found the river Canche awkward to contend with. A century or so later Haithabu, where the boats beached, was abandoned in favour of Schleswig, where they docked. Kaupang was abandoned in favour of Tønsberg, and Birka was deserted in favour of Sigtuna.[51] We cannot claim that such settlement shifts were entirely due to larger boats and increased shipping, for other factors like defence and river silting must also be considered. Yet, by the late eleventh century the harbours of northern Europe were very different in character from those that had welcomed either the Sutton Hoo or the Utrecht ship.

It is interesting to view the boats of this period against this model. Sadly the sample is all too small, though the vessels themselves are particularly valuable ones.

The Graveney Boat from Kent dates from the second quarter of the tenth century and was 14 m long and 3 m at the beam.[52] It was a heavy clinker-built boat with a relatively flat bottom and only a keel-plank, which had been beached on a bed of sticks beside a creak about a kilometre from the sea. The few finds from the vessel include a Rouen-type pottery vessel, some lava-quern ballast and the remains of hops. (The pottery suggests that the ship was a French rather than a Frisian or Anglo-Saxon vessel that was using the querns, obtainable in most ports, as ballast.)[53]

Two points need making about this boat. First, the Graveney boat indicates that keel-planks were still preferred to keels for specific purposes as late as the tenth century. This, once again, suggests that only a light sail could have been employed. Secondly, in terms of its carrying capacity (as well as its structure), the boat would hardly have been anachronistic in the seventh or eighth or ninth centuries. It therefore demonstrates the slow evolution of boats with deeper draughts able to carry larger cargoes – this point has some pertinence when we review the character of tenth-century long-distance trade in England, and must be critically weighed against the evidence of settlement shifts (see Chapter 9).

The six boats from Roskilde Fjord in Denmark dating from about 1000 magnificently extend our knowledge of Dark Age maritime craft.[54] These boats were deliberately sunk to block the entrance to the bay before Roskilde, and they include two vessels fundamental to our discussion.

Wreck 3 is a small merchant vessel some 13.5 m long and 3.2 m broad. It had a half-deck fore and aft, and amidships there was an open hold. Three oar-holes were found on the port and two on the starboard side. The craft, therefore, could be propelled by five men, though on most occasions we must imagine that its sail was used. It is usually considered to be a typical example of vessels engaged in Baltic trade; yet, apart from its small crew, it is typical of the coastal boats which two centuries previously were tackling the Atlantic seas north of Bergen. We can scarcely doubt that wreck 3 is the product, indeed the culmination, of several centuries of experimentation with small coastal trading vessels which could carry up to about 10 tons.

Wreck 1 from Roskilde was the ship of the future. This was a heavy boat about 16.5 m long and 4.6 m in the beam, and was probably a *knarr*, the kind of vessel used on the voyages to Iceland and Greenland. It too had fore and aft half decks with a central hold that could have accommodated nearly 30 tons, causing the ship to draw 1.5 m of water, compared with the metre that wreck 3 would have drawn when loaded. This load-draughted boat required two pairs of oarsmen fore and aft, but it was primarily a sailing boat that docked and was, we assume, seldom man-handled, unlike those that preceded it.

We can draw several conclusions from the surviving vessels of the early medieval period. First, it is far from clear, despite the terminology

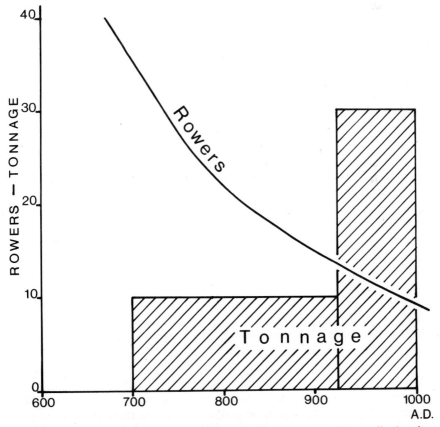

Figure 24 Sketch to illustrate the changing technology in boat-building, affecting the numbers of rowers and the cargo capacity of the vessels

expressed in the later literature, that there was always a clear distinction between long-boats and trading vessels. The Utrecht ship, the Graveney boat, the Åskerarr boat and the Roskilde wrecks 1 and 3 were clearly traders, but the tenth-century vessel from Haithabu was, in terms of its dimensions, a long boat. (How much weight we can place on this sole example of a vessel wrecked near an emporium remains in question.) Only technical evolution distinguishes Roskilde wreck 3 from the Kvalsund and Bårset boats. The implications of this are twofold. First, one merchant meant as many as twenty crew members before the tenth century. Secondly, bearing the crew in mind, cargoes must have been very limited; on the basis of Ellmers' calculations, in the order of 8 tons or less before about A.D. 1000.[55] Quite clearly bulky goods were out of the question (Fig. 24).

Secondly, there appears to be some ground for the belief that the Frisians used rather different boats from those employed in Scandinavia and England. *If* the Utrecht ship is typical of their craft, it provides a further reason for their prominence in the historical documentation. It also suggests that they may have been slightly more concerned with speed than with carrying capacity. (Tim Severin's experiments with an Irish curragh, however, quoted below, are revealing here.)

Finally, the Graveney boat illustrates that traditions died slowly, and that smaller craft were still being employed, as docks were being constructed in the refurbished harbours of north-west Europe. It was not until the twelfth century or later, with the rise of the Hanse, that a shipping system as complex as that developed by the Romans was to emerge.

At sea: time and motion

Crossing the North Sea or the Baltic has always been a hazardous experience in small craft. Yet the fourth- and fifth-century migrations attest beyond doubt the sea-faring spirit that conquered these seas. Indeed the ship was perhaps the symbol of these northern European communities, and of the proportion of wrecked vessels we are fairly ill-informed. That the merchantmen of the eighth and ninth centuries needed repairs after these journeys is clear from the prolific numbers of clench-nails from most of the emporia, as well as the ship-working tools from Paviken on Gotland.[56] Yet how long did these crossings take?

Contemporary or near-contemporary chroniclers have left us with some information about the travelling schedules of certain saints and adventurers. Bede's abbot, Ceolfrid, boarded a ship destined for France in the Humber on 4 July 716 and arrived on 12 August after the boat had put into port three times.[57] As we shall see, despite the large ship's company, this was a fairly slow trip. By contrast, king Alfred's(?)

account of (the Norwegian) Ottar's voyages in the north provide us with plentiful navigation details:

> From Skiringssal [?Kaupang] he said he sailed in five days to the port which is called Hedeby, which stands between the Wends, the Saxons, and Angeln and belongs to the Danes. While he sailed thither from Skirringssal, he had Denmark [i.e. Scania] to port and the open sea to starboard for three days; and then for two days before he reached Hedeby he had Jutland and South Jutland and many islands to starboard.[58]

Alfred also reports an account of Wulfstan, an adventuring Englishman, who tells of how it took seven days and nights under sail to journey from Haithabu to Truso.[59]

Clearly the value of these historical reports can be examined in the light of modern calculations and experiments based on the nautical data. Charles Green has carefully tried to estimate the North Sea crossings undertaken by the Early Anglo-Saxon migrants in vessels like that found at Nydam as well as the Sutton Hoo ship.[60] Green has postulated two routes, both emanating from Esbjerg and ending in East Anglia. The first ship follows the coast as far as Texel in the Netherlands and from there makes a crossing to Norfolk. The second follows the North Sea coast beyond the Hook of Holland to Flushing (located very near the small emporium at Domburg) on the island of Walcharen. His sea-faring informants suggested to him that if the Nydam and Sutton Hoo boats were rowed they could have averaged 3 knots for little more than six hours. This lead him to calculate a journey of some 12 days for the first boat, concluding, however, with a 24-hour open-sea crossing 'rowing steadily at 5 knots and steering an accurate course, in practice an impossible feat'.[61] The second boat would have taken 14 days and included an open-sea crossing of over 16 hours. These figures are useful, for they represent very slow journeys; but as it is more than probable that some sails were employed, crossings quicker than these should be envisaged. None the less, it seems valuable to quote Green's report for the final day's journey of his second vessel:

> May 7. Left Flushing at sunrise (04.00) and steered towards Harwich (roughly W by N½N). At first the tide set W and NW but later turned to SW. At the end of 6 hours rowing, the ship had advanced 30 miles direct and had been set some 7 miles to the SW of its estimated position. During the most of the next 6 hours rowing, the tide was setting NE, so that the ship's actual position was roughly some 5 miles NE of estimate. For the next two hours, the tide was nearly slack, first setting NE and then SW, so that the divergences from true course cancelled each other. Finally, in two to three hours, on the SW-running flood-tide, the ship reached Harwich at about 20.30. Sunset that day was at about 19.30, so that dusk was rapidly falling as the shore was approached.

With sail and convenient tides we might venture to suggest that the trip from Dorestad to Ipswich could be undertaken in about the same time. Quite clearly, using sail, it could have been achieved in two days. By contrast, Green's estimates suggest that as much as a week would have been needed for the journey to Haithabu from Dorestad, with

Figure 25 The Bantry pillar stone, Co. Cork, Eire (courtesy of Graeme Barker)

Medemblik and Hamburg presumably proving useful stopping-places en route.

For comparison with these simulated sailings there is evidence provided by the experimental ships. The Norwegian exhibit at the Chicago World Fair in 1893 was a replica of the ninth-century Oseberg boat.[62] This was sailed across the Atlantic without mishap, demonstrating the resilience and flexibility of the design in high seas, as well as the possible speeds that might be obtained. An average 10–11 knots, more than double that estimated for six hours' rowing, was easily attained under sail. We must bear in mind that the original boat was probably a special model – hence it became a burial chamber – and yet we still have some perspective of ninth-century long-boat speeds which would have halved the time taken by the Nydam boat rowed from Jutland along Green's courses. To this we may now add the more recent experiment by Tim Severin to build and sail a curragh from Ireland to America which has been just as illuminating.

Severin was concerned to recreate as far as possible the voyage of St. Breandan as recorded in a ninth-century manuscript, *Navigatio Sancti Brendani Abbatis*.[63] His vessel was constructed along traditional lines and was less than 12 m long and 2.5 m at its broadest. With a crew of 5 and all their equipment, the boat weighed about 5 tons. (We should note that St. Breandan was apparently accompanied by fourteen monks, presumably so that any rowing could be satisfactorily undertaken – as is depicted in the eighth-century Bantry pillar stone, a cross in Co. Kerry (Fig 25). Severin's daring voyage showed that a vessel with two masts (and sails) gave greater balance and he reports on its speeds as follows:

> The average day's run under sail was 40 miles, and a cruising speed of 2 to 3 knots was considered satisfactory. This required a wind F3-4 where the boat was fully laden. In ideal conditions of a following wind of F5-6 the log would register sustained periods of 5 to 7 knots. The maximum reading on the log scale was 12 knots and this speed was achieved comparatively frequently in heavy weather and high seas. . . .[64]

We may conclude, quite justifiably, that boats of this so-called Celtic tradition which effectively ran with the waves could be rather fast under sail. Indeed, they might even attain speeds similar to those of the long-boats, and easily attain the slower speeds reached by the early keel-plank type vessels which supported no large sail-areas. Moreover the stability and strength of this experimental vessel explains the challenging journeys that the Early Christian monks so fearlessly undertook.

All these experiments and calculations provide no more than a crude scale; yet they put time and motion into perspective, compelling us to be ever-critical of our settlement and artifactual data. One feature of this review has been the cargo capacity, and now it is apposite to examine the nature of the cargoes, the subject of long-distance trade.

Chapter 6

THE OBJECTS OF TRADE

The objects of stone age trade were always luxuries . . . at least things that men could have done without.

V. G. Childe[1]

At first there might appear to be a timelessness about Childe's observation. It is a recurrent feature of long-distance trade in archaic societies that prestige goods form a notable (often non-perishable) part of the exchanged commodities. But equally significant, as Malinowski and his successors in the field of economic anthropology have shown, is the *gimwali*, the exchange of specialist utilitarian items that tend to create more efficient production of surplus which in turn enables the acquisition of the prestige goods which attract the observer.

By later medieval standards the traded commodities of the period 600–900 are limited in range and quantity. We are fortunate in possessing historical (mostly observational) and archaeological data pertaining to these objects of trade. But while we cannot accurately assess the quantities involved in the trade, we can distinguish between prestige and utilitarian goods on the basis of their incidence within early medieval society (Table 3).

In this chapter we shall examine two aspects of the traded commodities listed above. First, a review of coinage in this period is especially apposite since bullion is one commodity that we can show was regularly moved about as well as stored. Secondly, an item-by-item review of the other traded commodities is necessary so that the object of the trading systems discussed in the preceding chapters is immediately apparent.

The archaeology of coins and bullion

Colin Renfrew has written that 'the presence of coins in a civilisation is a crucial one'.[2] Coinage seems to permit us direct access to the exchange system – or does it? The paucity of theoretical discussion about

Table 3

Archaeological		Historical
	Prestige goods	
coins as bullion		precious metals
precious metals		hunting dogs
decorated metalwork		hides
arms		arms
basins and cauldrons		spices
textiles: e.g. silk		textiles
ceramic tableware		wine
glass vessels, window panes, beads		dyes
precious stones		honey
	Utilitarian goods	
lava quernstones		'black stones'
honestones		foodstuffs
soapstone vessels		salt
linen smoothers		slaves

numismatics reveals the implicit problems. Coinage may seem an index of marketing systems, but a tenet of this book is that such a system is conditioned by statehood, and in early medieval north-west Europe the appearance of coinage clearly pre-dates this level of social complexity and organisation. In fact coinage appears to be a function of long-distance trade as it becomes regularised and more formally organised. We have also argued that in many circumstances coinage evolved as an index for the payment of blood-feud prices; therefore in these cases it is related to the process of increasing social segregation.[3] Coinage also evolved from the trading of bullion, which was used in the production of prestige goods – primitive valuables, which were important to the process of redistribution. Early money, unlike our own currencies, is, as Polanyi defined it, special-purpose money.[4]

John Collis in an important paper has examined the evolution of coinage and the mechanisms of minting.[5] His two models are summarised in Figs. 26 and 27 respectively. The first model examines the spread of coinage; he writes as follows:

In 1a I show six such systems (these might be territories, kingdoms etc.) with interlocking relationships. System 1 has already adopted coinage which is rapidly disseminated to all parts of the system including the overlap areas with systems 2 and 3. In 1b coinage, having been introduced into these systems as a new innovation, is rapidly disseminated to all parts of these systems. However, the coinage in system 1 has itself developed (e.g. drop in weight, typological development) and as the overlap areas also go through change, and as these areas are the innovation centres for the spread of coinage into systems 2 and 3, the new coinage of systems 2 and 3 will reflect the changes in system 1. Also there will be divergence between systems 2 and 3, each adopting different features of the coinage system 1 from either its earlier or later stage, as well as introducing their own idiosyncracies.

. . . In phase 3 system 4 adopts coinage much as 2 and 3 had earlier though again the coinage of systems 1–3 has developed further, and this is reflected in the coinage of systems 4 and 5. System 6, however, has not adopted coinage. Though it had been introduced into the system it answered no needs in that system, and was rejected by it. System 5 is in the interesting position of being coinage introduced from two different systems, and may adopt characteristics from either or both systems for its own coinage.

Collis concludes by discussing circumstances (Fig. 26d) in which four different minting conditions are introduced by two unrelated neighbouring systems. When we come to discuss the coinage from north- west

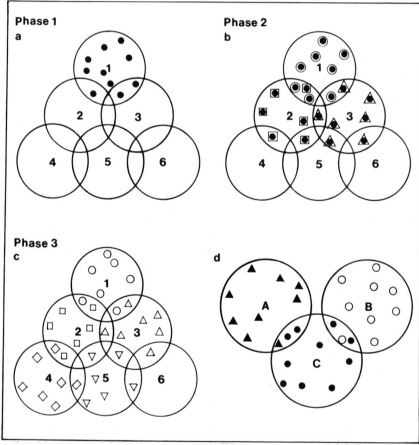

Figure 26 Models illustrating the diffusion of coinage through related territories (after Collis)

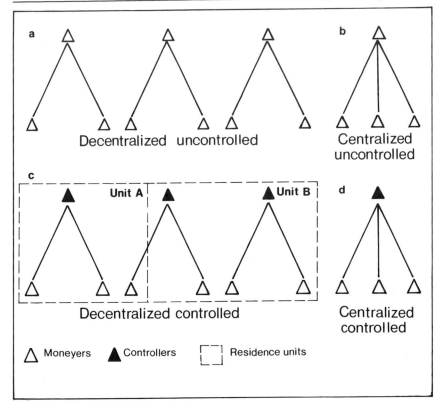

Figure 27 Models illustrating the organisation of coin production (after Collis)

Europe, we may envisage Merovingia and later Carolingia as the system 1 in this model, changing and leading to change through Phases 1–3.

Collis's second model is concerned with intra-territorial mechanisms of minting. He has defined two essentially different socities (Fig. 27): (1) a centralised social structure which approximates to a pyramid in terms of power and organisation, and (2) a decentralised society where within a defined territory there are several individuals of equal status (an oligarchy at its most perfect); in this structure power is based on familial ties or on social obligations such as patronage. In (1) minting may be centralised but uncontrolled (Fig. 27b), or centralised and controlled (Fig. 27d); and (2) it may be uncontrolled, in which case theoretically anyone with access to the requisite resources may produce coins (Fig. 27a), or controlled and therefore administered by a leading class or individual (Fig. 27c).[6]

A second theoretical paper on coinage has been published recently by George Dalton, doyen of the substantivist school of economic anthropology. Dalton has attempted to define primitive valuables, primitive money and early cash in what he has termed 'aboriginal societies'.

Primitive valuables 'were spent, transacted, paid out, but in non-commercial ways, that is, in political and social ways such as death compensation, bridewealth, and war alliance'.[7] By contrast, *primitive money* is defined as a medium in peripheral market exchange (cf. Chapter 1). Dalton includes cowries and slabs of salt as examples of this medium, and also items which might easily be imitated and therefore cannot be controlled by any central authority. *Early cash* is the product of early states and has been used for the payment of taxes or fines as well as in ordinary market-exchange. In effect, this tends to be a controlled medium which can be graded to tax indirectly if the coinage is marked with the insignia of authority. For this reason it is difficult to imitate, while rulers tend to legislate against forging early cash.

One further aspect of coinage is its changing character as primitive money becomes a form of cash: from possessing specific functions it becomes multi-purpose. We should have several expectations of coinage passing through such a trajectory.[8] First, we must expect primitive money to be restricted in its spatial distribution to those particular groups which require or share this medium. Cash, on the other hand, should flow more freely in and between the centres in which it is used. Secondly, we should expect coinage to be the subject of more rigorous controls as its use becomes more daily and general. Hence early cash should be marked more prominently than primitive money so that it bears a clear representation of the person authorising its use. Similarly the credibility of the issuing authority will be in doubt if standardised weights and metal measures are not met once the currency is in general use. If the user cannot be assured of such standards he will resort to other media of exchange, such as pure gold or silver. The creation of cash, therefore, calls for readily identifiable objects the value of which cannot be in doubt.[9]

In this section we shall examine briefly two areas of research on primitive currency. The first is the history of coinage in Early and Middle Saxon England, which is now well-established. During this period the development from coins as primitive valuables to early cash can be illustrated. The second area is the question of hack-silver and raw bullion.

Table 4 summarises the intricate history of Anglo-Saxon coinage. The earliest coin-types in Anglo-Saxon England are the bracteates – abstract imitations of coins made of gold. These were probably made in Denmark late in the fifth century, and also during the following century.[10] They were partly influenced by Byzantine solidi, which were reaching the Baltic region in considerable numbers at this time. (Some of the Byzantine coins came via the transalpine route described in Chapter 2.) The bracteates have an extensive distribution, but their frequent occurrence as pendants suggests that they were traded as primitive valuables, possibly between the diffused Germanic tribes. But their concentration in Kent, for example, also implies some significant

Table 4

Date	Coin-type	Metal	Use
6th century	bracteates	gold	primitive valuables
c. 550–c. 600	continental tremisses	gold	primitive valuables
c. 600–c. 625	" (civic issues)	gold	"/primitive currency
c. 625–c. 650	" + English imitations	gold	primitive currency
c. 650–c. 675	" + English imitations	gold	primitive currency
c. 690–c. 725	primary sceattas	silver	small denomination currency
c. 725–c. 750's	secondary sceattas	silver	extended currency
c. 780s	primary Offan penny	silver	restricted currency
c. 790s–796	secondary Offan penny	silver	? incipient early cash

trade between the Scandinavians and the Jutish community alleged to have settled there. Of course, many of these bracteates may have been melted down and reworked into native jewellery. We can only speculate whether the abstract ornamentation on the bracteates may have been a mark of some authority.

These types were probably superseded to some extent by the influx of Byzantine coins later in the sixth century.[11] At about this time gold coins were also first being issued in several regions in France and western Germany, and some of them reached Kent. Their frequent occurrence in the rich cemeteries of south-eastern England shows that they were still valued as primitive valuables important to the funerary rite. By this date, however, kingship in Kent was becoming more centralised and contact with the Merovingian courts was on a more formal basis, as we saw in Chapter 2. The importation of bullion, which was almost certainly turned into much of the fine jewellery for which Early Saxon Kent is famous, was an important means, we may suspect, of extending the role of Kentish kingship. It is therefore no surprise to find more gold coins dating from the early seventh century in Kentish and East Anglian cemeteries. By this time the Merovingian kingdoms were minting the so-called 'civic issues' on a lavish scale, possibly in response to the decline of the Byzantine influence in the west, and their issues in England mark an important commercial phase, though it seems likely that their use within England was still very limited. During the next two decades the adoption of coinage in England begins to take hold and, as Rigold has shown, far fewer imported coins occur in graves. Rigold has phased the history of gold coinage as follows.[12]

1. A phase that covers the second half of the sixth century, before c. 595 when St. Augustine landed; it includes orthodox Byzantine issues, eastern Gallic issues of Theodebert I; Gallic derivations of heavy

tremisses; Visigothic, Spanish or south-western French tremisses; Alemannic tremisses.

2. A 'Sutton Hoo' phase covering the very end of the sixth century and the first quarter of the seventh century; this principally includes Merovingian 'civic issues' and Provençal light coinage.

3. A 'Crondall hoard' phase covering the second quarter of the seventh century and probably the 650s as well; this includes debased Merovingian 'civic issues' and the very first English gold coinage.

4. A 'post-Crondall hoard phase' when a standard alloy of 30 per cent had become established, lasting until the 660s or 670s, when the switch to a silver standard was effected; principally English, though some continental types still found.

Rigold's phase 4 gold coinage was in fact heavily alloyed with other metals. These are pale gold issues which probably indicate the growing scarcity of gold for minting purposes. Rigold states that these issues were 'quite prolific' and that 'some types actually span the abrupt transition to silver – the so-called "sceattas", the earliest of which appear suddenly, on a *lower* standard (his italics) of silver than that which was to prevail as soon as silver coinage became prolific'. Both types of coin were largely restricted to south-eastern England, emphasising Kent's supremacy in international affairs.

The switch to silver pre-dated the Arab conquest of the western Mediterranean. It was an ordered change set in motion from the 680s in Merovingia, perhaps because supplies of gold were more difficult to acquire since Byzantine mercantile operations in the Mediterranean and beyond were severely restricted. Spectrographic and metrological analyses show the high degree of control maintained over these gradually devalued coins. The seventh century, however, was also a period of gold fever in Merovingia and north-west Europe generally. In part this was a consequence of Christian propaganda which was expressed in the form of elegantly ornamented crosses and pendants as well as sacramental vessels. In part it may have been a consequence of the apparently uncontrolled decentralised minting which marks the central decades of the seventh century in Merovingia – a period of near-anarchy in government. In switching to silver in the 680s, Pepin II was bringing some order to bear on the widespread civic minting, as well as creating a more readily available currency. Gold, however, continued to be used throughout the remaining centuries of the millennium, but for objects that were essentially primitive valuables, such as prestation rings which bear the names of their owners or the name of the giver.

This switch to silver has many implications. Besides the abandonment of the gold standard, it probably marks the effective beginning and widespread use of a Germanic system of weights and measures as opposed to the Roman system used previously. In Kent, the tremissis was valued at one-third of a (Byzantine) solidus, as it was elsewhere on the continent. This Byzantine measure was roughly equal to 20 Kentish sceattas or one whole Kentish *scilling*. Thus the coin reform of the late seventh century introduced to north-west Europe a small denomination calculated from its own traditional weight systems based on the barley-grain rather that the siliqua of the locust-tree, otherwise known as the carat.[13] Grierson, in particular, has drawn attention to the variants of this Germanic weight system. In Wessex, for example, a gold tremissis issued in Kent was worth only ten silver pence – or, since the West Saxons were late in minting coins, half an ounce of silver.

The adoption of a silver standard, however, seems to have been for economic reasons. It reflects the growth of commerce within the Germanic areas, where their weights and measures were ultimately more useful and appropriate than those derived from the classical world. Moreover it was clearly a reform aimed at controlling exchange from Merovingia centrally, as well as a means of stimulating it. Pepin's other great economic action appears to have been the foundation of a 'new' settlement at Dorestad soon after the annexation of the Rhinemouth area in the 680s. It brought a swift response; the Frisians issued sceattas, and the primary series of sceattas was also issued in Kent, some in imitation of the Frisian coins.

The first minting of these new Kentish coins is not easy to place chronologically. Rigold believes that the minting was initiated by king Wihtred in the first few years of his reign, probably in 690.[14] (The gold tremisses in their pale form, he believes, were issued until 694, when they were withdrawn after the massive blood-price payment to the west Saxons on the murder of their prince, Mul.) Rigold's attribution of these primary sceattas to Wihtred rather than Hlothere, his predecessor, can be confirmed if we refer to Collis's model. If system 1 is envisaged as Merovingia, system 2 as Frisia and system 3 as Kent, we should predict some delay in the minting of coins in Kent, while their coastal distribution in Kent (especially eastern Kent) tends to confirm their major function as media in long-distance trade.

These sceattas in Rigold's primary series (with a high silver content) must have been exchanged for the raw silver still used as a measure of value in other English kingdoms. Their incidence, however, in the initial phase at Hamwih, Saxon Southampton, though in small numbers, suggests that outside Kent these coins were used only for international purposes. Altogether it tends to confirm Kent's singular trading activity with Frisia and the Rhineland at this time (see Chapter 2).

The extension of the sceatta series to other parts of England has become known as the 'secondary series'. This series was initiated sometime in the 720s; and Wessex may be regarded as system 4, Mercia as system 5 and Northumbria as system 6. Each kingdom began minting coins over the next quarter century with a high level of silver, and after an interval each appears to have debased its own sceattas progressively (see below). Metcalf, the leading scholar concerned with these coins, believes that this secondary sceatta phase marks an economic boom which effectively embraced the coastal areas from the Humber to the Exe as well as the heartland of Mercia.[15] This was the period when king Athelbald of Mercia was '*rex non solum Marcercium sed et omnium provinciarum quae generali nomine Sutangli dicuntur*' ('king not only of the Mercians, but of all the provinces which are known by the general name of the Sutangli'), as well as a man of international reputation.

The many coins of this period from Hamwih, Saxon Southampton, illustrate this secondary series debasement: the earlier BMC type 39 which was probably minted here has a high silver content, ranging from 82 to 92 per cent. By contrast, the later BMC type 49, found in considerable numbers, has a silver content of only 61 to 66 per cent. Milliprobe analyses of about 20 per cent of the known coins have shown an even greater step-like debasement of certain Northumbrian issues, so that while the coins of king Eadberht (737–758) are shown to be of alloys similar to the Hamwih coins, by the reign of king Aelfwald of Northumbria (779–788) the issues are only about half silver: $48\frac{1}{2}$ to $52\frac{1}{2}$ per cent. It is strikingly reminiscent of the step-like gold debasement of the previous century (Fig. 28). However, as tin was beginning to be added to whiten some alloys in these debased coins, all issues in southern England were abruptly terminated.

Metcalf believes that the end of the secondary sceatta series was the result of a silver shortage, but this seems improbable for three reasons. First, the Northumbrian kings continued to mint sceattas intermittently throughout the next two or three decades, during which time southern England was virtually without coins. Secondly, there seems to be a correlation between the minting of coins in southern England and the phases of activity at Hamwih.[16] This may be a dangerously circular argument, yet there are grounds for believing that international trade ceased or, at least, declined to a shadow of its previous scale from about 750 until the last decade of the eighth century. We shall consider this argument again in subsequent parts of this and later chapters. Thirdly, when king Offa of Mercia, Aethelbald's celebrated successor, issued the new heavier coins of the last quarter of the eighth century they had a high silver content. Metcalf counters this last point by proposing that Offa gradually imported silver and was thus after some time able to achieve this purity.

The more satisfactory explanation of events is the simplest one. The use of sceattas after about 725 in most parts of England was almost certainly conditioned by their primary use in long-distance trade. And while Metcalf has rightly argued in a recent essay that the secondary sceattas may have been used at fairs and peripheral markets, this use, as a primitive currency, was restricted.[17] The immense concentration of

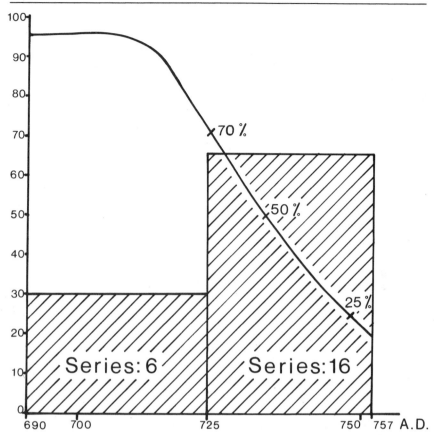

Figure 28 Sketch illustrating the numbers of series for the primary and secondary sceattas respectively, set against the apparent decline in the silver purity of these coins

sceattas at Hamwih emphasises beyond doubt their international significance. This was apparently ended when Pepin III in 755 reformed the continental coinage, much as Pepin II had done in the 680s, to reassert some authority over coinage which was gaining ground, we must assume, as a useful medium in regional Carolingian transactions. Pepin's new currency was issued with a wider, thinner flan, and his coins had a higher silver content.[18] This reform coincided with the death of king Aethelbald of Mercia. It is possible that the Mercian king's demise and the subsequent struggle for supremacy afterwards created a phase in which long-distance trade was no longer either possible or relevant. Equally, it is possible that Pepin was more interested in intraterritorial than in international commerce.

Of course, the dating of sceattas is far from precise, since they seldom carry the names of kings, or any clues to them. Therefore they must be treated with caution in spite of the amount of research which has been devoted to understanding them. Furthermore their purpose remains obscure. The variety of designs employed on the coins, ranging from imperial motifs to abstractions of Anglo-Saxon images, leads us to believe that these were special-purpose artifacts, while the large numbers associated with minsters such as Richborough, Reculver and Whitby point to ecclesiastical use in some quantity. The absence of kings' names and mint-marks on most of the coins, and yet the clear presentation of the Northumbrian kings' names on the series, suggests that the royal use of sceattas was limited. There is certainly a striking lack of standardisation in the designs which would have made them very hard to use. There is also a wide variation in the weights of the coins, in contrast to the variation permitted in the Late Saxon period. This, of course, may mask regional differences and relate to the different systems employed in Kent, Wessex and Mercia; it remains to be tested. Similarly, we need to know whether this weight variation undermines the sequence of decreasing silver content suggested for the secondary sceattas. All these questions demand more detailed research. At the moment the degree of standardisation, the perplexing variability and the range of dispersed and concentrated patterns for the individual series emphasise the problems of primitive currency.[19] These coins may have been a means of maintaining relationships between groups on a crude yet regulated basis, but there is much to be done to prove the hypothesis. With the introduction of the penny, our interpretations of coinage become clearer and we reach a point where the currency has a strong resemblance to our own.

Offa's reform of the coinage has also been extensively discussed in the literature. Indeed Blunt's celebrated paper on the coinage of Offa splendidly summarises the main characteristics of this important period.[20] In brief, Blunt argues that the new coin, the penny, was introduced by two Kentish kings ruling jointly under Offa's hegemony. In fact these kings, Heaberht and Ecgberht, minted very few pennies which appear to be in line with Pepin III's 755 reform. The alloy of these coins had a high silver content, which was in excess of 90 per cent in the few examples analysed. These so-called group 1 Offan coins are generally attributed to the 770s and are limited to Kent in a pattern similar to the primary sceattas which were similarly restricted in distribution.

The group 2 Offan pennies mark a significant change, as they present the king's bust on the obverse, 'sometimes of a quality of workmanship that entitles one to believe that an attempt at portraiture was being made'.[21] This was evidently an exercise in propagating the power of the Mercian king, now styled '*rex Merciorum simulque aliarum circumquaque (in circuita) nationum*' ('king of the Mercians and at the same time of the other surrounding tribes'). These coins also represent a significant upgrading of the weight and increase in the size of the flan, as a result perhaps of Charlemagne's reform in about 790.[22] The group 2 coins are widely distributed throughout southern and eastern England, though more have been found on the continent. Blunt favours a date around 790 for their inception, a time when Offa was very much engaged in the problems of continental trade, as the letters exchanged with Charlemagne illustrate.

There is, finally, a third group of Offan coins. This is distinguished from the previous groups by its heavier weight, which is 'distinctly over 20 grains', in comparison with those of the other two groups, which average about 19 grains.

The secondary series of Offan pennies marks the beginning of a century of minting at a standard weight. Not until king Alfred upgraded his pennies late in the ninth century, and also experimented with half-pennies and third-pennies, were any further changes to occur (see Chapters 8 and 9). Offa's second group of pennies was probably also intended as a form of early cash; the control of their production, for example, is apparently more regulated than was the case with the earlier sceattas. The number of coins minted by Offa would obviously be one key feature of the development.

Metcalf has attempted in several papers to calculate the numbers of coins for this early medieval period.[23] He has used a random sampling technique, known as Brown's formula, which was devised to estimate the hammered coinage issued during the reign of Elizabeth I in the sixteenth century. This estimation essentially depends on first identifying the number of dies in use, calculating what sample of the total population of dies these remaining ones must be, and then multiplying the total population of dies by the number of coins that may theoretically be minted from one die – and evidently were minted in later medieval England. Metcalf has favoured figures of up to 10,000 coins from each die. Thus 'if the original total of obverse dies was of the order of 135 to 150 (and it can hardly have been less), the number of pennies (primary sceattas) struck within the thirty-five-year period covering the reign of Wihtred will have been something like $2\frac{1}{2}$ to 3 millions'.[24] He then considers Offa's coinage and calculates that 2,500 dies ±500, each producing 5,000 coins in the last decade or so of the eighth century, results in a currency of between 10 and 30 millions.

Metcalf's work is extremely valuable, but there appears to be a conceptual flaw, to which Grierson has drawn attention.[25] Quite clearly, Metcalf has assumed that each die was fully used and, as we have seen, there is no reason to suppose this to be true in the case of primitive money. It is as likely that only one sceatta was minted from Wihtred's moneyer's die as that 10,000 were. Exactly how more feasible calculations could be made is unclear. Grierson argues the case for lower figures, not only for the sceattas but for the Offan pennies too. Figures in the order of half a million and 1 to 3 millions respectively seem instinctively more satisfactory, but Metcalf is right to persist in finding some formal means of justifying one's instincts. In the case of primitive currency, however, in contrast to early cash, this is difficult to achieve, and remains a theoretical problem badly in need of definition.[26] With Offa's coins a new monetary era was embarked upon, and several of his issues were possibly minted in much greater numbers and with standardised silver content, weights and designs in contrast to those produced by sceatta-moneyers.

Only England, Frisia and Carolingia, however, were using currency in any marked form before about 800; and beyond these regions, while long-distance trade was in operation, central authority exerted only minimal control over it. In these circumstances raw materials must have been the primitive money, and while metrological laws may have been enforced (thus explaining the commonplace discovery of balances and weights), the system probably prevented the accumulation of wealth in the hands of central persons.

Several authors have demonstrated the existence of bullion and hack-silver for use in long-distance trade during the Viking period. Recently, however, Bakka has argued that the system stems from the fourth century in Norway, while Skaare has shown that the tenth- and eleventh-century Vikings were very sensitive to the purity of the silver they had plundered and then cut up into pre-determined values.[27] Similarly, Richard Warner has indicated the existence of denominations in the hoards of hack-silver found in ninth- and tenth-century Scotland and Ireland.[28]

Birgitta Hardh has examined the evolution of the hack-silver system rather further, showing that it is ultimately an extension of market transactions in Scania (which was then part of Denmark, and is now southern Sweden). She has shown that the heterogeneous hoards of the early tenth century were replaced in about 970 by more homogeneous hoards principally composed of plundered coins. These hoards prevail until the mid-eleventh century, when coins issued by the new Danish urban mints begin to predominate any coin assemblages (see Chapter 9). Hardh demonstrates that during the course of a hundred and fifty years silver, initially kept for re-working into primitive valuables, attains an intrinsic value as a primitive currency. By the eleventh century hack-silver has become the force of the early market: a form of early cash.[29]

The slightly anarchic overtones implicit in the use of hack-silver and bullion have been skilfully woven into the Late Saxon poem describing the infamous battle of Maldon. A Viking spokesman is sent to the defiant Saxon earl Bryhtnoth, and he says the following:[30]

> The swift-striking seafarers send me to thee,
> bid me say that thou send for the safety
> rings, bracelets. Better for you
> that you stay straightaway our onslaught with tribute
> than that we should share bitter strife.

To the civilised Anglo-Saxons who then used coinage, the ring-money was further evidence of the barbarous nature of their enemy. It was the establishing of some centralised authority over a community based on a highly decentralised primitive currency that was the real challenge faced by the Danish and Norwegian kings whose men were involved in this and other battles in England at the time.

We may well wonder precisely how exchange was effected in the closed environments of the Scandinavian emporia, where the use of bullion in its raw form prevailed. We can only speculate on the inefficiency of bullion and possibly its role in delimiting the scale of exchange. There is evidently a great deal still to be understood, and, like the gold ingot (as yet unpublished) from Dorestad, where coins were also in use, it remains perplexing.

The evolution of currency is very much a function of systemic 'inter-connectedness'. It appears in part to have been a response to an international system, as Collis's model illustrates. Yet it also evolves as a requirement of strong leadership itself intent on regulating commerce for its own ends. Minted coins, unlike bullion, are a more efficient means of accumulating wealth if their use is successfully enforced, and thus coinage ultimately contributes towards the attainment of goals which the institutional means of society are intended to delimit. Value indices, however, are naturally a product of ranked communities, for these are the principal methods by which large communities interact. It is therefore a direct progression to some form of primitive currency; but beyond this primitive character the evolution is by no means certain. Without at least the theoretical notion of early cash, however, it is impossible to articulate an economy of any size, and therefore, as we shall see in Chapter 9, its inception is a fundamental attribute of competitive markets and state societies.

The archaeology of traded commodities

Coinage was probably a medium of exchange and on occasions also bullion in international commerce. It was the most precious form of metals, though with a function that varied regionally and through time. The main precious metals other than gold and silver were tin and lead. Nor must iron be overlooked. Lead weights have been found in south-eastern England[31] in the Early Saxon period and may have been ingots; from Kaupang there is a small lead ingot which would probably have been turned into the scale-pan weights used by merchants in Norway at the time.[32] Pure tin is seldom found, though its incidence in certain types of Anglo-Saxon sceattas has recently been demonstrated.[33] It was also applied as the thinnest foil on the pots familiarly known as Tating ware, which were mostly made in the middle Rhineland and were traded throughout northern Europe (Fig. 10).[34] Iron currency bars from

Vestfold in Norway and from Norrland in Sweden indicate the intrinsic value of the metal.[35] In particular, it was probably esteemed for its use in weapons, but of course it had a general use.

The extensive distribution of specialist decorated metalwork has long been established in the early medieval period. Werner's maps of the late fifth- to sixth-century radiate brooches in northern Europe, for example, illustrate the movements of such specialist jewellery, while the Sutton Hoo ship burial brings together a rich assemblage of metalwork from diffused origins representing a myriad artistic styles. Ypey has identified Anglo-Saxon metalwork in the Dutch cemeteries, while the (Carolingian) Tassilo chalice is probably of Middle Saxon manufacture.[36] Vierck has taken this kind of stylistic analysis a stage further and pointed to the pieces made by the seventh-century Neustrian gold-moneyer Elegius, bishop of Noyon and Tournai, whose gold coins are also well known. Each of these studies presents a remarkable insight into the specialist craftsmen of the time, and the local and inter-regional movements of their products. Recently, however, the discovery of the smiths' shops at Helgö has enabled us to plot the movements of this metalwork, providing, as we shall see in the next chapter, a real basis for interpreting the regional context of a workshop. Smiths have also been identified at Ribe, Haithabu, Dorestad and Hamwih: at the first two of these sites moulds for dress-jewellery have also been found.[37]

The Hamwih smith was probably engaged in the production of more prosaic metal items. Keys are one such object commonly found in north-west Europe in the early medieval period. Many of these keys were for caskets, but larger examples have been found with barrel-locks which they fitted.[38] There has been some speculation that keys were a speciality of the smiths in the Meuse valley from the later Merovingian period. A number have been identified in the local cemeteries there, while several were found on the beaches which had previously been the dune-sites of Domburg and Westenschouwen.[39] In view of their general skills with iron, an indigenous Viking-period production in Scandinavia may account for the superbly artistic keys found at Birka and other sites.

There has been an extensive discussion about the trading of weapons in northern Europe during the early medieval period. Certainly the Rhenish sword blades were famed not only in the western world but in the east also.[40] These were so-called damascened swords with the pattern-welded structure which made the blades especially strong and durable. Such swords with 'the wavy pattern reminiscent of an adder's back' may well have inspired the frequent references to 'serpent-patterned blades' which figure in the Icelandic sagas. The most famous of these weapons are the Ulfberht swords, named after the legends stamped on to the blades. Similarly named swords are known throughout the Viking period and must be some indication of the prestige of the great sword-smiths, while their extensive distribution implies that these valuables were traded. Sword-smiths, of course, operated in all the states around

Carolingia, but these particular weapons with their mark of sound craftsmanship were clearly much in demand. Indeed for a brief period Charlemagne put an embargo on their shipment when the Danes were in rebellion against him.

There are two major groups of cauldrons and basins which have fortuitously survived from the period in north-west Europe. A small group has been found in the Meuse valley and a far larger and more varied group is known from Norway. Outliers exist also. A few basins from eastern England date from the sixth century, while Viking-period basins contemporary with some of the Norwegian vessels have been found in Gotland.[41] Because of their prominence in the production of basins and cauldrons from the later medieval period, it has been suggested that the Meuse Valley smiths made all these containers. But in view of the Norwegian iron ore deposits and the fame of their smiths, the Scandinavian vessels should be attributed to Scandinavian craftsmen unless it is proved otherwise.

The direct evidence for textiles is pitifully slight. The best collection was recovered from the graves at Birka, where fragments of silk, as well

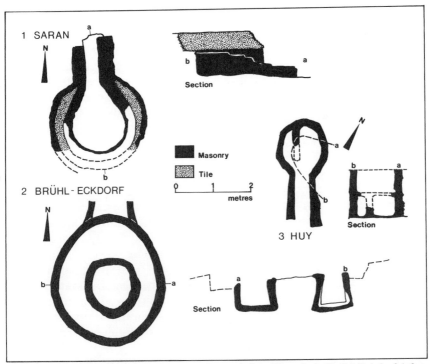

Figure 29 Three early medieval kilns: Saran (after Chapelot); Brühl-Eckdorf (after Janssen); and Huy (after Willems). The Saran (Orléans) and Brühl-Eckdorf (near Cologne) kilns are probably ninth-century, while the Huy kiln (near Liège) is seventh-century)

as cloaks in other materials, were recovered. Such small woollen fragments are not particularly significant in themselves, but from cemeteries of Early Saxon date, as well as from Viking cemeteries, including Birka, tiny fragments of gold-threaded garments have been found.[42] Evidently the funeral attire of many early medieval women was splendidly elegant, which suggests the importance of textiles in commerce at this time. Display was an important index of rank, in a rank-conscious society; we may note the changing dress of the Jellinge dynasty in western Denmark during the tenth century, when this dynasty assumed control of an incipient state. By contrast, in view of the Haithabu and Dorestad finds, the production of leather goods, and shoes in particular, were an important specialist output which must not be underestimated.[43]

There have been many references to the trading of pottery in the early medieval period in previous chapters. Mass-replicated table-wares from the (low hills of the) Vorgebirge in the middle Rhineland near Bonn (Fig. 16) dominate the assemblages from Dorestad and (to a lesser extent) Haithabu, and were traded elsewhere along the North Sea littoral, as we have seen in Chapters 2 and 5 (Fig. 5).[44] French Carolingian wares were also widely traded, as were Slavic wares, some of which were made in the region of Mecklenburg.[45] The most unusual and widely traded pottery was Tating ware.[46] This pottery (Fig. 10) occurs in only two forms: pitchers and small jars, most of which are decorated with thinly applied tin-foil. Thin-section analysis has demonstrated that several of the various fabrics were made in the middle Rhineland, probably in the region of the Mayen potteries. There was some imitation of this ware, however, presumably because it was widely sought. It may have been imbued originally with some Christian significance – hence the Maltese crosses in tin-foil – but its occurrence in pagan graves as far east as Russia, and the considerable numbers found on trading sites, suggest that it was traded in its own right as well.

Glass is more difficult to provenance than pottery, especially as a number of 'glass-houses' re-using Roman and early migration period glass have been found. Later Merovingian and Carolingian houses have been found in the neighbourhood of Trier and at Macquenoise in the north-west limit of the Ardennes. It was from these centres presumably that the glass vessels came which were found, for example, at Ipswich and at Dorestad, as well as the superb vessels from Sweden dating from the Vendel period onwards.[47] The discovery of glass-bead manufacturing centres at Paviken, Ribe, Helgö, Haithabu and Kaupang has necessarily complicated the picture.[48] That the vessels themselves were locally manufactured along with the beads has been considered, but is generally doubted. Jankuhn, however, has argued that the bead industry was originally diffused from Haithabu, though the evidence now appears insubstantial.

Analyses of a few of these glasses has pointed to the presence of a

Figure 30 The buddha from Helgö (courtesy of Statens Historiska Museum, Stockholm)

potash component, which has lead to the speculation that this at least was imported from the eastern Mediterranean to the glass-houses of the middle Rhineland. It remains to be seen whether this can be demonstrated for a larger sample of vessels, or whether re-used Roman glass has misled the investigators.[49]

Bede describes how Frankish glaziers came to Jarrow to make the multicoloured panes that have been retrieved from recent excavations.[50] Similar panes have been found at the nearby monastery of Wearmouth founded at the same time, as well as at Escomb some 50 km or so away – at the Saxon church of Repton in the Midlands, and at the royal mill at Old Windsor, Berkshire. The vestigial remains of glass furnaces of seventh-century date at Burgh Castle, Suffolk, and at Glastonbury of ninth-century date, imply that monastic communities were also keenly patronising glaziers to fenestrate their new stone buildings.

A further by-product of the glass-houses is the linen-smoother, definitely a utilitarian artefact, in contrast to the usual prestige wares of the glass-houses.[51] These thick lumps of glass were probably the end pieces of blown glass. Glass linen-smoothers were presumably preferred to pebbles in textile production, though we may doubt that they were more efficient. An early medieval distribution map shows that they are widely found in late Merovingian and later contexts. As a by-product of the glass-trade, they are found in the emporia – for example, at Hamwih and Dorestad. The incidence of such objects on inland rural sites such as the Saxon village excavated at St. Neots, England, however and in the tenth- to eleventh-century souterrain at Treguennec in Brittany, goes some way towards confirming the model of utilitarian object distribution outlined above.

Precious stones and exotica are perhaps the classical items in this kind of long-distance trade. Baltic Sea amber was worked at Ribe,[52] and was also probably quarried near Whitby, Yorkshire, at this time, though its use in ornaments was infrequent. (An entire cache of Baltic amber has recently been found at Kiev.) The fashion of setting cut garnets in the finest jewellery must have brought these precious stones northwards from the Mediterranean world during the sixth and later centuries and created a significant trade. Yet these, of course, were insubstantial exchanges, involving few people and relatively modest quantities. Exotica like the Coptic vessels, cowrie shells and Byzantine spoons were the staple of the sixth-century transalpine trading system which began in Theodoric's reign (see Chapter 2).[53] After this phase, Mediterranean and oriental objects are rarities until the Arabs began to influence the course of Baltic sea commerce from the later eighth century. Perhaps to this phase can be attributed the northern Indian buddha of sixth- or seventh-century date found at Helgö, which has a twin in a private collection in Kashmir (Fig. 30).[54] In the intervening centuries, when north-west Europe was a closed system, exotica are rare. Note has therefore been taken of the turtle-bone (a species of north African

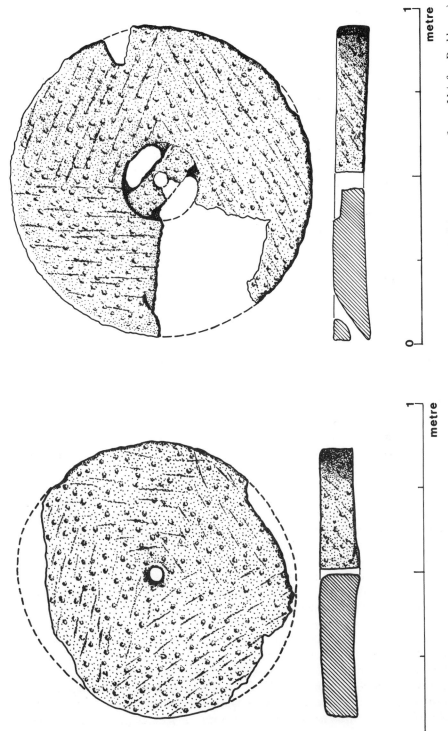

Figure 31 Two examples of Niedermendig lava quernstones from Dorestad: left, lower stone of type V; right, upper stone of type V (after Parkhouse)

animal) from Hamwih, and the Avar sword reportedly sent to Offa by Charlemagne.

Utilitarian items

The range of archaeologically defined utilitarian items is limited. Cooking-pots were seldom traded over long-distances before the twelfth or thirteenth centuries; iron as ore, or in the spade-shaped bars known from Vestfold and Norrland, give us but a fleeting glimpse of this highly significant industry. We have made reference to the linen-smoothers, which were probably a minor by-product of a prestige trade, but their distribution is not established. The staple utilitarian items from this period are the quernstones, honestones and soapstone vessels. Their petrology permits them to be readily characterised and traced to an unequivocal source.

Are the 'black stones' (*petrae nigrae*) mentioned in Charlemagne's letter to king Offa quernstones? If they are, it demonstrates the real force of the trading system – a motivation at production level which, in effect, stimulated the trade in prestige items. Lava quernstones certainly have 'black' volcanic grits and were extensively traded at this time (Figs. 31 and 32).

There were two major-production centres. The Merovingian and Carolingian centre lay in the Eifel mountains near the villages of Mayen[55] and was doubtless an industry of some organisational complexity, being a scarce resource of enormous production significance. The other main quern-quarries lay in Norway and produced Glimmerstein stones which were traded around the Baltic. There were, of course, other quern-quarries in northern Europe. They probably existed in northern France, possibly in eastern Brittany. The Hamwih evidence also points to querns from areas in southern England. The Tamworth mill in Mercia – possibly a royal mill – had a number of lava querns, but also a quantity of gritstone querns, likely to have been made of stone, from the Sheffield region.[56] The Early Christian Irish evidence is among the best studied. Evidently neither the Carolingians nor the Norwegians impinged on the various local industries producing small hand-mill querns. Querns from the Mourne mountains, for example, served the farmsteads of Co. Down and Co. Antrim, essentially the tribal areas of the Dál nAraide and the Dal Riata respectively.[57]

The lava querns were shipped in large quantities, often in roughed-out form to Dorestad and Haithabu. At both sites they were finished off. There is a little evidence to suggest that they were also dressed at Ipswich, though the available sample is substantially smaller than from the other two sites. The pattern of finds may be seen to conform to the trading model presented in the previous chapter. Briefly, lava querns seem to be a staple of the Frisian trading system. They are found in

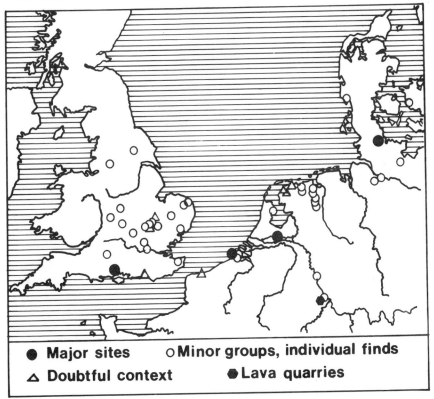

- ● **Major sites**   ○ **Minor groups, individual finds**
- △ **Doubtful context**   ◑ **Lava quarries**

Figure 32 The location and distribution of Eifel mountain quernstones (after Parkhouse)

quantity in Dorestad, Ipswich and Haithabu; they occur also at Medemblik and Ribe, and in many other sites within the catchments of those settlements. The production of the Norwegian Glimmerstein, however, effectively debarred the Frisians from the Baltic trade in this essential commodity. Similarly, the strikingly small number of lava querns from Hamwih underlines the significance of the court-traders from northern France at this time. It is too early to generalise satisfactorily about the distribution of lava querns in England. But they have been found on Middle Saxon sites of all kinds – hamlets, villages, mills, monastic and royal settlements – in the Thames valley, Mercia and eastern England generally. It remains to be seen whether any significant distribution is found for Wessex.

Honestones for sharpening iron tools were traded over equally long distances and, such is their frequency in all rural medieval sites, were clearly a commodity of singular importance. The mica-schist hones of Norway came to dominate the later medieval market in north-west Europe, so it is hardly surprising to find a specialist industry in operation in the early Viking period. We can only speculate about the relationship of this industry to the iron ore and metalworking industries. Indeed a boat with a cargo of hones was recently found a little up the coast from Kaupang, and was almost certainly a vessel that had earlier left that site.[58] (Part of this shipment, however, may have been ballast, which would explain why it was not salvaged.) Ellis has made a preliminary study of the Hamwih hones, and his report indicates some diversity of sources, both local and continental, for the pieces found there.[59] Similar diversity is often found on Irish royal sites such as Garranes, Lagore Crannog and Knowth; here inter-regional (tribal) exchange at least is becoming demonstrable. Clearly more research is needed, but when it is done the study of hones will be of some real significance in documenting regional, inter-regional and highly centralised trade and production respectively.

The importance of Kaupang in the trade of Vestfold iron ore and Glimmerstein quernstones has already been pointed out; its proximity to the soapstone quarries at Hisåsen and Austre Vimme suggests that it may have been paramount in the early stages of the trade. Soapstone vessels are the one cultural item which typifies the Vikings, whether they settled in the Shetlands, Co. Kerry, Dublin, York, Greenland or even Newfoundland.[60] The trade was probably at its peak in the tenth or eleventh centuries, but soapstone vessels arguably of ninth-century date from Haithabu, as well as from other sites in Jutland, indicate a cultural preference for more durable containers over the crude hand-made pottery.

The historical perspective

There is an interesting divergence between the archaeologically documented commodities distributed by the early medieval trader and those documented historically. For the most part, we hear of the prestige items as having been given as gifts, or remarked upon with admiration, while our knowledge of the utilitarian items usually comes from documents dealing with the fiscal arrangements at the source of production.

Textiles were prominent in the trade between the continent and England. In Charlemagne's celebrated letter to king Offa there is a reference to *sagae*, the cloaks which were a speciality of the English weavers.[61] There are also several references to *pallia fresonica*, which may have been Frisian-made garments, or at least the vestments they handled.[62] Anglo-Saxon, Frisian and Carolingian village sites show plentiful evidence of weaving, including the huts and the industrial equipment (see Chapter 7). The art of embroidery was also well-developed in the Anglo-Saxon and Norwegian worlds, as the *casula* from the monastery of St. Harlinde and St. Relinde at Measeyck in Belgium and the Oseberg boat tapestry demonstrate. The *Liber Pontificalis* records that king Aethelwulf gave pope Benedict III a silk dalmatic with gold stripes and an alb of silk embroidered with gold.[63] The significance of the textile and clothing trade to clerics and kings in a world very much concerned with personal display, whether in life or death, is beyond doubt.

The dyes for colouring the garments are a further question. Many were oriental in origin, though neither history nor archaeology tells us much about them. A charter of king Dagobert permitted the inhabitants of Quentovic to take dyes to the fair he established at St. Denys.[64] We must suppose that this isolated reference represents a rather active exchange in the commodity.

The trade in leather is rarely documented. The increasing evidence of cattle specialisation, however, particularly by the Gotlanders, leads to the conclusion that leather must have been traded. The number of leather items that survive, especially from tenth-century and later urban contexts, points powerfully to its important place in early medieval society (see above).[65] Yet we hear only of Irish monks in the Loire valley during the seventh century trying to trade it.

Lead is a precious metal which is mentioned often in the texts. In 852 some English lead was noted as it passed through Quentovic en route for the abbey of Ferrières.[66] Archbishop Wilfred was probably using local Pennine lead to roof his remodelled minster at York in 700, while Alcuin sent tin (Grierson thinks this a mistake for lead) to archbishop Eanbald II of York to cover the bell-tower of the minster.[67] (If it was indeed lead, it was sending coals to Newcastle; if it was tin, its use to roof the campanile seems odd.)

The goldsmith's status in society, often referred to in contemporary poems, is best judged from the rank and power of the seventh-century smith, bishop Elegius. The Exeter Book – probably a late ninth- or tenth-century compilation – states that a certain goldsmith possessed large estates, though by then objects of gold were rare and valuable indeed.[68]

There are many incidental items which, like the goshawks, so valued by later Plantagenet kings, recur in the surviving documentation. Hunting-dogs were taken along to the Loire with the leather by the Irish monks. Bede, in his great history of the English, mentions spices; presumably they were brought northwards by the Frisians, who are known to have been handling them in Mainz.[69] This kind of reference cannot be accurately evaluated. Honey, however, was a luxury of some importance. It was, after all, the only sweetner known at the time, which may explain its allegedly guarded trade. Bee-keepers figure as a select class in the laws of king Ina of Wessex, and we may suspect that their products were traded in controlled circumstances. We can only speculate whether the merchants from Quentovic were trading honey of English origin when they visited the fair at St. Denys.[70]

The importance of the wine trade is also difficult to assess. In Anglo-Saxon England wine was drunk by 'old men and wise ones',[71] the rest had to be satisfied with ale or water. Alcuin sent wine, with the tin, to Eanbald of York; we may assume that it was a Vorgebirge vintage. The reference to its consumption in an Irish monastery perhaps implies its value and scarcity. And while we need not doubt its staple value in Carolingia, beyond these confines – if the traded pottery, at least, is to be trusted – it was seldom consumed and then only as a delicacy.

Utilitarian items

In a strict sense, the trade in human cargoes, often on a large scale, was explicitly designed to increase local production by the cheapest method. Slave-trading was possibly the single most important trade in early medieval Europe. As we have seen in Chapter 2, it may have been a fundamental force activating the sixth-century north–south trade. Slave-trading was certainly important during the seventh century, but it began to decline when the church reacted strongly against it in Anglo-Saxon and Carolingian society. Charlemagne's wars with the Saxons and Avars undoubtedly reopened its value, while it was a motivating force behind the Viking raids which began late in the eighth century. The Vikings' calculated onslaughts on assembled populations during the ninth century show how great an emphasis they placed on the trade. It lubricated the trade with the Arabs, to the east and to the south-west. In part, it was the sheer pagan horror of the trade that created so vehement a reaction to the Vikings from contemporary Christian chroniclers. The sale of 10,000 slaves in Cordoba's market-place in five years shows just how colossal this irksome commerce had become, and puts the fear of the Vikings in some perspective.[72]

Salt, the only satisfactory preservative known, was a major requisite in all societies. The power that stemmed from control of salt-working is formidably demonstrated in the later medieval period by the rise of the Hanseatic League, which commanded the salt mines of Luneburg in northern Germany. The freedom from toll in the 'port' of London granted in 716/717 to the bishop of Worcester, who had several salt-furnaces, is a minor illustration of the early medieval power of salt.[73] The brave resistance of the monks at St. Philibert on the island of Noirmoutier near the mouth of the Loire, matched only by the persistence of the Vikings in holding the island during the central years of the ninth century, reminds us forcefully of the untold wealth the monks may have accumulated from their working of the extensive salt pans. Baiesalt, as it later became known, was already traded widely along the Loire and into the heartland of the empire.

There are scarcely any references to the movements of foodstuffs. In Chapter 7 I shall attempt to reconstruct the movements of subsistence products, using the distributions of other, non-perishable objects of regional trade. International movements of foodstuffs on any scale seem improbable in view of the boats' limited capacities. But as the middle Rhineland became more and more specialised as a region of vineyards we must presume that grain had to be imported, as it had been imported in the Roman period from southern England. There is a casual reference to this by Ermoldus Nigellus, writing in the mid-ninth century,[74] who describes the shipments of wheat being exported up the Rhine from Alsace. We must of course be wary of over-emphasising this singular reference, and yet it seems an obvious corollary of the later eighth-century Carolingian economic reforms which are discussed in Chapter 8.

In conclusion, we should note that our discussion of the boats dating from the seventh to ninth century indicates that the volume of commodities was strictly limited. The 900 amphorae, for example, from the seventh-century wreck at Yassi Ada discussed in Chapter 5 were apparently never matched by the Frisian or Rhenish vessels plying northwards from Dorestad. Boat sizes suggest that these North Sea cargoes were at most a quarter of the cargoes carried by the Byzantine merchantmen. Cargoes were of 6 to 8 tons at most and were supplied irregularly, so that commodities arrived in small batches. The small scale and limited range of the traded commodities is illustrated by Charlemagne's letter to Offa. The two most powerful men in western Europe are discussing a much troubled trade agreement, central to which is the exchange of quernstones.

Chapter 7

SUBSISTENCE STRATEGIES

The settlement pattern – the arrangement of population upon a landscape – may be taken as the material isomorph of the entire mode of production in its broadest sense, and of the core features of social and political organisation.

B. J. Price[1]

With the inception of competitive markets, the artisan and bureaucratic classes necessarily require a more complex agrarian regime. Foodstuffs have to be produced and traded to feed those engaged in non-subsistence pursuits. As a result, there will be increasing specialisation of the economy which may not have been fully mobilised before. Landholding will become more important, especially land which for ecological reasons was previously largely ignored. This revolution is as fundamental a part of the process of urbanisation and state formation as the eighteenth-century agricultural revolution was of the industrial age. It is now a commonplace that agricultural specialisation is linked to the institutional means of bringing potential surpluses to life.

The critical phase, of course, is when the elite organisations, who have been concerned primarily with the transfer of prestige items, begin to use their position to administer and manage surplus. In north-west Europe, in the first millennium, this change coincided with the development of the emporia.

The evidence available to tackle this highly significant problem is sadly limited, however. The historical record illuminates only one section of the producers – those concerned with major landholding. This evidence baldly contrasts with that revealed since 1945, by archaeology. Yet, as we shall see, the archaeological data are all too limited also. In particular, sites have been excavated in isolation, and little interest has been shown in their dynamic function. Only within a regional framework will the force of the evidence be powerful enough to answer the questions that are most interesting.

Similarly, as archaeologists, we have yet to grasp the full significance of the faunal and plant assemblages. For example, while they may show what the inhabitants of a particular site were eating, data on the local economy are far from conclusive. A regional perspective on the dietary data is called for, which should be developed in conjunction with the environmental history and the presence of field-systems and, in particular, be related to the morphology of settlements and the vernacular architecture.

We must emphasise that the absence of this kind of data tends to undermine this section of the book. What follows, in effect, are notes and variations on the theme. But some dynamic perspective of the all-important first signs of specialisation can be gleaned if we review the settlement data, analyse the basis of surplus in the early medieval world and its archaeological expression and, in particular, examine the nature of intra-regional exchange – the prosaic aspect of trade.

The archaeology of rural settlement

The archaeology of rural settlement in Merovingia and Carolingia is still at an early stage. Two contrasting forms of settlement seem to have existed. The documentary sources, on the one hand, indicate that the principal form of agrarian organisation was handled by the *villae*. These were large estates held by the aristocracy or the church. Estates might be distributed over considerable areas; for example, the abbey of Stavelot-Malmédy held land in Belgium, the Ardennes and the Aisne valley and rights to certain tolls on the Loire.[2] Many historians have shown that the *villae* were complex structures with large populations, most of which contained a substantial work-force. It remains to be discovered to what extent these great farming institutions were the successors of their Roman-period counterparts. Archaeology could certainly illuminate the question, but so far only small-scale explorations have been carried out on Carolingian villas, apart from the great imperial complex at Ingelheim in the middle Rhineland.

Elite settlements such as Büraberg to the east of the Rhine area are now well documented archaeologically, as are tenth-century burgs,[3] but these are not the kinds of settlement which we imagine from the following contemporary description of the Royal villa at Annapes (which lies on the border of Flanders and Artois):[4]

> We have found the fisc of Annapes a royal palace built of very good stone, with three chambers, the house surrounded by a gallery with eleven small rooms; below a cellar and two porches; inside the courtyard seventeen other houses built of wood with as many rooms and the other dependencies in good condition: a stable, a kitchen, a bakehouse, two granges, three storehouses. A courtyard provided with a strong palisade, and a gate of stone surmounted with a gallery. A little courtyard also

surrounded with a hedge, well ordered and planted with trees of different kinds.

Equipment: a set of bedding, linen to cover the table and a cloth. Tools. Two copper basins, two drinking vessels, two copper cauldrons and one of iron, a pan, a pot-hook, a firedog, a lamp, two axes, an adze, two augers, a hatchet, a scraper, a plane, a chisel, two scythes, two sickles, two iron-tipped shovels. Plenty of wooden tools.

Farm produce: old spelt from the previous year: 90 baskets (=12 muids) from which 450 measures of flour can be taken. Barley, 100 muids. From this year: 110 baskets of spelt; 60 have been sown and we found the rest. 100 muids of wheat, 60 have been sown and we found the rest. 98 muids of oats. One muid of beans, 12 muids of peas. From the five mills: 900 small muids; 240 muids of which have been given to the prebendaries, and we found the rest.

From the four brewhouses, 650 small muids.

From the two bridges, 60 muids of salt and two sous. From the four gardens: 11 sous, three muids of honey. From dues: one muid of butter.

Bacon from the previous year, 10 smoked porkers. 200 this years' porkers, with sausages and lard. This year's cheese, 43 loads.

Livestock: mares, aged, 51; three-year-olds, 5; two-year-olds, 7; yearlings, 7.

Horses: two-year-olds, 10; yearlings, 8; stallions, 3. Oxen, 16; donkeys, 2; cows with calves, 50; heifers, 20; this year's calves, 38; bulls, 3. Old pigs, 250, young ones, 100; boars, 5. Ewes with lambs, 150, yearling lambs, 200, sheep, 120. She-goats with kids, 30; yearling goats, 30; he-goats, 3; geese, 30; chickens, 24; peacocks, 22.

Contrasting somewhat with this description is the archaeological evidence. It is clear, of course, that the Germanic tribes penetrated Roman Gaul and introduced their own settlement types, including to some degree their traditional economy. In particular, the nucleated village, comprising the long-hall and sunken-huts, is the ubiquitous feature of this colonisation. The small community of perhaps half a dozen farm units at Gladbach near Cologne is a classic seventh-century example. A similar settlement has been uncovered at Mayen near the quern quarries, while substantially larger villages of the same period have been found at Brebières near Arras and at Liebersheim in southern Alsace. At this latter site only sunken-huts, structures usually connected with industrial activities, were found. This, of course, may be an indictment of the excavation, but these rubbish-filled huts leave little doubt about the material wealth of the community. A great deal of pottery and a rich faunal assemblage were also uncovered. At the nearby settlement of Ensisheim, dating from the eighth century, a potter's workshop was found; his products appear to have been distributed within this sub-region north of Basle.[5]

Further to the north, the excavations at Warendorf in Westphalia have revealed a substantial village of farm-houses, each with its own lock and key and with material assets which place it within a local and regional exchange framework during Charlemagne's reign.[6] The same kind of village-morphology is now apparent in Denmark, where village greens have been identified as early as the later Iron Age.[7] At Vorbasse the long-houses are neatly demarcated one from the other by their own enclosures. There is a regularity and uniformity of size that is reminiscent of later medieval villages. The only difference is one of scale. The early medieval long-house dweller had rather more property and a rather larger house than his medieval counterpart. Accompanying most of these long-houses are sunken-huts, in which industrial activities such as weaving were performed. These structures, as Randsborg has explained, are better lit for work than the barn-like halls traditionally best fitted to the telling of stories at night time.[8]

Three points must be made about this archaeologically demonstrated type of settlement. First, there is a farm-unit, which is fully apparent in these villages. Van Es has distinguished this unit in the Roman period in Holland.[9] It merely comprises a major dwelling hall, an outbuilding (sunken-hut), possibly a granary and in some circumstances, a well, all surrounded by a fenced enclosure (Fig. 33). Secondly, this is the basic self-sufficient farming unit which was in existence in the last decades B.C. and is clearly a characteristic of the Roman-period villages beyond the *limes*, as the villages of Wijster in Holland and Feddersen Wierde in north Germany attest.[10] This tends to confirm the slow socio-economic

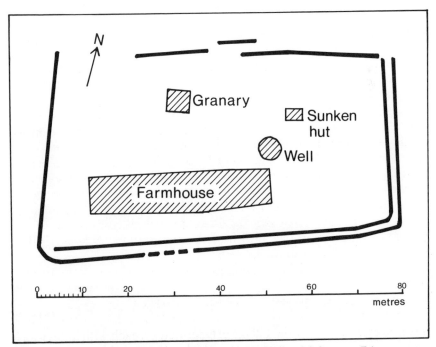

Figure 33 Model of a farm unit in Roman-period Holland (after van Es)

progression of these Germanic communities during the first millennium. The third feature of the sites is their overall size. Hayo Vierck has pointed out that they seldom exceed six or eight units, six or eight

Figure 34 Aerial view of the excavations at Chalton, Hampshire, showing part of the sixth- to seventh-century village (courtesy of Department of Archaeology, University of Southampton)

farms.[11] Using Randsborg's cemetery data, this is a settlement comprising between 40 and 100 persons.[12] We might further refine this information by establishing two settlement sizes: a small hamlet of two to four farms and a major village like those already discussed. The two sizes have particular significance when we turn to consider the Anglo-Saxon settlement evidence in England.

From England there is growing evidence of both village-sizes, and with the same units surrounded by the fenced enclosure, the *gewade*. Millfield in Northumbria, currently under excavation, is an example of the smaller village; so is Maxey, Northamptonshire, and even Witton, Norfolk – a settlement in an altogether marginal context. West Stow, Suffolk, is the best-known example of the larger village, with at least four halls in the excavated area attended by numerous sunken-huts. Chalton (Fig. 34) and Bishopstone, perched high on the southern chalk downlands, are also larger villages, numbering as many as six units, though with few ancillary buildings. Catholme, Staffordshire, is an interesting example of a smaller village that progresses to a larger one in the period *c.* 500–900, the addition of new farms being discernible.[13]

The structure of these settlements has remained the same. It was a socio-economic structure with distinct Celtic origins, and so it is essentially similar to the native Roman-period villages, which must have continued in some areas and yet remain an archaeological enigma. The migrant farmers, however, even in this period of climatic deterioration, adapted to the warmer English climate. Their homes, like those of the native Romano-British, were not designed to accommodate their stock in the winter, as along the North Sea littoral. Instead, this classic type of architecture – the long-house with a byre at one end – usually associated with the Angles, Saxons and Jutes, was left behind.[14]

By contrast, we should briefly examine the Late Celtic zone in western Britain. In these areas, as in pre-Roman Britain, the nucleated settlement is rarely found. Instead the defended or undefended extended-kin farm remained the rule. The most familiar type is the rath: the fortified farmstead. Raths are in fact a regional term in Ireland, and to a lesser extent in Wales, for this kind of settlement unit.[15] Stone-walled structures are familiarly known as cashels, island examples being often known as crannogs. Other names persist as well, such as the 'round' in Cornwall and Pembrokeshire. All conform to the well-known socio-economic mode of the Celtic world and appear to extend from the early Iron Age to the seventeenth century in western Ireland. On most of these sites there is sufficient economic evidence to indicate the farming regimes; for example, mixed farming is documented in the Co. Down raths of north-east Ireland, while the famous cashel at Cahercommaun, Co. Clare, in highland western Ireland has a 97 per cent preponderance of cattle in the faunal assemblage and is surrounded by great kraals (Fig. 35).[16] On most sites there is evidence of iron ore smelting to make farm tools, but only on hierarchically select sites evidence of specialist craft production.[17]

Surplus and settlement segregation

The West Saxon laws of king Ina dating from the end of the seventh century or early in the eighth give some insight into the organisation of agriculture and, indeed, the realisation of 'surplus'. The laws require that:[18]

> He who has (a holding of) 20 hides shall show 12 hides of land under cultivation when he means to leave.

> He who has (a holding of) 10 hides shall show 6 hides under cultivation.

> He who has (a holding of) 3 hides shall show one hide and a half under cultivation.

Further to this, the food-rent required by the West Saxon king from every 10 hides was 10 vats of honey, 300 loaves, 12 ambers of Welsh ale, 30 ambers of clear ale, 2 full-grown cows or 10 wethers, 10 geese, 20 hens, 10 cheeses, a full amber of butter, 5 salmon, 20 pounds of fodder, and 100 eels.[19]

Two points seem to emerge from these laws. First, we are able to see that the West Saxon king was concerned with production and, in particular, determined that the landscape should be carefully divided between what was cultivated and what was under pasture. The second point concerns the size and production implications of this food-rent. Sawyer has recently drawn attention to its size;[20] yet according to calculations made as a result of studies of peasant agriculture the rent is, in fact, very modest indeed.

Drawing on agricultural guides to early market economies, Graeme Barker and Derrick Webley have calculated recently the kind of livestock and cereal outputs that might have been achieved on a large Roman villa estate in Somerset.[21] In this instance a 15,000 acre estate worked by about 50 to 60 families was being considered, and its goal was obviously to interact in a marketing system to make the most profit from output. The figures used by Barker and Webley can be scaled down to a 10-hide (1,200 acres) estate, of which 720 acres, according to Ina's laws, was supposed to be cultivated.

First, 720 acres under cultivation in Wessex were almost certainly divided into one-third wheat and one-third barley or a similar crop, with perhaps one-third left fallow for hay. One-third of the cultivated land's produce would have been required for seed, so it would be the product of 320 acres that might be harvested for consumption. Barker and Webley estimate about 6 cwt per acre and allow 1 lb per person as a daily ration. Thus one acre would feed approximately 2.5 persons for a year, and the theoretical crop might feed up to 800 persons.

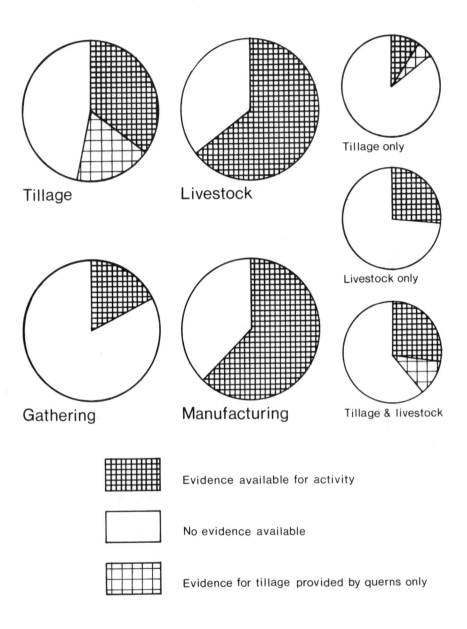

Tillage

Livestock

Tillage only

Livestock only

Gathering

Manufacturing

Tillage & livestock

Evidence available for activity

No evidence available

Evidence for tillage provided by querns only

Figure 35 The economy of the Irish rath (after Proudfoot)

Secondly, hay would be required for the stock, and this might come from 240 acres if a maximum of 240 cattle and 240 sheep were kept. These would need about 160 and 80 acres of hay respectively. This would be a high-production goal, because the manure from the stock would fertilise rather less than 300 acres, and thus a good proportion of the arable ground could not be sufficiently maintained. This suggests that the arable component of Ina's laws is much too high.

Thirdly, to cut the hay for this stock, some 240 acres would require 25 persons, if we follow Barker and Webley, who estimate that each person might cut just under 10 acres. This figure, in fact, is close to the estimated populations of many Anglo-Saxon hamlets.

These rough calculations suggest that the Anglo-Saxon villagers were quite affluent. At the threshold of statedom, the farmer apparently enjoyed unprecedented wealth as a result of environmental resources, a modest population level and a socio-political climate that gave every ceorl a stake in the future of his kingdom. Indeed this underlies the changes discussed in the next chapter, for these were not the exploited, overworked peasants who suffered the hardships so vividly described by cultural anthropologists like Marvin Harris, nor were they the feudalised communities of Carolingia.[22]

Furthermore, the king also would have benefited very satisfactorily from the food-rents. His food-stocks would have been considerable if he chose to enforce the laws efficiently, for his retinue, as we shall see, was small. We must speculate, in anticipation of future research, on the communal warehousing of these rents; perhaps as much as half was stored as a buffer against calamities. Equally, as we shall discuss below, we can only speculate on the warehousing of these food-rents to feed the nascent urban communities – the emporia. This speculation is reinforced by the simplest calculations. The seventh-century Mercian survey known as the Tribal Hidage assesses the kingdom of Wessex at 100,000 hides; the figure is generally assumed to be rather high, since Mercia was rated at only 30,000 hides.[23] The net food-rent, however, from the Mercian hides, if the West Saxon laws applied there, equates annually to 30,000 vats of honey, 90,000 loaves and 36,000 ambers of Welsh ale. When we also consider the slow but inexorable extension of colonised land, the food mountain owed in theory to the West Saxon kings must surely have been of EEC dimensions, and yet still a modest tax. Herein lie the reserves to support an emporium containing as many as a thousand persons for several months.

The description of the royal fisc of Annapes quoted above, as well as several *polyptiques* pertaining to certain Carolingian monasteries, indicate a similarly high production. There, however, it was apparently achieved with a large and subservient labour force.[24] French historians claim that on these estates the workers were rigidly controlled and equipped with primitive technology. They argue that this exploitation was extended during the tenth century, the distinctions between free and servile workers shading into one another as more and more labour was required. But the process of land reclamation in Flanders was accelerated in the tenth century, while the colonisation of upland areas, in the Eifel mountains for example,[25] also took place. This tenth-century expansion must be attributed to the emergence of urban communities, but its roots lie in the previous centuries.

The technological question remains a matter of some debate.[26] Whether the wheeled, heavy plough was prevalent in seventh- or ninth-century Carolingia, as Professor White argues, is far from clear. If it was, production might have been exceeded with the evidently large work forces. So we must ask why the high production was warranted in the first place. Again, we have only two major hypotheses to account for the apparent food-mountains. First, they may have been intended to buffer the community at large in times of war and climatic deterioration – both significant problems in the period. Secondly, the emergent urban institutions had to be fed. The palatial complex at Aachen, for example, was constructed entirely on the largesse of the nobles in Charlemagne's empire. It shows the resources that the emperor's palaces could expect to draw upon. This can be extended to include all the emergent feudal powers who were accruing officers to handle manifold duties, while the evident growth of the ecclesiastical population would have to have been met by increased produce. We are involved here with the very complexities that face all students of emergent 'primary states', and, as if to emphasise the complex variables, recent research has shown that these centuries experienced climatic deterioration. Work on Greenland data has suggested a slight climatic deterioration from *c.* 400/500 until *c.* 800/900, when the climate improved (deteriorating again in the later thirteenth century).[27] The impact of a drop of two or three degrees centigrade would obviously be most significant on large populations which were highly structured. We need look no further for confirmation than the evidence from the fourteenth century. Such climatic changes would only have shortened the growing season by a modest amount in much of Carolingia, while perhaps making certain upland areas 'marginal' for cereal production. Such a deterioration, however, would hardly have affected the smaller population in Anglo-Saxon England, or indeed pre-Viking Denmark, where there was probably plenty of room for expansion.

However, as far as the Carolingian economy was concerned, these are but notes on two critical variables, and fuller details will be necessary before we understand the need for such intensive production in this pre-market economy.

Rural reorganisation in Carolingia, Anglo-Saxon England and Denmark accompanied the emergence of urban communities. A symptom of these changes is to be found in the increasing use of documentation to define the extent of property holdings. Ganshof, for example, has maintained that there was an unmistakeable rise in the use of the written word to legalise land transactions within Carolingia after 780. This coincides with the expansion of the Carolingian church between 750 and 825 when it tripled its property. Similarly, the proliferation of land charters in England and the advent of bookland are features of the later ninth century and subsequent centuries. In Denmark runestones are used to define property boundaries and lineage rights just as the new market places call forth rural production on a new and economically significant scale.[28] Settlement shifts and the restructuring of settlements may also be attributed to this phase. The Carolingian monastery of St. Gall, for example, prepared a formula which could be used to shuffle secular and church property so that land-owners acquired contiguous rather than widely dispersed blocks of land. In England field-survey has emphasised the number of Middle Saxon desertions as aggregated settlements were created in the ninth and or tenth centuries.[29] (We should note in passing, however, that this fieldwork has value only in a regional context, for the process of shifting settlements continues on an individual level throughout history: there are, for example, sixth-, seventh-, eighth- and ninth-century desertions.) This process of nucleation was clearly proceeding at different rates, and in particular was a characteristic of agriculturally rich zones. It is no surprise, therefore, that to this period can be attributed the origins of the English manor. Historians have argued this from their sample of histori-cal documentation; archaeologists can demonstrate it more objectively with the evidence from sites like Goltho, Lincolnshire.[30] Here a previously isolated Middle Saxon farming settlement becomes the focus of a village in the Late Saxon period that expanded until its later medieval desertion. We may predict that the observed nucleation at Wharram Percy, North Yorkshire, occurs at the same time and was brought about by a nascent manor.[31] The excavated manors at Goltho, Sulgrave and Portchester Castle suggest that rapid segregation was introduced into the village morphology as local power became estab-lished.[32]

We have yet to establish what happened to the farm unit, though as we have seen the size of the villages themselves escalated – a process indicated to some extent by the sudden growth in Late Saxon church sizes. Randsborg has examined the same process in Denmark, where the earlier villages were taken over by what he terms magnate farms.[33] So far the relationship of these to the emergent medieval village is not clear, but evidently the traditional rural structure was being superseded.

In Scandinavia, the climatic optimum made possible the renewed colonisation of marginal land (in the period *c.* 500–900), as the excavated (eleventh-century) village at Lindholm Høje in northern Jutland demonstrates.[34] As in Flanders and the Rhineland, so a positive new phase of land colonisation sweeps across northern Europe hand in hand with the new systemic variables, and lasts essentially for nearly two centuries. By 1086, when Domesday Book was compiled in England, the arable acreage was an estimated 93 per cent of the total under plough in 1914.[35]

Economic data from the emporia

In real terms there is an obvious dearth of quantified economic data from rural settlements. Indeed we possess too shallow a picture of the hierarchy of rural settlement within a regional framework in the immediate pre-market phase, although the studies of the present generation of archaeologists bode well for the future. It is enormously disappointing that the excavated evidence from royal sites in Britain, Ireland, Carolingia and Scandinavia amounts to so little. Our ability to explain the food-rents, for example, and to discern regional patterns of agrarian economy is sadly limited.[36] The only major assemblages of data are those from the consumption end of the production chain: the assemblages from the emporia.

At this moment the faunal and plant assemblages from Hamwih, Ipswich, Dorestad, Haithabu, Ribe, Kaupang, Löddeköpinge, Helgö and Paviken are being studied for imminent publication. There will be much to discuss in these results, which will be available in perhaps five years. But from the interim reports some preliminary comments can be made.

First, there is an apparent contrast between the faunal assemblages from Hamwih/Ipswich, and Haithabu/Ribe. In the former butchery probably took place within the settlement, as is demonstrated by the incidence of all parts of sheep/pig/cattle skeletons from pits within the emporia. In Haithabu and Ribe, however, Randsborg has drawn attention to the incidence only of joints of meat, suggesting that the animals were butchered before they reached the trading-sites.[37] This has interesting implications. The former pattern is one which was generally maintained until the twelfth or thirteenth century in England and which effectively meant that livestock might be driven over considerable distances to feed the urban community. Only in the later medieval period in England was there a switch to supplying butchered meat to the towns in the fashion already extant at Haithabu and Ribe by the ninth century. This made it far more important for the settlements in the immediate environs to provide food for the urban population. The system might be organised through a ring of settlements with a regulated supply pattern, linked to villages further afield. Or these inner ring settlements might assume the burden of supply themselves – much, of course, as the later medieval urban-dominated landscape suggests that it was the responsibility of catchment-area villages. Whatever the case may be, this second mode of supplying the emporia required rather more organisation than the first when livestock were driven to the town. It also placed a detectable socio-economic emphasis on the inner ring of settlements while the emporia existed in a territory without any other urban competition.

Of course, it is possible that stock was kept literally around the emporia, in the rich meadowland surrounding Hamwih, Ipswich, Haithabu, Ribe, Kaupang, Löddeköpinge and Birka. When the wall around Haithabu was constructed, the entire enclosed area was far from built-up; similarly the fence or small wall around Löddeköpinge would have retained stock driven into the site for the seasonal gathering. At Dorestad, however, the existence of long-houses with byres seems to indicate that the inhabitants were part-time farmers as well as traders, a phenomenon that is quite familiar in the later Viking world although, as Randsborg has shown, the structures at Haithabu and Ribe are distinctly urban in character and very different from rural buildings.[38]

In addition to the markedly contrasting supply systems, the Hamwih sheep, as has been noted, are abnormally large – larger than either their earlier or their later medieval counterparts.[39] The reason is not entirely clear. In the first place, we assume that they were the pick of the West Saxon flocks which formed the food-rent exacted by the West Saxon kings. If, however, they were supplied by local farms and the feeding of the urban community was in private hands, as it was in the later medieval period, the emergence of a class of magnate farmers in the environs of Southampton ought to feature in the historical documentation. These farmers would have been the very first to urge that their right to land-tenure was secure and documented. To follow the theme in one more direction, we must briefly take into account the evidence from Wicken Bonhunt, Essex.[40]

At Wicken Bonhunt, a village lying close to the Essex–Cambridge border, Keith Wade excavated a major Middle Saxon village with a series of structures and associated pits, ditches and wells, but with little evidence of the farm-enclosures discussed above. Notably this site produced a rich array of imported pottery (it is more than 70 km from the coast), as well as a massive quantity of Ipswich ware. It also produced an equally large quantity of cattle bones, amounting to many cwt and including a marked number of skull fragments. Furthermore, there is some suggestion, if the place-name evidence is accepted, that it might well have been a royal farm. In sum, the evidence points to a cattle-processing centre. We may therefore speculate whether it is at all significant, and indeed whether Wicken Bonhunt is a rare example of a royal food-rent collecting centre. Once more we can assert that only within a regional perspective will these questions be answerable.

Marine resources also illuminate to some degree the process of specialisation. Clearly the inhabitants of Haithabu were as fully geared to the exploitation of this resource as they were to obtaining meat, but in contrast we have the evidence from Hamwih and Ipswich. In these settlements the marine assemblages are very varied, and only in the ninth- or tenth-century rubbish pits from Ipswich is there incidence of herring-bones in quantities that are characteristic of the later medieval diet around the North Sea. To this transition period we must attribute the arrival of the deep-water drift net in England – a technological invention, however, which had been used effectively to the advantage of the citizens of Dorestad, who were supplied with North Sea fish caught in northern Frisia and around Zeeland, to the west (Fig. 36).[41]

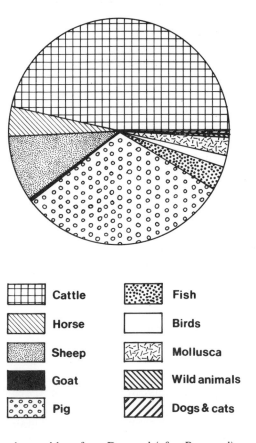

Cattle Fish

Horse Birds

Sheep Mollusca

Goat Wild animals

Pig Dogs & cats

Figure 36 The faunal assemblage from Dorestad (after Prummel)

The marine fauna from Hamwih, including a great many eels and oysters, tends to emphasise the varied diet of the occupants of this settlement. We must wait to see whether a changing diet through time can be identified, or whether it is possible to distinguish various levels of consumption within the settlement. But we rest assured that these English and Scandinavian sites were comfortable ports of call, extending even further perhaps the semblance of affluence that we have already attributed to the rural settlements of this epoch. As if to emphasise the point, there is a brief phase of shell-middens along the Hampshire-

Sussex coast-line dating from the eighth or ninth centuries.[42] A prehistoric interpretation of their presence would suggest that the agrarian regime was experiencing some stress and was in need of supplementary protein; yet, as we have seen, the argument cannot be sustained. Instead, it is further evidence of the wealth of almost every part of Anglo-Saxon England before the ninth century.

Intra-regional exchange

The degrees of specialisation within these pre-market based economies should be reflected in the patterns of regional exchange. Quite simply, specialist farmers would have to trade their produce to acquire goods or food that they did not have. Most of these goods, however, are perishable and therefore difficult to identify in the archaeological context. But it is possible to construct a model of such exchange patterns based on the trading of non-perishable artifacts, and this is best documented for those artifacts which were produced by craft-specialists in the rigorously organised urban communities. As we have already seen, with the growth in the scale of the settlements under royal supervision the number of servicing craftsmen will also have grown. These artisans must have constructed houses and provided necessary everyday equipment, as well as trinkets and specialised goods. If we accept a model of centrally controlled settlements, these trinkets would probably have been redistributed as tokens or as largesse in return for the food-rents which in part, of course, maintained the courts. Alternatively, these trinkets or utilitarian artifacts may have been exchanged directly by the artisans for foodstuffs; or entrepreneurs may have been involved in the process; or, finally, we may detect no relationship whatsoever between one class of commodity and the other. The thesis central to this book, of course, espouses the first model, as we have seen in Chapter 3, though only within a regionally designed framework will we really be any the wiser.

Many artifacts were either made or finished off in the emporia. These range from prestige goods like glass beads, jewellery and certain types of pottery, to quernstones and perhaps leather goods and bone items. Two case studies briefly exemplify the value of this data, and enable us to examine further (though not to test) our model.

The first example is provided by the smiths' shops at Helgö on the island in Lake Mälaren. The site was evidently concerned with the production and distribution of prestigious metal-work, and the patterns of finds which originally emanated from this centre are most illuminating.

By 1972, 227 mould fragments for the headplates of relief brooches, 338 for foot-plates, 526 for clasp buttons and 315 for dress pins had been found. Thousands of other mould fragments have also been found and are in course of publication. Of these remarkable finds, the excavator

Holmqvist has been rightly cautious. 'The variety of the forms', he writes, 'is in fact so great that, if the original products had been found scattered throughout the country one would have been compelled to think of them as having been derived from a number of different *workshops*.' Some positive patterns of distribution, however, emerge from the data.[43]

Fig. 37 illustrates the distribution of several clasp button variants as they have been distinguished by Lamm. There are clear concentrations in the cemetery groups to the north of Helgö, which are still strictly in the Lake Mälaren region and within the confines of Uppland. A few others have been found further north in Norrland and may represent some token of exchange (finished products) for the Norrland iron ore, which evidently came to Helgö in the form of spade-shaped bars of iron.

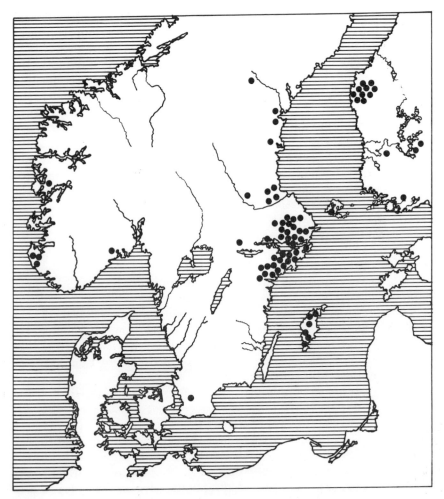

Figure 37 The distribution of clasp buttons from Helgö (after Lamm)

Finally, we should also note that a small group of this particular type of Helgö-produced metal-work has been found also in Finland.

An interpretation of these clasp button patterns – and here we have just referred to one example of the metal-work – suggests a regional exchange pattern for the majority of the metal-work, travelling up to about 100 km from source. Beyond this, the metal-work appears to take on a directional mode and may well be a receipt for scarce commodities given in exchange; hence the apparent isolated extra-territorial concentrations of finds.

Until the data is quantified and viewed in a total assemblage of jewellery, it is perhaps difficult to emphasise the value of the model. In contrast to metal-work, however, pottery is never (or rarely) re-used, and its modest intrinsic value in most societies is such that it provides a useful indicator of regional trade. Two Anglo-Saxon examples clearly provide rather useful information about intra-regional exchange.

Ipswich ware was first identified in 1957 as a result of rescue excavations in the town that revealed kilns and their wasters (Fig. 38).[44] The production of this pottery appears to have been a specialist industry of some magnitude. Four fabrics have been identified microscopically, and the typology has been discussed at some length. Essentially, the pottery was made in developed Early Saxon forms from the early seventh century onwards; it was well-fired and proficiently finished. It is

Figure 38 A range of Ipswich ware vessels from Ipswich (courtesy of Suffolk County Council)

the few unusual forms that have attracted attention, however. These include various types of bowls, lugged pitchers, some of which are highly decorated, and a few bottles which seem to be similar to continental types. Further imitation of certain French Carolingian traditions has also been suggested recently.[45] The principal reason for its importance is the scale of production, the range of forms almost unknown in the other very localised Middle Saxon potting industries, and the extensive distribution of Ipswich ware which may be 'not only a quantitative measure of the industry, but also perhaps be an indication of the "zone of influence" of Ipswich' at the time.[46]

Several other points about this anomalous production can be considered. First, large quantities of the ware have been identified at Sedgeford in Norfolk and Wicken Bonhunt in Essex (both about 100–120 km away from Ipswich), and also at sites in London.[47] It remains to be seen whether other sites nearer to Ipswich itself will produce such quantities, but the present evidence implies a possible distributional preference for certain sites. Royal patronage of the industry has also been postulated as a result of the discovery of an unusual sherd from near Cox Lane in Ipswich. This is a sherd with a face-mask very similar to the one on the whetstone from the early seventh-century ship burial at nearby Sutton Hoo.[48] At present the distributional evidence clearly needs to be examined more thoroughly to establish the character of its fall-off from Ipswich. This highly centralised industry, however, supplied a zone that coincides with the known territory of East Anglia, as well as a few pots to centres beyond those boundaries. So far most of the extra-territorial finds have been of the specialist decorated pitchers, but before this factor can be safely interpreted we need to examine all the evidence thoroughly.

The exceptional nature of the industry is perhaps emphasised by the very localised trading of other Middle Saxon wares, as well as their conservative range of forms. From Hamwih, for example, there is a major assemblage, but it contains only two Middle Saxon pitchers. The two major industries represented in this assemblage comprise only cooking-pots and jars. One tradition may have been manufactured near the downland, some 20 km from the settlement, while the other ware was probably made in Hamwih itself (Fig. 39).

The former ware (Hamwih Classes 2/4) was clearly traded around the Hampshire basin, though the distances involved are no more than could be walked in a day. The Class 3 ware, which was probably made in Hamwih, has seldom been found outside the settlement. It is a pattern oft-repeated in Middle Saxon pottery studies. It perhaps suggests the presence of specialists who operated on no great scale and for only specific communities. The implications are of a structured industry, where only the Ipswich ware potters seem to be at variance with the pattern.[49]

If we were to assess the patterns of various other artifacts produced in

Figure 39 Two hand-made class 3 vessels from Hamwih dating to the early eighth century (courtesy of Southampton Archaeological Research Committee)

the emporia, we should probably find that their distribution was much the same. The coins minted at Haithabu in the ninth century have a sub-regional distribution; we may wonder whether the glass and metal objects which were also produced there were distributed over the same area.

Future research should also illuminate the regional extent of Ribe's influence in the ninth century and the question whether its catchment lay in northern and central Jutland until Aarhus was founded at about the beginning of the tenth century. Two general patterns emerge from this preliminary examination, however. First, there is the regional pattern for the trading of prestige goods and valuable utilitarian items, and secondly a localised market for the trading of more modest utilitarian artifacts – effectively the products of individuals operating without competition and patronised by one community and its immediate environs. A web of kin-related exchange might explain this second pattern,[50] while institutional mechanisms (cf. Chapter 1) account for the regional pattern. Equally, the regional pattern may indicate the area from which certain emporia were drawing their food resources, while the sub-regional pattern of emporia-produced manufactured goods may approximate to the area supplying food for the urban community.

These movements of artifacts clearly contradict the existence of a closed economy in the period 600–800 and provide a basis at least for proposing that there was modest trading in specialist foodstuffs. This would have been organised either by the secular or the ecclesiastical leaders of the community. But the evidence for a market-based economy, as we have seen in Chapter 3, simply does not exist beyond the borders of Carolingia. Within the empire itself the intensive production on documented *villae* points to the possible prevalence of the market principle operating through periodic markets. This is confirmed by the incidence of a potting industry which, from the seventh century, was clearly geared to mass-replication of a range of wares.[51]

Perhaps the most eloquent early evidence of production for Carolingian markets comes from a ninth-century document which may be a copy of an earlier one – the *Capitulare de Villis vel Curtis Imperialibus* – which lists the complex farming regime operating on an imperial *villa*.[52] The capitulary suggests the same enormous scale of activity that we saw earlier in the description of the royal fisc at Annapes. Every dimension of pastoral and arable agriculture is considered, while the upkeep of the farm is scrupulously reckoned. So strict is the system that stewards are warned not to let farm-hands waste their time at markets (no. 54). The weekly or monthly market must have been in the mind of the bureaucrat who drew up the document, for there remains the negative evidence that there was no permanent urban revival on any scale before the end of the ninth century.

The rigorous concern with monetary control in the empire (and frequent reissuing of capitularies on coin-using) shows Charlemagne's concern for the regional exchange of commodities. The apparent centralisation of the middle Rhineland pottery industry, probably during the eighth century, points to a similar interest in the control of a critical industry. Indeed this industry, so closely associated with the wine-trade, may be eloquent expression in itself of the emergence of specialist producers.[53] In effect, we are witnessing from about 793 (if not before), when Charlemagne declared his first edict on coin-using, the slow creation of a market-based economy within the empire. And as a result we must assume that there was a steadily increasing interest in rural production and rural specialisation with estates aiming to intensify production to supply urban communities. It is not surprising, therefore, that Alsatian grain was being shipped up the Rhine in the mid-ninth century, presumably to feed the communities of the middle Rhineland (see Chapter 6).

By contrast, periodic fairs must also have provided the mechanism of intra-regional, as well as inter-regional, exchange in the communities beyond Carolingia. The seasonal fairs in Scandinavia remain an enigma before the tenth or eleventh centuries. Only the discovery of Löddekö-pinge casts some light on this important institution. Whether such gatherings occurred in Anglo-Saxon England remains equally obscure. The distribution of pottery types, for example, with the exception of Ipswich ware, suggests that no great emphasis can be placed on fairs or assemblies. Metcalf has argued that fairs can sometimes be identified for this period by the pattern of sceatta-finds.[54] It is certainly true that these inland coin-finds tend to occur on hillforts, or close to territorial boundaries. It is also true that there are many examples of later medieval fairs being held within prehistoric fortresses. Some even continued until the nineteenth century and were observed by the novelist Thomas Hardy. Yet a more probable explanation for these coin-losses, bearing in mind the administrative purpose of sceatta-minting, lies in the meetings of moot-courts, many of which also met at prehistoric sites, for these were traditional landmarks in the landscape and, indeed, landmarks upon which the division of the landscape has been based. The same evidence for assemblies and fairs meeting at prehistoric locations is known from the Late Celtic literature; yet a similar archaeological obscurity surrounds this significant institution.

In conclusion, we can still only speculate that there was a low level of intra-regional exchange. The villages themselves endorse the view of agrarian self-sufficiency which has confused previous economic interpretations; yet there was a surplus to be articulated, provided the institutional means of activating it chose to do so. Despite the climatic deterioration between 500 and 800, beyond the empire lived a well-fed population with abundant opportunity to colonise new areas. With the market, however, there came new pressures on the land to produce food regularly for large numbers permanently involved in non-subsistence activities. This put pressure on the holding of land and gave it a new value – a value which is a general law of market-based societies and of which we are well aware. With the market came an agrarian revolution and rural segregation, and after this, ironically, the peasant farmer was not to experience the same affluence again until the arrival of the next revolution nearly 900 years later.

Chapter 8

SYSTEMIC CHANGE: THE NINTH CENTURY

Floruit egregium claro diademate regnum:
Princeps unus erat, populus quoque subditus unus.
At nunc tantus apex tanto de culmine lapsus
Cunctorum teritur pedibus; diademate nudus
Perdidit imperii pariter nomenque decusque,
Et regnum unitum concidit. Sorte triformi
Induperator ibi prorsus jam nemo putatur;
Pro rege est regulus [sic], *pro regno fragmina regni.*

Florus of Lyons[1]

The glory of one nation, people, crown
All now dispersed, disgraced and trampled down.

tr. Colin Haycraft

Every age experiences its dramas. The drama of the ninth century, however, is without question vividly encapsulated in the elegy of Florus of Lyons. The century witnessed the last major European invasions and migrations (except for those to America in the past hundred years), and it also saw the disintegration of the empire which Charlemagne had forged. Yet surprisingly most of these traumas took place between the end of Charlemagne's monumental reign in 814 and the rise of king Alfred late in the 870s. In the central decades of the ninth century, between the reigns of the two greatest early medieval monarchs, the socio-economic framework of Carolingia, Anglo-Saxon England and the Scandinavian territories experienced a critical morphogenesis. Such was the force of change that by the year 900 western Europe seems to have set a course out of the Dark Ages and in the direction of the 'medieval world'.

Of course, we cannot truly attribute this change to a mere fifty years: the process, as we have already seen, lay deeply embedded in the preceding two centuries. Moreover we must not fall into the trap of attributing the change to that oft-quoted single cause – the Vikings.

Their role was within a grander, more extensive systemic development. To understand the emergence of the truly urban society that has characterised western Europe since about 900, we must seek a model of change which can be tested, and which possesses a general value for the many component regions of western Europe at this time. These will prove important, for the archaeology of the ninth century is still dismally sparse, with plentiful hoards only from this area. The characterisation and explanation of change has been a major concern of recent archaeological theory. The debate in recent years has focused on two areas. The major difference has been between those who favour monocausal and those who favour multivariate explanations. The debate has assumed an added significance in the many papers on the origins of primary and secondary states. Quite obviously, monocausal explanations are not universally applicable, and for this reason Lewis Binford and Kent Flannery in particular have drawn attention to multivariate appraisals of past cultures. They have espoused the use of systems-thinking derived from the science of cybernetics, this being a dynamic way of modelling change with reference to variables that are universal to all or most cultures. As Flannery has written:

> the use of a cybernetics model to explain prehistoric change, while terminologically cumbersome, has certain advantages. For one thing it does not attribute cultural evolution to 'discrepancies', 'inventions', 'experiments' or 'genius', but instead enables us to treat prehistoric cultures as systems . . . it allows us to view change not as something arising *de novo*, but in terms of quite minor deviations in one overall part of a previously existing system, that once set in motion can expand greatly because of positive feedback.[2]

The inception of systems-thinking in archaeology has been a feature of the last dozen years; now, however, it has come under attack, and its scrutinisers claim that this multivariate model will never explain why change takes place – that it merely describes change. In effect, this second area of debate focuses on the law-like possibilities of past human activity and seeks to construct a model that has predictive ability, a stage beyond 'descriptive mechanics'. 'We have no scientific idea . . . of why these channels become overloaded in certain cases and not in others, nor why there is so much variability among complex social systems,' writes Stephen Athens, who is concerned with transcending mere description.[3] He and others have begun to assert that one universal parameter conditional on all societies should be examined – the energy base. The new paradigm seeks to extend the ecological perspective of culture. Yet, while we cannot deny the great value of exploring this new theoretical approach, equally we must recognise that it requires plentiful data to monitor the energy base and only then will a series of expectations emerge regarding the character of specified dimensions of complex systems. Such data must prove elusive for complex societies, for there is little scientific anthropology to draw upon, and the archaeological research required will necessitate a considerable restructuring of field priorities.

At present the ecological model appears to be a goal for future research rather than an applicable construct in which to evaluate data of the kind presented in previous chapters. It may be true that systems-thinking does not explain, but it contains an explicit means of qualifying societies. This is powerfully demonstrated in Renfrew's *The Emergence of Civilisation*, a study devoted to change in the Cyclades and the Aegean in the third and second millennium B.C.[4] Renfrew divides culture into sub-systems defined by human activities: the subsistence – technological, social, symbolic or projective – and trade and communications sub-systems. It is in the interactions between these different sub-systems that culture change is produced, and Renfrew has invented the *multiplier effect* to describe these positive mutual interactions. This is 'a special kind of positive feedback; reaching across between the different fields of human activity' and ultimately invoking the morphogenesis of the system.[5]

The power of morphogenesis, so apparent in the past, is invoked largely because human culture is a homeostatic device in which change will be minimised. Wherever possible, existing activity patterns will react to counteract innovation. The 'multiplier effect', where sub-systems enter into a mutual deviation amplifying relationship, is needed to overcome this innate conservative homeostasis of culture.[6]

The multiplier effect in action: the primary states

Charlemagne's empire was the achievement of nearly three decades of campaigning to maintain and extend control over areas bequeathed to him by his father and grandfather. His coronation in 800 marks the triumph granted to him by years of conquest, and it clearly distinguished him from his Merovingian forebears. His intention to emulate the grandeur of the Romans was satisfied. This was no empty act of vanity; the new emperor tried immediately to control his territory more efficiently and to expand its legislative powers insofar as was consistent with empire. The programme of new laws confirmed the obligations and rights of all his subjects, and yet the repeated issuing of these tracts suggests that the administration made less impact on his contemporaries than it has on historians.[7] It was in these circumstances that Charlemagne was evidently trying to stimulate a market-based economy, developing the pre-existing system of peripheral markets. The founding of new towns in Westphalia, the expansion of industry in the Rhineland and the reforms of the coinage point to this emergent market system.[8] It may well have been designed with capital and materials acquired by long-distance trade with the satellite territories which have been reviewed in the previous chapters. This trade reached its zenith during Charlemagne's reign. The scale of these operations should leave us in little doubt of their importance.

Whether silver was obtained from the Baltic, for example, as capital to invest in the development of the reformed Carolingian currency remains, and probably will remain, an enigma. Sture Bolin has presented a strong case, using metrology as the basis of his thesis (see Chapter 1).[9] Those historians who have objected to Bolin's views have pointed to the absence of Arabic coins within the empire without recognising that these would have been melted down on entry into the state, not least because of their heathen images.[10] The Carolingians, of course, may have simply been seeking Scandinavian furs as well as Frisian and English cloaks, yet there would seem to be a limit to the need for such commodities in circumstances where demand for such luxuries was probably restricted to a small elite. Spectrographic analyses may reveal the answer in the case of the coins, but in the end what we need most is more information on the range of goods imported into Carolingia. At the moment we can only question whether Charlemagne would have ignored the flow of oriental silver into the Baltic and whether the series of incidents relating to the foundation of Haithabu by king Godfred are isolated occurrences or incidents relating to a Carolingian policy now lost to us.

Charlemagne seems to have been well aware of the legislative problems involved in administering such a massive area. Moreover we cannot doubt that he was well aware of the plight of his Roman forebears on whose state he was, to some extent, modelling his own. It was perhaps for this reason that he decided in 806 to split the empire between his three eldest sons. This of course was a means of maintaining Germanic inheritance traditions, but, equally, it was a policy which avoided civil war. The death of his second son, Pippin, king of Italy, in 810 and of the eldest, Charles, in 811, forced him to bequeath the empire to his third son, Louis of Aquitaine. This action must have been all the more unacceptable to the old man, since several regional potentates rebelled against him in 811.[11]

Louis the Pious succeeded his father in 814, and three years later he pledged that he himself would be succeeded by his eldest son, Lothar. This was encouraged and confirmed by the court elite. After the birth of a third son, however, Louis changed his mind, and in 828 he took his wife's advice that his newest-born child, Charles, should be included in a division of the empire. The result was a civil war, in which Louis lost all semblance of central authority after 830. On his death in 840 the empire entered an intense phase of civil war, which was ultimately resolved at the treaty of Verdun in 843, when the empire was divided between Louis' three sons. This internal fission took place as Viking raiders systematically attacked the Carolingian coastline, creating further social and economic disruption. In these circumstances, as one writer has recently suggested, 'central authority was more of a pious reminiscence than an effective reality'.[12]

Yet the division was already apparent in economic terms, as was shown in Chapter 5. A sharp divide seems to have existed between the extensive Frankish trade across the English Channel and the trade stemming from the Rhineland. The division may have been encouraged by the Carolingian monarchs who regarded the Frisians as a means of trading with areas hostile to the imperialists. Yet it reveals the continuity of the two Merovingian kingdoms, which were largely reinstated as independent entities as a result of the Verdun treaty in 843. It also shows that the Rhineland was becoming increasingly specialised in agricultural and industrial production, in contrast to the Frankish economy, which appears more diverse in character and less developed. The division was one encouraged by the Carolingians themselves, since they favoured their Rhenish palaces at Ingelheim, Aachen and Nijmegen. These buildings were designed to be consistent with the achievements of the monarchy and also, to some extent, with the recreation of a past image. They housed the (inadequate) administrative staff[13] and the artists who were responsible for the contemporary renaissance.

Yet it is equally clear that Charlemagne in his later years tried to compensate for this centralisation in the Rhineland by disseminating some of the skills developed there. The skills achieved by the manuscript illuminators and the ivory and metal-workers were transferred to the regions of his empire, ultimately to the detriment of the art which, during the course of the ninth century, becomes less imaginative and less dynamic in form. This kind of regionalisation went hand in hand with Charlemagne's bid to increase his patronage of the church.[14] As a result the church acquired even greater tracts of land and achieved wealth at the expense of the later Carolingians.

The same pattern of Rhenish development followed by regionalisation is evident in the pottery industry. In the later eighth century the Rhenish industries began to produce new forms with sagging bases, very different from the traditional flat-based wares.[15] The difference persisted until the new types were copied in the tenth century by the Frankish potters. On the other hand, we know that the south Italian (and Roman) tradition of painting pots was initiated north of the Alps in about 800. Whether the first Carolingian red-painted vessels were products of the Vorgebirge kilns near Cologne is not yet clear, but the technique was soon being used also by potters in Alsace, Trier and the Beauvaisis.[16]

We must conclude that Charlemagne's failure was to have created a polity without the necessary mechanisms to administer and control it. If the economy could have been consolidated the area might have been fused into a unit which a strong leader could control. There were contradictions. Power became focused in a core area, while the monarch sought to express a cultural unity.

The division of the empire in 843 left the Rhineland in the hands of Lothar and Louis, and Neustria in the hands of Charles the Bald. Because of the dynastic failure of the eastern Carolingians after 855, attention has been focused on Charles, who seems to have resisted socio-economic collapse and even to have brought about some expansion of Charlemagne's economic aims. He certainly stressed coinage reforms in his edict at Pitres in 864, while his unmistakeable concern for the vulnerable urban communities is shown by his call to them to refurbish their fortifications.[17] These monastic and secular communities were slowly expanding their regional involvement. Archaeology, however, has yet to illuminate the period, though it has shown that the trading settlements were in decline even before the signing of the treaty of Verdun.

The coins issued by Louis the Pious at Dorestad confirm that the site remained important for some years at least into the 820s.[18] Furthermore, the recent series of dendrochronological dates taken from wine barrels which were reused as wells points to a date-range between the 680s and the 830s (Fig. 6).[19] The sample is small, but when the evidence is considered in conjunction with the evidence of coins it goes against the theory of Dorestad's decline, which is usually attributed to the 860s when the Rhine is thought to have silted up.[20]

The new series of dendrochronological dates points to a turnabout in Dorestad's economic condition in 830/40; that is, the decade of the major assaults by the Vikings on Dorestad.[21] It was also at about this time that Hamwih, Saxon Southampton, began to decline. A recent analysis of the coins from this site shows that they were concentrated in the eighth century, with an outlier around the end of the eighth or the early ninth century. Very few coins dating from after about 810 have been found in the excavations since 1946 (see Chapter 6). Of more significance, however, has been a seriation analysis of the changing proportions of local pottery in selected pit-groups within the settlement, which has demonstrated two clusters of activity coinciding with the two coin peaks.[22] The later pit-group cluster, however, is quite as significant as the first, and incidentally illustrates the differing loss-rates for the eighth-century sceattas and the subsequent pennies. This second cluster of pits appears not to extend beyond the second, or perhaps the third, decade of the ninth century. Effectively, the settlement was largely deserted of its commercial agents when, in 842, Nithard reports that '*Per idem tempus Nortmanni Contwig depredati sunt inibique mare trajecto Hamwig et Nordhunnwig similiter depopulati sunt*' ('At this time the Vikings pillaged Quentovic, and from there crossed the sea to ravage Hamwih and North Hamwih in the same way').[23]

The thrust of the evidence points to a decline in commercial activity before the main wave of raids in the later 830s and following decades. Furthermore, it implies that the raids were directed at emporia of diminishing importance. This perplexing picture has been splendidly rationalised by Klavs Randsborg's recent research.[24] His reinterpretation of the silver hoards from Scandinavia and Russia indicates a peak in Arabic silver around the period *c.* 790–*c.* 820/30, followed by a dramatic fall-off in the remaining decades of the tenth century. This view controverts the thesis propounded by Bolin (and subsequently developed by Sawyer),[25] that the fall-off in silver occurred only after 850. The fall-off created a social imbalance in the Scandinavian system, calling for a new injection of wealth to maintain homeostasis. The injection was achieved by increasing the previously spasmodic raiding of the Christian territories, and perhaps by dealing more with the western Moslems of Spain than with the silver-rich emirs of Tashkent. Moreover it generated dissension among the silver-starved Viking chiefs, which was partly responsible for the migrations that date from this time to Scotland and Ireland in particular.

Why, we must ask, did not Louis, and subsequently his son Lothar, push more manufactured goods northwards to fill the breach left by the oriental trade? No doubt largely because the Carolingians could not offer the precious metals which the Danes coveted. Moreover the direction of the economy was probably forsaken during the civil war. The merchants themselves were probably tied to the very courts that were engaged in the warfare. Some merchants, of course, did venture northwards, but their numbers must have been depleted by the Viking piracy, as in the raid on Hamburg in 845. Finally, the treaty of Verdun gave the *pagi* of Mainz, Speyer and Worms to Louis, while Lothar gained the northern stretch of the Rhine valley. Much of the wine-growing area thus came into Louis' hands and control of its trade to Frisia and beyond into Lothar's. The subsequent division of these areas in 855, when Lothar died, merely complicated the situation and must have rendered an efficient economic system impossible to sustain.

To some degree these explanations also account for the decline of the northern French trade aimed at Hamwih. Civil war and subsequently the Viking penetration of the English Channel must have destroyed the sense of security enjoyed by earlier Carolingian merchants. The temporary achievement of Charles the Bald, who commanded the area west of Flanders, failed to outweigh the Viking menace which by the 840s was threatening the heartlands of France and Wessex.

The multiplier effect in action: the emergence of a secondary state

England had seen the growth of a centralised authority in eighth-century Mercia under Aethelbald and Offa. Offa had created a special kingship which gave him a personal status in Europe but in real terms proved to be no more than a cyclical event (see Chapter 10). The power he gained in his last years, which was manifest in the propaganda character of his coins, may in fact have come from the control he exerted over long-distance trade into England – the trade on which Charlemagne was designing his imperial economy. King Ceonwulf of Mercia was to continue to exert control over this trade, as his early ninth-century coins from Hamwih and Ipswich seem to attest. But by 850 the growth of political power in Wessex had eclipsed the Mercian ambition. Before we outline the historical details, however, we must examine the archaeology, for recent results have demonstrated an important change in the settlement pattern.

As we have already suggested, there is new evidence pointing to the demise of Hamwih, Saxon Southampton, as a trading station in the early ninth century. The details are not as precise as those available for Dorestad, but the absence of coins and a seriated clustering of pit-groups have combined to indicate it. Martin Biddle's major campaign of excavations in Winchester have, therefore, as we might expect, detected renewed activity there in the course of the ninth century. There is also some evidence which seems to show the aggregation of the dispersed Middle Saxon farms in London, and the ultimate creation of a wharf during the ninth or early tenth century.[26] Similarly there is charter evidence from Canterbury pointing to tenemental divisions there by 839.[27]

It appears that the pattern of organisation within Wessex was changing with the formation of new centres which mostly performed administrative functions. These, we may contend, are the solar central-places of an incipient state. There is little archaeological evidence to amplify this hypothesis, for the principal industrial take-off dates from the end of the century.

The two West Saxon kings who dominated Anglo-Saxon politics in the first half of the ninth century were certainly in a position to exert new authority over their kingdom. Egbert and then Aethelwulf succeeded in conquering the entire length of southern England in the 830s and 840s, stretching from eastern Cornwall to Kent and at times including Winchester, London and Canterbury. Under their control was a large population and a workforce that had operated at Hamwih. Moreover by the time Alfred issued his laws the notion of kingship had been aggrandised to the cost of the clergy and ceorls (see Chapter 10). Indeed by 839, with the mention of a *cnicht's* guild in Canterbury,[28] there are signs of a growing separation between the king and his traditional duties towards his people. This corporation implies that the West Saxon king no longer provided the security that these knights required, so that they sought corporate security – a feature of the tenth century and later. And, as if to assert the new royal authority, Charles the Bald permitted Aethelwulf to marry his daughter, creating a liaison which Offa, in the end, had failed to achieve for his family.

It appears that the West Saxon kings had begun by compensating for the decline of Hamwih – their source for acquiring prestige goods – by extending their territorial control. This expansion, however, created the need for new administrative controls, which further amplified the distance between leaders and their community. In effect the West Saxon lineage was slowly accumulating centralised wealth and authority which could be separated from the institutional demands of kingship. Whether these kings set out to capitalise their resources remains to be seen from further excavations in Winchester, Canterbury and London, but they certainly provided a powerful platform on which king Alfred was to build.

The Viking raids on England, which escalated in the 840s, must have shown further the need for centralised leadership.[29] It was at this heart of the West Saxons that the Viking conquerors of eastern England aimed in the 870s. Having annexed half of England late in the 860s and removed the kings of the conquered Anglo-Saxon territories, they purposely struck out at the young king Alfred.[30]

The West Saxons under Alfred suffered a series of defeats until, in 877, Alfred was forced to flee to the marshes on a western edge of his kingdom. From this base the king led an attempt to quash the invaders which culminated in the battle at Etheldun in 878. By then the Danes seem to have wished to settle, so the offer to cede them half England – the Danelaw – and the condition that they accepted Christianity were terms that were as advantageous to the invader as they were to the alleged victor of the engagement.[31] But Alfred quickly built upon his victory, establishing in his territory a network of forts and burhs, from which no one was more than 20 miles, and creating a new standing army and a navy.[32] He was therefore to meet further Viking aggression with aggression. And, as Asser tells us, he was also to build new towns, as well as encourage the growth of towns that were already in existence. Archaeology has substantiated this. Clear urban development inside Winchester's Roman walls, for example, dates from this period, while the laying-out of the new burhs – communal refuges – was a policy exacted by a powerful leader.[33] Alfred clearly paved the way for the reconquest of the Danelaw by his descendants and the emergence of the market system at the same time (see Chapter 9). For the first time kingship had broken the traditional Germanic bonds and emerged in a new guise.

Table 5 Ninth-century raids recorded by the Anglo-Saxon Chronicle[34]

789	3 ships of Northmen in Dorset
836	35 ships (25 in some versions)
840	33 ships (34 in one version)
843	35 ships
851	350 ships; 9 ships captured later that year
875	Alfred fights 7 ships and captures 1
877	120 ships lost at Swanage in a storm (or in a mist)
878	23 ships

882	Alfred fights 4 ships; 2 captured and 2 surrendered
885	Alfred's fleet encounters and captures 16 ships, but is later defeated by 'a large naval force'
892	The *here* crosses from Boulogne, 'in one journey, horses and all', in 200, 250 or 350 ships according to different versions of the annal
893	Northumbrian and East Anglian Danes collect 'some hundred ships' and go 'north around the coast'
896	6 ships
896	20 ships perish along the south coast

Ninth-century change

Writing of the formation of the state, Malcolm Webb points out that 'tribal egalitarianism would gradually vanish even as it was being appended, without awareness of the nature of the change, and the final achievement of absolute control would at that point seem merely a minor alteration of established custom. The consolidation of governmental power would have taken place as a series of natural, beneficial and only slightly (if at all) extra-legal responses to current conditions, with each new acquisition of state power representing only a small departure from contemporary practice.'[35] The real events of the ninth century are for this reason concealed by the dramas. Social and economic change in these two areas had been effected at least by 900, when the Vikings were beginning once more to engage in commerce with the Arabs.

Charlemagne, in seeking the goals of statedom, attempted to capitalise on the vast resources available within his empire and in the territories beyond his boundaries. By investing in long-distance trade he probably anticipated that this would help to bring the regional markets to life, and these he could control by strictly regulating their medium, silver currency. The system would enhance the wealth of his family and sustain his dynasty. Instead, the system was too large and, because of the stratified structure needed to administer its widely separated regions, bred social fission. Though it appears to have taken off, the economic system was apparently dependent on trade either to the north or, quite possibly, with the Arabs. The inter-connectedness of the sub-systems is nowhere better demonstrated than here, as the Carolingian communities spiralled into a nightmare of events, which triggered more and more problems in the generations following the death of Louis the Pious in 840.

By contrast the Anglo-Saxons, like the Vikings, reacted positively to the loss of the economic input which was being mobilised by their kings. The West Saxons extended their domain, while the Vikings compensated by pillaging, although some sought to colonise new areas improved by a milder climate.[36] The Saxons built from their capital slowly until power was firmly centralised. The promotion of craft specialists and the accumulation of wealth were, we assume, the foundations of Alfred's achievement.

These developments came about almost silently in England and with some sense of loss on the continent. Can we model them from the energy base, as it is documented at the moment? And are we able to determine the trajectory through which this energy base passed? There seems no answer yet. If we collected the evidence of the ninth and tenth centuries, the trajectory, as we saw in Chapter 7, would be clear, but this would be to confuse the intricacies which make the cultural model interesting. Moreover such a bland appraisal of change would conceal the rather different processes that brought about the tenth-century urban revolution in Carolingia and Anglo-Saxon England.

Chapter 9

MARKET PRINCIPLES AND PLACES

What of the cities and towns he restored, and the others which he built where none had been before?

D. Whitelock[1]

Implications of the market place

The ninth century probably experienced the greatest socio-economic changes of the medieval period. One result of these changes was a growing appreciation of the world as is made clear in Alfred's introduction to his version of Orosius' history: Book 1 presents a panorama of the known world. The implications of the changes, however, come in the multifarious documentation that has survived. These, as before, take the form of annals, chronicles and so on, but also include a rich legislative vein that asserts rights: rights to borough status, to holding markets, to establishing guilds, to lands, and so on. These come in the form of charters, capitularies or runestones and indicate beyond all doubt the changing social relationships which are in the process of being formed. Above all, documentary history assumes a greater command, because its volume and sample of material is so rich. Yet, as we shall see in this chapter, there are also more general points that can be established about the market-based societies which emerge before 1000 A.D., not only contributing to our historical perspective of medieval society, but permitting us to evaluate synchronic processes.

Carol Smith's models provide us with an incisive means of predicting the course of the competitive market, especially when reviewed in conjunction with Skinner's and B. W. Hodder's work in Asia and Africa respectively. Moreover they enable us to examine the evolution of markets which stem from the two origins predicted by Hodder:[2] the first from direct participation in long-distance trade, and the second from the division of labour, to some extent, in response to long-distance trade and to central authority.

In Carolingia we have seen how Charlemagne sought to develop a market-based system by founding markets, centralising resource industries and, after reforming the coinage, commending its use to all. This course was pursued hand in hand with a particularly active long-distance trading network, which extended around the North Sea, as we saw in Chapter 2. In effect, Charlemagne established a partially commercialised system which operated through solar central-places like Mainz, Strasbourg, Rheims or Tours, and periodic markets. It was a system which his successors attempted to sustain once the international market, and possibly the silver base for his economic initiative, fell away. The impact of this initiative on the emerging secondary states beyond Carolingia is interesting. There, when central authority was paramount, it acted to effect a market-based system which also grew first from a solar central-place base with some peripheral markets. This was enacted, not as a result of long-distance trade, but from the socio-economic platform that it must in part have provided over several decades. And it was built around the administrative nodes which a new polity also required.

Craft specialisation in the emporia was perhaps the actual platform for the emergence of competitive markets. Yet we should stress that these craft activities are only integrated to underpin a competitive market system when this system in England and in Scandinavia is vigorously encouraged by central authority. The central role of power in the development is beyond question. It is this which effects the spatial organisation of the new system, including its artisans, which articulate the system. Central authority is also essential to the expansion of the system and then to its adaptation to other systems. These are factors which historical archaeology is beginning to illuminate with some precision.

There is the question of arranging craft-specialists. We have seen that Charlemagne appears to have collected his middle Rhineland potters into craft villages;[3] yet we are equally familiar with the multiplier phenomenon in urban life, where artisans practising different crafts can each enhance the others' activity.[4] On this theme, Bruce Trigger has written that 'the proximity of related trades encourages greater independence and hence more specialisation. For example, in such situations the production of tools and the working up of raw materials for various crafts can be left to other specialists, whereas if each craft is geographically separate workmen normally prepare their own tools and materials.'[5] It is this pattern of production which typifies the Late Saxon pottery and industry, for example, with individual potters operating in emergent towns, in contrast to the Carolingian pattern (see below).

There is also the question of engaging the rural response to craft specialisation. In the initial years – for solar central-place markets – this response need only be a modest one, as we saw in Chapter 7. But as the urban population in competitive markets grows, resources greater than those available to artisans with allotments will be needed. Moreover rural production is as much a craft specialisation as shoe-making, shield-making or potting. Increased woollen sales, increased leather sales, increased timber sales, increased inter-regional exchange of vegetables, cereals and stock are features of a new economic environment. A milder climate facilitated production during the tenth to twelfth centuries, while increased social distancing, combined with its market value, put a greater emphasis on land-holding and led inevitably to a new emphasis on rural management involving technical intensification.

These changes were activated against a background which was demographically and economically harmonious if, for example, it is compared with the Third World situations that are reviewed by modern anthropologists, geographers and human ecologists. There were still ecological niches to fill, and population levels were yet to rise without problems for several centuries (Fig. 40). Agricultural and economic intensification were not the direct result of increasing population but, as we shall see, a socio-political response to systemic circumstances.

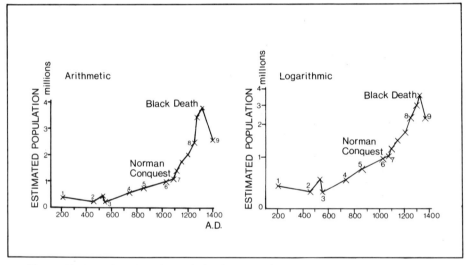

Figure 40   An estimation of population in Anglo-Saxon England (after Wailes)

Competitive markets: the new patterns

Clearly two most interesting aspects of competitive markets are the differential speeds at which they are formed and the evolution of the tiered system of markets which, for example, Skinner has distinguished in recent studies of Chinese regional exchange. It is becoming possible to approach both questions with the degree of time depth that only the archaeologist and historian has available to him.

In the Roman period the extension of urbanism to England has been studied by Ian Hodder, who has illustrated the non-random pattern of later third- and fourth-century towns.[6] Hodder shows that each area was served by a near-perfect hierarchy of markets. This pattern, however, may owe much to the preceding pattern of forts fundamental in the first place to the conquest of England. That these came to perform a dual militaristic and economic function is becoming clearer, as their civilian *vici*, beyond the walls, attest. These were industrial zones and, it appears, market places. Yet the transition from a military to a fully urban pattern is a slow one that takes over two hundred years to create.[7] By contrast, the Late Saxon urban process, given great stimulus by Alfred in the 880s and 890s, was a rapid affair and has induced Martin Biddle to comment that 'the very fact that the setting up of towns on this scale was then contemplated is an indication of the expectations men then held of their potential success'.[8] Biddle has recently published an excellent survey of Anglo-Saxon urban archaeology, and from that basis we must make an appraisal of the questions that concern us.[9]

The hierarchy of urban communities and their chronological evolution can be determined to some extent by the documented incidence of moneyers operating in each one, if critically assessed in conjunction with the topographic and material history of the particular sites. We are especially fortunate in possessing a remarkable list of West Saxon moneyers in king Athelstan's Grateley laws (*c.* 925–40). These read as follows:

> In Canterbury there shall be seven minters, four of them the king's, two the archbishop's, and one the abbot's. In Rochester three, two of them the king's and one the bishop's. In London there shall be eight, in Winchester six, in Lewes two, in Hastings one, in Chichester another, in Southampton two, in Wareham two, in Dorchester one, in Exeter two, in Shaftesbury two, in each other burh one.[10]

The laws also reaffirm, with certain caveats, those of Athelstan's father, Edward the Elder, who early in the tenth century stated that 'if anyone buys outside a market town, he shall forfeit the sum due for insubordination to the king'.[11] Athelstan's modification of this law, so that only larger transactions were legally obliged to take place within burhs, illustrates not only royal concern to be realistic about trading but also an already lively concern with marketing by peasants evidently evading the system. This could not be tolerated, since royal control was aimed at taxation using coinage – in the first place through market tolls (we assume), and later by taxing the coinage itself.

Before evaluating the Grateley laws it seems valuable to allude briefly to this taxation of coinage, since it illuminates the Saxon economic strategy and the importance of this source. This has been argued by H. B. A. Petersson, who has followed Bolin's work on Roman coinage closely, showing that there is an indisputable chronological decline in the average weights for issues of kings Edgar, Edward (the Martyr) and

Ethelred the Unready. He has suggested that the intrinsic value of the coins was progressively reduced in each issue period until those struck just before a recoinage contained only its bullion value of silver. Petersson claims that 'there can be only one conclusion: the late Anglo-Saxon penny was a charged coin, over-valued in relation to its metal content by $33\frac{1}{3}$ per cent. The conclusion is evident for the entire period between king Edgar's monetary reform and the Norman conquest. A supposition that the value of the Anglo-Saxon penny did not depend on its intrinsic worth, but on the word of the king, is without doubt explained by this.'[12]

Petersson's work confirms – if confirmation were really needed – that royal control over coinage was imperative. For this reason it is apparent that the Grateley laws, decreed before the over-valuation was effective, permit some crude ordering of southern English centres, for these mints must be some economic expression of the predicted exchange and hence the revenue which was Athelstan's target. This is no new idea. With typical perception Sir Frank Stenton drew attention to this point in his great history of Anglo-Saxon England.[13] More recently Metcalf has contested the validity of the argument. He points out that it is not the amount of coin minted in a borough that may be an index, but the amount in circulation.[14] He once again uses die numbers multiplied with a hypothetical minting number – 10,000 or half that minted by Edward I's dies late in the thirteenth century – to calculate the circulating coins. In this case, the logic is sound, unlike that proposed for pre-market coinages, and the results satisfactory. But until all the mints have been assiduously studied by numismatists the quantities remain to be discovered. David Hill, however, has used the lists of moneyers, including the Grateley figures, to prepare a ranking for Ethelred's reign spanning the last quarter of the tenth and first quarter of the eleventh century.[15] Hill has discerned the fluctuating pattern of moneyers in each burh between 930 and 1060 and used Danegeld tribute figures – ransom paid to the Danish invaders – to create an ordered ranking of markets. This is illustrated in Fig. 41.

Hill's ranking, however, inevitably obscures certain levels of urban development, taking the tenth and eleventh centuries together and leading to similar results for an early burh like Southampton and a short-lived *fluctburg* like South Cadbury. The hierarchy reads rather like an anthropological report based on ethno-history. The Grateley laws themselves surely hold the simplest key.

The laws indicate a major tier of markets which had been the solar central places in the previous century, then primarily serving regions in an administrative capacity. These comprise Winchester, London and Canterbury.[16] In the second part of the tenth century, however, and thereon afterwards, the pre-eminence of London becomes incontestable, as Hill's table indicates. This is indicated not only by its high number of moneyers as well as its own heavy tribute to the Danes in 1018 –

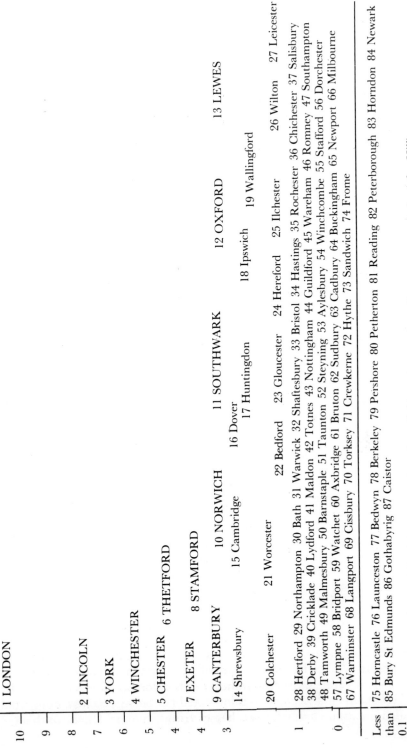

Figure 41 The ranking of Late Saxon mints, using numbers of moneyers as an index (after Hill)

amounting according to the Anglo-Saxon Chronicle to about 12 per cent of the country's Danegeld – but also by its immense topographic expansion detailed by recent investigations.

To this tier can be added Lincoln, York (Fig. 41), Chester and Thetford, which were in the Danelaw when the Grateley laws were prepared. At various times Oxford, Exeter, Stamford and Norwich also join this rank.

During the tenth century the second tier comprises Chichester, Southampton, Wareham, Lewes, etc. – towns with one to two moneyers when Athelstan prepared his list – and later embraced towns which Hill has recently referred to as 'shire towns' like Worcester and Gloucester. These towns are the first-phase burhs, most often set either within refurbished Roman-period defences or new fortifications.

The third tier comprises the smaller markets which emerge after Athelstan's reign as the higher tiers are expanding and in response to the king's rigorous monetary reform.[17] These appear to be insubstantial market-places, usually with only one moneyer. Hill has discussed these in Somerset. Perhaps we could include the hill-top burh of South Cadbury, founded in 1010 in place of Ilchester when the Viking incursions were at their height and lasting until about 1017 (see below).

A further, remarkable insight into this third tier of markets has been published by F. Neale in Philip Rahtz's report on the Saxon palace at Cheddar.[18] Neale draws attention to the following passage in the Axbridge Chronicle, a fourteenth- to fifteenth-century compilation which must be a copy of an earlier manuscript probably originating from London.

In the times of Athelstan, Edmund, Edred, Edgar and St. Edward burhs were established on the royal estates; the King and his court were to live off the royal estates, progressing round the country.

There shall be Governors in each Borough, who at that time were called Wardemen, that is Port Reeves, Constables and other officials who in the name of the king were to supply victuals, to wit wheat, wine and barley, sheep and oxen, and other cattle of the fields and fowls of the air, and fishes of the waters, for the time that the King with all his following ordered a stay in the appointed Borough. But if it happened that the King did not come there, then all the supplies were to be sold in the market of the aforesaid Borough, and the money received there-from shall be carried to the King's treasury . . .

This three-tier pattern seems fairly clear, with London drawing apart as a separate level by the end of the tenth century. We must of course stress the regional and chronological shifts within the lists of towns founded by the Late Saxon and Danelaw kings. Yet it is interesting that Edgar and Athelstan appreciated this ranking to some extent, which shows that the

non-random pattern achieved in southern England at least was the goal
of central government.[19]

Edgar's fourth law code states that thirty-six persons shall be chosen
as witnesses for every borough, while the following code states that only
twelve should be chosen for small boroughs. As Hill shows, Ethelred
then made the same distinction in the fourth law code compiled by him,
but this time in every principal town there will be three moneyers and in
every other town one – in both cases a ratio of three to one.

But in contrast to the contemporary view (and that offered by David
Hill) there is the archaeological evidence presenting topographic detail.

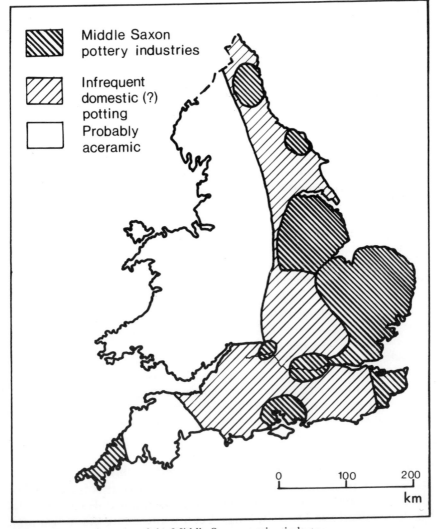

Figure 42 The character of the Middle Saxon potting industry

It has been established that the first tier of markets experienced an explosion of activity. Extensive development at York, Thetford, Lincoln, Norwich and Oxford have all been demonstrated, with early attention being paid to the delineation of tenements. The extent of Late Saxon London has already been mentioned, while its substantial new wharfs are a feature which required considerable investment.[20] Martin Biddle has distinguished the laying-out of the street grid at Winchester early in the tenth century (as well as in other West Saxon towns) and the subsequent evolution of the densely tenemented city.[21] Alfred consecrated a new minster in his capital next to the tiny seventh-century old minster shortly before he died. Biddle believes that this was designed as a 'burh church' and would have been much larger than the adjacent Early Saxon building.[22] Even so, the old minster was radically enlarged in the 970s as if to maintain pace either with urban demography or urban wealth, or possibly both. This expansion inevitably includes a remarkable industrial revolution consistent with the determinants outlined by Trigger. Rows of artisans' shops have come to light in Thetford, Lincoln and York. In particular, mass-replicated goods abound. The Late Saxon pottery industry is perhaps the best-studied example of this industrial development, with the establishment of potters in almost all first-tier centres early in the tenth century and in second-tier settlements very soon afterwards.[23]

In southern England the industrial process appears to be eloquently expressed in the form of the pots themselves: the potter's wheel seems to have been a tool which was slowly mastered and to which Middle Saxon 'hand-made' forms were often horribly adapted (Fig. 42). These late ninth- or early tenth-century wares are mostly characterised by their half hand-made, half wheel-made, wholly and crudely trimmed vessels which bring the earlier forms into a new age and to a larger populace. By the time three or four generations of local potters had mastered the wheel, the wares are wholly (or very nearly) wheel-made and in a wide range of forms. In the Danelaw pottery production evolved in a rather different way. Here is was founded on the Ipswich ware tradition discussed in previous chapters. The wheel-made Late Saxon wares proficiently extended the Middle Saxon range of forms, including some French Carolingian forms in their repertoire. This was achieved on a massive scale and with great speed late in the ninth century.[24]

Excavations have also revealed the topography of the second- and third-tier settlements. But nowhere have these towns been given the attention devoted to the major tier. At Wareham excavations have revealed a rural character in parts of the interior until the middle or second half of the tenth century. The nucleus of this vastly defended burh seems to have lain around the minster of St. Mary's, which sits on the banks of the river Frome. In the second half of the century, however, industrial buildings had extended all the way up the High Street, and the subsequent century or so seems to have witnessed the town at its full medieval extent.[25] Excavations in Chichester, Lewes, Wallingford, Gloucester, and Northampton and many other towns have also established this development, effectively from an agrarian nucleus often founded around a monastic or royal settlement, to an urban centre by 1000 A.D. The same piecemeal development is apparent in Southampton, a burh which appears to have been a mere shadow of the former emporium (see below).[26]

The archaeology of the third-tier settlements is rather more obscure. Burpham, for example, has been shown to be entirely agrarian in character. Here was an early fortified site which never gained a moneyer but appears, in the light of recent excavations, to have maintained an agrarian settlement at least. Axbridge in Somerset, another early foundation, certainly has an eleventh-century mint and occupation, while South Cadbury is perhaps the most interesting excavation of this level of market – one that in fact had shifted in emergency circumstances.[27] These were agrarian communities which seem seldom to have grown very large and yet maintained markets at least by the early eleventh century, filling in gaps in the servicing areas of the two earlier tiers.

Randsborg in his recent *The Viking Age in Denmark: the formation of a state* has made a similar study of the urban process, again intrinsically linked to the total centralisation of power. Here, however, he has had to use the archaeological evidence more explicitly, for there are very few references to the Viking centres before the later eleventh century.[28]

It is especially interesting that the emporia tend to merge into the beginnings of the competitive markets, with Haithabu being active until the early eleventh century, after which it is superseded by Schleswig. This was partly a response to the second phase of Arabic interest in the Baltic Sea when Kufic silver once more permeated all levels of Scandinavian society. But unlike the first phase a century before this boom does not seem to have spilled over into the North Sea. Carolingia and England at least appear to have been more concerned with national affairs, which may explain Ribe's enigmatic role in this renewed activity. The recent excavations located the ninth-century emporium but found no evidence of tenth-century activity.[29] Probably the site experienced a recession and its role was performed by a new foundation at Aarhus.

Excavations at Aarhus have shown that this settlement, like Haithabu, was planned from the beginning with plank-covered streets, small timber sunken-huts and a near-circular rampart enclosing an area about 250 m in diameter.[30] This was evidently a royal centre and one that was involved in the Baltic trade, as Slavic pottery and Norwegian soapstone vessels attest. Aarhus links the commercial and urban activity of the eighth and ninth centuries to the emergence of markets in the later tenth century. When Adam of Bremen was travelling in the Baltic countries during the eleventh century, however, he regarded Aarhus as a *civitas*, in common with the other town foundations of the later tenth century and later, rather than as a *portus*, the name reserved, interestingly, for Haithabu and Ribe.[31]

Adam also included Odense along with the other towns, but there is a suspicion at least that this was another royal planned town and, contrary to opinion, earlier than the royal strongholds such as Trelleborg, Fyrkat and Aggersborg, with which it has been compared.[32] It certainly has tenth-century origins and was the seat of a bishopric by 988.

These are the solar central places – the major tier of markets – performing administrative, regional and international functions. Their role, however, was almost certainly conditioned by the incidence of long-distance trade, and its cessation once again, in the 930s, must have gravely threatened the stability of the Danish community. Harald Bluetooth and his son Svein Forkbeard, however, asserted a new domination on the loosely cemented Danish polity. This process was initiated in the second half of the tenth century in the phase of intense silver famine, before the renewed raids on the Germans – rich now with Harz mountain metal – and the Anglo-Saxons. Both warrior kings must have been familiar with the establishment of the German markets under the Ottonians, a feature of the reign of Otto the Great, and doubtless the Danish kings appreciated the economic investment of towns. Similarly they must have been familiar, for example, with the flourishing urban communities which had been created in half a century in the Danelaw in England.

Roskilde was founded by the 980s and was certainly a king's seat in the next century. Dendrochronological dates also suggest that Lund was founded some time late in the tenth century, although tradition persists that king Canute was responsible for planting the town early in the eleventh century.[33] With the earlier settlements these two later foundations comprised the first tier of markets founded by 1000, and were well spaced out to serve the provinces that were being politically bound together. At this juncture these are functioning as solar central places, with no competition in existence between them; but very early in the eleventh century a second tier of centres was established. These were Alborg and Viborg, the latter being the thing-place and a natural choice for a periodic or permanent market-place; later in the century Ørbaek, Slagelse and Ringstead were also created, and by the time Adam of Bremen visited the country all these centres were also mints.

Randsborg, who attempted to rank these centres as mints, used the familiar *Kriterienbündel* discussed in Chapter 1. He awarded points for (1) a bishop's seat, (2) a royal mint, (3) a thing, and (4) a *civitas*, as defined by Adam of Bremen, suggesting an industrialised centre in contrast to a village. The poll that emerges is interesting, since the towns of Viborg, Odense and Lund have 4 points, Aarhus, Ribe and Roskilde 3 points, Alborg and Ringstead 2 points and Slagelse and Ørbaek 1 point each.[34]

Here Viborg's earlier administrative role outweighs the powerful urban growth at Aarhus, unquestionably the more significant medieval market. The poll, however, is a valuable and objective experiment.

At this juncture it is interesting to compare the settlements, especially in the light of our review of the Anglo-Saxon towns. It is more than apparent that while Aarhus and Lund both figure in the first tier of towns their topography is very different. Aarhus, like Haithabu, is a planned settlement which seems to have been densely populated from its beginnings. Within a century or so, inhabitants were spilling out beyond its walls, as they did at Haithabu. One reason may be the densely occupied, highly active and wealthy Jutish community, but this hardly seems sufficient. By contrast, Lund, while it has a distinctive artisan community, vividly exposed by the recent archaeological investigations, was a relatively small town in demographic terms, with a population of possibly 200 in contrast, for example, to the 1000-plus estimated for Haithabu.[35] Moreover it takes the form of a slowly evolving centre, developing first from an agrarian character with many open spaces within its urban limits. This point is emphasised by the recent reconstruction drawings published in Martensson's excavation report – illustrations that underline its early origins.[36] Similarly, Jan Ekman's recent monograph on the fauna attests a high proportion of wild animals – as much as $38\frac{1}{2}$ per cent, though fish comprise a significant part of this figure.[37] The contrast is splendid, being between the urban communities which have a gateway function in the first place, and those which interact specifically for the regional market. They are indices of the two different systems. It is emphasised by the abandonment of Haithabu, probably after Harald Haldrada's sack in the 1040s and the occupation of a more modest town at Schleswig nearby. Furthermore there is a similar comparison to be made with Sigtuna, the modest industrial and administrative centre which develops in place of Birka on the north shore of Lake Mälaren in central Sweden. Probably the same contrast exists also between Kaupang and its urban successor, Tønsberg. Like Lund, old Oslo developed slowly around an administrative and communications focus early in the eleventh century.[38] Moreover, as at Ribe, Aarhus, Roskilde, Schleswig, Lund and Sigtuna, we can here see the influence of the church in the propagation of the market principle. Its role, like that of the kings, appears to have been a powerful force. In the first place the Christian missionaries must have realised the wealthy rural vein to be tapped and also appreciated that their power lay in isolating the communities rather than permitting the dangerous pursuit of long-distance trade, with all its concomitant spiritual connotations.

Between these examples of market origins in the secondary states and the circumstances experienced in the primary state of Carolingia, there is a striking contrast. While historians have made numerous studies of the evolution of the tenth-century market in France and Germany, it is a subject that has really lacked systematic archaeological research.[39]

Dutch and German archaeologists from an early date have with great skill excavated many urban interiors, but the overall impression is still rather confused. By contrast, in France urban archaeology is at an infant stage.

Market-charters demonstrate the ninth-century origins for the many centres which lay in the hub of north-west Europe, between the Loire and the Rhine, but at what rate these expanded is not clear. Nor is it absolutely clear that the later tenth-century charters issued in western France and in North Germany are a true reflection of the process which, within a further century, had resulted in politically explosive urban communities that had far outgrown the modest examples discussed in the secondary states beyond.

Dorestad and Quentovic clearly failed, and sondages in Rouen attest a slow growth there in the tenth century.[40] Tiel replaced Dorestad and by the eleventh century was flourishing as an entry point into the Rhine; Wissant unsuccessfully made a bid to succeed Quentovic.[41] The systematic work on the Dutch coastal 'burg' towns has shown that their

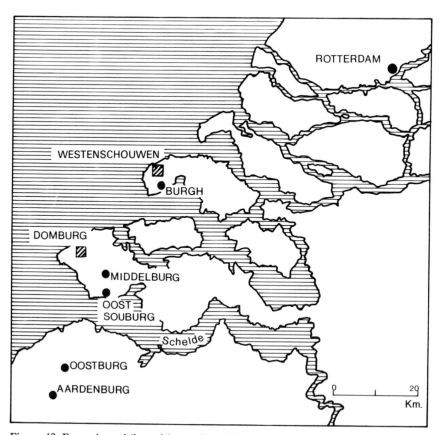

Figure 43 Emporia and 'burgs' in northern Flanders (after Trimpe Burger)

expansion came in the late tenth century. Trimpe Burger, for example, following his investigations at Oost-Souburg, Middleburg and Aardenburg, has shown that these communal refuges (?) were re-occupied (Figs. 43 and 44).[42] By this time the reclamation of Flanders was advancing to the great advantage of communities like these.[43]

Yet whether we can uniformly accept the slow growth documented by

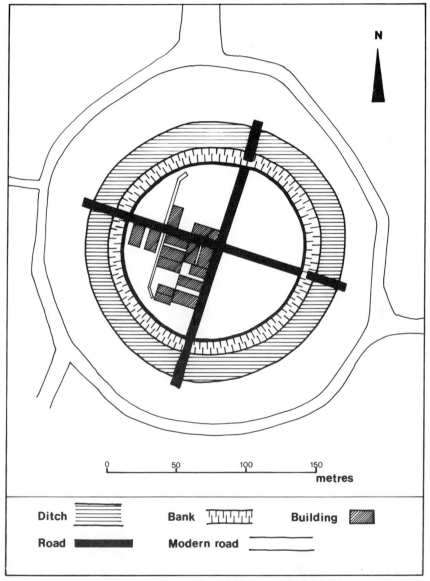

Figure 44 Schematic plan of Souburg showing the later tenth-century urban topography (after Trimpe Burger)

the historians remains in doubt. The commonly held view is that the emergence of feudal lords combined with weak leadership restrained economic growth. Certainly the few examinations of the Frankish denier which have been made, notably those from the tenth-century Fécamp hoard, show that it was poor in silver – a consequence of decentralised minting.[44] Yet historians may simply be overlooking the process of urban expansion and remarking on the rash of secondary-centre foundations late in the tenth century (when they were attributed legal status), rather than identifying the origins of the entire system. The opening of the Harz silver mines in the 970s combined with strong Ottonian leadership in Germany without doubt stemmed the tide of events. This stimulus was the life-blood of what must clearly be a string of second-tier markets dating from this time, as well as of the established Rhenish and Flemish towns. By the eleventh century these latter communities were expanding their influence and beginning to pose a formidable presence on the international market.

We can now discern an early growth in key centres in the ninth century although its real character remains for the most part enigmatic. The tenth-century expansion of towns like Bonn, Cologne, Trier, Mainz, Frankfurt and Strasbourg was indeed one reason for the fresh colonisation of upland areas in the central Rhineland as rural production sought both to re-align itself with the new economic requirements and to cope with the social and demographic developments.[45]

One feature remains strikingly clear, and that is the slow evolution of a well-documented craft – the pottery industry. This industry seems to have been centralised late in the eighth century and remains so for the rest of the first millennium, and indeed until recent times. These potting communities were located short distances from key market centres like Cologne, Bonn, Aachen, Paris and Orléans and took advantage of natural resources, though often in what might seem to be marginal contexts when they were founded.[46] The production of these industries, as for example the Badorf-Pingsdorf centres in the Vorgebirge Hills west of Cologne, seem to have expanded in the tenth to the twelfth century to maintain supplies to the new urban communities. Yet in view of the contrasting organisation of the Anglo-Saxon and emergent Danish potting industries, we cannot but question the efficiency of these Carolingian-Ottonian communities. They seem to be at variance with the principle cited by Trigger earlier in this chapter and with the continuity of the resource-control phenomenon by which Charlemagne in all likelihood sought to uplift his economy. We can only speculate whether this inefficient patronage of potters is a reflection of the malaise inherent in this primary state as it was divided to become Germany and France. (It is interesting to note, if nothing more as yet, that geographers like Hodder have tended to stress the existence of specialist industrial communities in market societies as a response to weak central authority.)[47]

In concluding this section we must return to Skinner's five-tier system of markets outlined in Chapter 1. To recapitulate, he has distinguished:

1. minor or incipient standard markets
2. standard markets
3. intermediate markets
4. central markets
5. regional markets

The bottom level he also calls the green vegetable market, where there is no concern with horizontal exchange of peasant-produced goods. These are not at all clear before 1000 and are almost certainly a product of a vigorous and complex system. Of course, the sources we have available to us may not identify them, since their topographic and administrative character would be minimal. The standard markets may correspond to the third tier of Anglo-Saxon markets – centres which develop late in the sequence. Intermediate markets seem to be the secondary centres which emerge in both Anglo-Saxon England and the Baltic countries fairly soon after the establishment of the central markets. The central market, strategically placed on the transportation network with wholesaling functions, may develop with the first tier of centres around administrative nodes, but these are probably a feature of the flourishing system where communications have grown to be significant and where large distances exist between the original first-tier settlements, the regional markets. Towns like Oxford and Stamford are examples of central markets. The regional markets are the major centres, the initial nodes in the competitive marketing system ultimately derived from administrative foci and thus creating a very different settlement arrangement from that pertaining to a redistributive network dominated by gateway communities if the central power is in the position to engage in long-distance trading.

The anatomy of the early medieval market

It is profoundly interesting that while the West Saxon Alfred was to see some at least of his economic plans succeed in his own lifetime, the fragmentation of the Carolingian empire was probably leading this established economy into a period of stagnation. The concept of power in controlling a market economy seems crucial. It must have been at Alfred's instigation that the half-penny and third-penny were briefly (prematurely?) issued, perhaps in imitation of Charlemagne's creation of the *obol* – the half-denier – a century before.[48] Alfred also upgraded the weight of the penny in an enigmatic reform which gave greater silver credibility to his coins and brought them into line with Charlemagne's reform, also a century earlier.[49] The question of where the silver came from to support this new economic gesture has never even been asked, let alone answered. Probably English reserves served the king satisfactorily, since there is no evidence of any significant long-distance trade by which he might have acquired bullion. Alfred's shrewdness, however, which included an awareness of European geography, probably extended to the European economy and, equally, to recent monetary history. But we can only speculate whether Ottar the Norwegian or Wulfstan the Englishman informed him, when they visited his court, of the second phase of silver input into the Baltic that began suitably as Alfred was conceiving his coin-reforms and the expansion of his urban communities. Some of his new wealth may have passed to the Danish half of England, the Danelaw, which Alfred had ceded in 878 to king Guthrum. And it is not at all unlikely that this rather remarkable king at some stage exacted some tribute from his new neighbours, for in the last years of his reign his power was incontestable. To understand these critical years more fully we shall depend on excavations in centres like York and Lincoln, so that we may discover exactly what investment the Danes were making late in the ninth century and whether this was derived from imported bullion or indigenous wealth.

The pattern of town-founding and the emergence of market tiers, of which king Edgar in particular was aware, points to the successful tenth-century economic policies of successive English kings. In the first half-century the level of direct selling was perhaps limited, but later the role of the market seems to have become more pervasive, with coinage ('early cash') frequently occurring in all classes of habitation. It was this indigenous wealth generated so skilfully in a century of growth that undoubtedly drew the Danes back to England late in the tenth century. This time, under the same Svein who had himself engendered an urban programme, they sought to intimidate England into subsidising the Danish transition from a silver-rich society to a market-based community. The English response is most interesting and confirms the accumulated wealth of the nation and, in particular, the role of the market in bringing it about.

The threat to the southern English markets was met by creating a number of emergency burhs. Professor Dolley first drew attention to these as curious numismatic evidence came to hand in the 1950s. The valley burh of Wilton was temporarily replaced by the Iron Age fortress of Old Sarum. Leslie Alcock's investigations within the hillfort at South Cadbury revealed the character of the emergency burh which probably replaced Ilchester. Here a church and a major defensive refurbishing were found. Cissbury, a hillfort in Sussex, appears to have been the *fluctburg* for Chichester, while Dolley has speculated that EANBYRI, as yet unlocated, was the short-lived replacement for Dorchester. The role of the market by king Ethelred's time had become fundamental to his society, and it had to be protected at all costs. Once again the southern English burhs were fortified, as is shown by recent excavations at

Southampton, Wareham, Shaftesbury and Oxford. And the defences of Ipswich may date from this period.[50] Ethelred, as Sawyer has shown in a celebrated paper, was defending the 'wealth of England'.[51] The list of payments made to the Danish invaders gives some indication of the country's fortune – a list fully emphasised by the immense flow of Anglo-Saxon silver around the Baltic Sea territories.

991	£10,000[52]
994	£16,000
1002	£24,000
1007	£36,000
1009	£3,000 [53]
1012	£48,000
1014	£21,000
1018	£72,000 + £10,000 from the people of London

The figures reported by contemporaries are commonly regarded with some caution; yet there is no disputing the substantial ransoms repeatedly paid for England. What part of the overall English revenue it represented remains contentious. Metcalf has argued that the Long Cross penny issue dating from between 997 and 1003 may have been worth between £50,000 and £62,500, while Sawyer has envisaged a higher figure perhaps exceeding £100,000.[54] David Hinton has usefully drawn attention to the Domesday Book tax record which amounts to an annual revenue of £70,000 without either Winchester or London's contributions – figures that are strikingly similar to the £72,000 (without London's contribution) recorded by the Anglo-Saxon Chronicle in 1018.[55] Despite this taxation England still prospered, or so it seemed to Sawyer in 1965.[56] Certainly the eleventh century saw a growth in urban development, and this may stem from Edgar's and Ethelred's market-founding, based around their own estates as David Hill has shown, the principle being that a market is a source of income greater than the agricultural value of the land and thus a good investment.[57]

Yet Sawyer has claimed that the wealth of England lay in its revitalised international commerce, drawing on the opening of the silver mines in Germany. Here of course is a fundamental issue of this book, and we must take the occasion to see how long-distance trade was affected by the institution of markets. Sawyer has argued that the English treasury could not have afforded the heavy burden imposed by the Danes – that its wealth was dependent on selling woollen vestments and obtaining bullion in return. More recently Metcalf has repeated this case, listing once again the spasmodic references to German and Flemish merchants in London. Metcalf uses the archaeology with little conviction to sustain his thesis, while Sawyer drew upon Gerald Dunning's studies of Anglo-Saxon trade with the continent.

Dolley, Gem and Hinton have recently joined the debate and each has found a case for a period of 'austerity' between about 975 and 1020. Dolley has suggested that 'a rise in the price of silver, consequent on embarkation on a deliberate and nicely calculated policy of fluctuating over-valuation of silver coin even more than on the renewed Viking depredations, meant that fewer and fewer private individuals could afford to patronise a silversmith as opposed to a jeweller turning out ornaments in bronze and pewter, the latter an alloy that does not appear to have been in general use before the tenth century'.[58] Hinton has expanded this point, showing that the eleventh-century Cheapside hoard from London, containing pewter ornaments among others, is an assemblage designed as trinkets for the wider market, while he has confirmed the apparent dearth of precious metals for a time after about 975.[59] He rightly attributes this partly to changing attitudes towards display – a view consistent with Rathje's cost-control model (outlined in Chapter 1) – as the state develops new production-distribution modes. Moreover Dolley's point has been amplified by Gem in a review of the pattern of church-building in Late Saxon England.[60] Gem has demonstrated the stark contrast between England in the first quarter of the eleventh century and the continent, particularly France, where churches were being constructed and refurbished on a major scale – a scale consistent, incidentally, with the investment of capital and the establishment of order which led to the swift expansion of the continental economies. Finally, it should be noted that Petersson carried out spectographic analyses of certain Late Saxon pennies ranging in date from Edgar's to Harold's reigns. He discovered that the high content of Edgar's and Ethelred's issues were followed by a deterioration which lasted until some time during the reign of Edward the Confessor.[61] The statistical value of this observation, like the previous ones, may be limited; yet the sum of evidence clearly urges us to be wary of Sawyer's theory. This, however, can be tested if we examine the evidence Sawyer drew upon – the archaeological evidence of trade.

We have already discussed the nautical archaeology in Chapter 5. There we pointed out the limited data available for new boat designs before the latter half of the tenth century. One consequence, however, of the new designs illustrated by the Roskilde Fjord boat no. 1 was the added emphasis put on sailing craft with stout keels, which required a smaller crew. The archaeological correlate is that less traders' debris will be found in ports but the level of traded goods will increase – perhaps threefold, if this boat is an accurate representation of the new shipping fleets. (Still, these boats are modest by later medieval and Roman standards.) Furthermore, we have seen that the adaptation to sail-power conditioned the ports into which the boats might venture. Fewer oarsmen could not drag thirty-ton vessels on to beaches, as was possible before; instead wharfs were called for. London's wharf would appear to date from the early tenth century, although the dendrochronological dates are awaited with much eagerness.[62] Elsewhere wharves are not commonly found at this date, perhaps because the investment was very high.

The settlement evidence from Southampton and Ipswich shows that these two major foci of the Middle Saxon period had contracted remarkably. Indeed tenth-century Southampton was a mere shadow of its former self, comprising a ditch-defended promontory to the west of Hamwih – a settlement consistent with the second-tier burhs developing in competition with neighbouring markets where once it had been paramount. But probably the royal villa was maintained throughout and this was the chief focus of continued occupation here, as well as the reason for Canute's gathering of the English nobles in 1014.[63] The imported material indicates trade on a vastly diminished scale and only across to Rouen and its catchment area.[64] The same deterioration afflicted Ipswich also where, in comparison with the substantial Middle Saxon imports, few exist for the Late Saxon period. Moreover the town slipped to the fourth centre – and possibly the fifth, if Dunwich were better accounted for – in eleventh-century East Anglia, after Thetford, Norwich and Cambridge.[65] Yet it is equally clear that Norwich, despite its rapid expansion to possibly 80 ha by 1066 and a population of about 7,000, was also little involved in international trade. At least this is the tenor of the absent imports. Dunning was wrong to imply lively Late Saxon trade-routes, for the flood-tide of excavations have shown that these do not exist. Virtually all the imported wares he discussed can be attributed to the post-Conquest period. Indeed, the near absence of imported pottery – traded pottery rather than traders' debris – is striking in comparison with both the earlier and later patterns. In part, if the thesis presented earlier turns out to be verified, it may be the result of successful potteries in England, as well as of smaller numbers of traders. Yet the twelfth-century finds from London, Norwich and Exeter, for example, emphasise the point; the Late Saxon absence of imported pottery is beyond dispute. Moreover there are few finds from York or Lincoln, and few from Chester. (Chester, a major mint, is often said to have dominated Irish Sea trade during the tenth century; the absence of material evidence for this always seems to be overlooked, and the political contacts between York and Dublin are allowed to outweigh the negative evidence. There seems little doubt that Dublin took off economically only at the very end of the tenth century, under Sihtric of the Silken Beard, after the Chester mint had been booming for some decades (see Chapter 10).)

This is not to dispute the evidence for low-key international trade. A few tenth-century imports are known from London, while eleventh-century pots from Oxford and Southampton are also known.[66] Moreover valuable utilitarian items, such as lava querns from the Mayen area, continued to be imported, as Parkhouse has recently demonstrated.[67] But by 1000 the wealth of evidence points to a modest involvement in long-distance commerce. London may have been the exception, and the necessary bullion may have been brought through its newly raised port.

But the boom in English woollen trading could not have been funnelled so effectively through this one port.

The austerity, and the hiatus in trading across the North Sea, suggest that England's wealth lay in the capital that was already in the land. It lay in its few silver mines in the Mendips, the Pennines and in Flintshire; it lay in the vast reserves of church silver and in personal jewels; and it may have come from the treasury stocks which conceivably were built on tribute taken from the Danes as their half of England was annexed by Edward and Athelstan. In particular, this wealth was mobilised by activating the indigenous rural properties of the country, and by manufacturing goods in emulation of those available on the continent. This feature certainly characterises the course of the pottery industry, as lead-glazed wares and fine table vessels came to the fore in the third quarter of the tenth century. We might conclude that the end of the silver recession was probably brought about by participation in the European market, perhaps in the reign of Edward the Confessor, and that the marshalled wealth was fully capitalised by the Norman invader king William, who drew up a tax register to confirm just how rich he had become. Growth continued, with a firm platform into the later medieval centuries – a growth fully substantiated by the archaeology of most English towns.

Once again we must look beyond the particular value of this example to the shift from redistributive economic systems to explicitly market-oriented systems. A further example exists, as we have seen, in Scandinavia.

The impetus for the formation of the Viking state in Denmark appears to have come from the demise of the second phase of Arabic trade to the Baltic. This cessation resounded all the way back along the trade-route, through western Russia to Asia Minor, where 'silver coins, previously struck at more than a dozen towns, became rare after 970 and had completely disappeared by 1027/8. Baghdad and the other territories under Buwachid rule had stopped striking silver by 1009/10.'[68] Harald Bluetooth may for a time have elicited some German silver from his contacts with Otto the Great (d. 973), but in the 980s relations between the two territories deteriorated and there was a series of minor invasions and counter-invasions, resulting ultimately in the seizure of Harald's throne by his son, Svein Forkbeard.[69] Svein established a firm mastery over his kingdom after the Scandinavian territories were crucially divided at the battle of Svold in 1000 and thereby made it possible to campaign in England. Svein was evidently seeking to build up his treasury in order to afford the urban process, and as a result there are remarkable concentrations of German and Anglo-Saxon coins in eastern Denmark, the area over which his sovereignty was wavering.[70] Clearly these coins were being introduced into the regional network in preference to hack-silver, and therefore their users were careful to check their value, as the pecking of the German coins illustrates.[71]

Once achieved, this system is remarkably regional in character, with a marked absence of imports. The Aarhus excavations have produced few imported pots, and as yet none from the Rhineland dating from this period, while the same is true of Lund. The indigenous character of the industries is very apparent from the recent investigations in Lund, though a small collection of Stamford ware may reflect the close ties maintained between the two areas when Canute was king in both lands.[72] Similarly Canute brought English moneyers to assist the progress of his indigenous minting, and he may have brought English architects to design some of his urban churches.[73]

In view of the well-documented expansion of the German trading-communities at this date the absence of Rhenish materials is most striking. A century later, the Pingsdorf wares, for example, brought under the auspices of the Hanseatic League, begin to occur and ultimately to flood into the market. They are present in Aarhus and Schleswig, for instance. But in the meantime the regionally organised industries were growing and the land-based wealth was being realised by the Scandinavian kings. This pattern in Denmark is repeated in Oslo, and it is a feature of Sigtuna, the market on the shores of Lake Mälaren which succeeded Birka in the eleventh century.[74]

There is a great deal of historical evidence suggesting that it was not until the late tenth or eleventh century, with the firm establishment of a market-based economy, that long-distance trade once again thrived. This time it was to thrive in the hands of power groups bonded together in guilds, but again the stimulus came from the Rhineland and, to a lesser extent, the area between the Rhine and the Loire. The Rhenish traders may first have directed their interests towards England, perhaps in the reign of Edward the Confessor, and only later towards the emerging Baltic Sea nations. This new European wealth was the setting for its great Romanesque churches and a foundation-stone of the Crusades.

In each area the market had taken advantage of a mild climatic phase and steadily increasing population and was generating production to the advantage of kings, magnates and at first even farmers. The regular incidence of coins in the first market phase on many classes of site illuminates this fact – as perhaps does Svein's desire to flood his prospective market with captured silver. Tenth-century Goltho in Lincolnshire has produced a number of pennies, like eleventh-century Lindholm Høje, a village on 'marginal' land, and each illuminates the response to the economic mode. Similarly tenth-century coopers' houses at Coppergate, York (Fig. 45), have produced pennies from their floors, as have the early tenth-century smiths' shops in Petergate, Lincoln. Mutually amplifying, the country and the market were growing together in favourable conditions evoked by centralised authority. The system afforded expansion if it could be directed, and certain, almost textbook principles seem to have been followed.

First, we can see the pattern of market evolution and its controlled

Figure 45 View of the coopers' workshops at Coppergate, York (courtesy of the York Archaeological Trust)

development of the rural wealth. Secondly, the expansion took place by valuing the determinants recognised by Trigger and encouraging a range of artisans in each centre, rather than creating state-controlled specialist communities. This required a strong leadership, choosing in the long-term not to control scarcities, though rigorously maintaining land-holdings. Thirdly, it clearly needed a satisfactory bullion base to be at all successful, but we may doubt that this was acquired through international commerce, because this hindered the indigenous market-based development and perhaps concentrated wealth, as it inevitably did, in few hands. Lastly, it appears that long-distance trade was not countenanced until the emergence of the system of tiered markets and the accompanying social evolution it entailed. By these means great monarchs were bent to the will of circumstances and with economic determination created an urban society where before a redistributive economy had effectively misused the resources which they knew existed from their Roman heritage.

Chapter 10

THE EVOLUTION OF STATES

Few problems in the repertory of social science are at once more provoking and less accessible to direct research than those concerned with the evolution of the political organization of human society in general and with the origins of the state in particular.

M. H. Fried[1]

Throughout this book we have alluded to the emergence of more complex social arrangements, concluding finally with the crystallisation of state societies. Social and political evolution are intrinsically related to the successive production-distribution stages. This chapter, therefore, recapitulates these socio-economic conclusions in order to reveal the patterns of social evolution experienced in this critical period and to emphasise the synchronic properties of these patterns. We must begin by examining briefly definitions of the state, and also of the preceding social horizons, before drawing attention once again to the data we have investigated. It is equally important to examine the failure of certain areas to respond to these patterns; in particular, we shall make a brief review of the early Christian Irish circumstances – in the words of Arnold Toynbee, 'an abortive civilisation'.

   In parenthesis we may assert that the primary aim of this chapter is to eliminate the often inaccurate comparisons drawn with other territories when debating medieval state formation and market origins.[2] This chapter also provides a suitably irreverent appraisal of a subject which has too long been the domain of the particularist, prepared to glance only at the odd African context and then express mild disdain for its illiterate character. Unquestionably the power and the weakness of these west European situations lies in the existence of documentation which, in conjunction with archaeology, can provide an eloquent picture of the past. The weakness has been the consistently held view (more tacit than published) that because a few monks expressed their thoughts on parchment these early state societies were different from most others (for example the Mesopotamian and Mesoamerican states).

Writing is obviously an important feature of emerging states, but we must not be deceived by what is transmitted; the transmission is only one element of cultural behaviour and often determined by socio-economic circumstances.[3]

The state

Kent Flannery in his paper on the evolution of civilisation regards the state as strong centralised government with a professional ruling class largely divorced from the restrictions of kinship. He considers it to be highly stratified and diversified, with residential patterns based on occupational specialisation.[4] A further important feature is that the state has a monopoly of force. In his book *Primitive Social Organisation*, Elman Service has laid particular stress on this feature – a key to understanding states.[5] The reinforcement of power by this monopoly of force necessarily entails taxation in order to maintain the force. This, of course, has a string of systemic consequences.

We can further qualify Flannery's definition by establishing that the state must effect a stable or permanent hierarchy which can withstand the disruptive effect of succession struggles.[6] As a result, leaders of states assume a sacred character, or at least some special investiture with connotations of status. Several anthropologists have been intrigued by this and it is therefore valuable to cite the comments of one important paper on this subject. Roy Rappaport has argued that 'whereas previously authority was contingent upon its sanctification, sanctity now became the instrument of authority. Coercion is expensive and difficult, and compliance and docility are achieved more easily and inexpensively through first the encouragement of religious experiences . . . and second, inculcation of the belief that the world's evils are a result of the worshipper's own sinfulness rather than a matter of external exploitation or oppression which the worshipper could possibly resent.'[7] This, of course, marks a new concept in leadership, with social distance intervening between the state's leader and the populace, where previously their interdependence was incontestable. The consequence of this is the inception of strong feelings of ethnicity or nationalism by 'citizen members' of the state.[8] The sense of corporation becomes important as groups rearrange their social bonds and thus adapt to the new horizon where previously the force of kinship was pervasive.

States are expensive levels of organisation to create and maintain, as Rappaport and others have pointed out. They require a 'high-energy infrastructure in order to function efficiently'[9] and, through positive feedback, to create growth. States need bureaucracies to handle the increased administration and a standing army; they need buildings to house them and they need to levy taxation efficiently – at first. The result, to quote a recent essay by Gall and Saxe, 'is to increase complexity . . . to continue to diversify structurally each part increasingly specialised to exploiting different sources of available energy or to administering, transferring and/or transporting this energy among the parts' (of the state system).[10] By this means buffers are created against the kind of perturbations which systemically delimit the expansion of many 'cyclical chiefdoms'.[11]

Yet it seems positively less ambivalent to adopt the criteria which Flannery and others have espoused (discussed above), for the natural economic expression of this system is the market. Only the market offers the high energy circulation that will sustain a complex infrastructure.

Chiefdoms and cyclical chiefdoms

Chiefdoms are the prevailing characteristics of the social organisation in early medieval Europe. These had existed beyond the Roman *limes*, as Tacitus showed and as Lotte Hedeager has recently demonstrated for Denmark.[12] These structures seem to have persisted into the migration period, the directors of the migrations in certain cases assuming power from their bold initiatives. We may suspect, however, that complex ranking was a regulator of the centralised authority invested in these Teutonic kings, and that to many of them the church proved an even greater regulator of power when it intervened as a major pillar of the community where previously the kings had retained monolithic theocratic status.[13]

In these contexts the development of increased centralised power is in essence a response to factors such as growing population, communal perturbations and the need to acquire utilitarian items integral to efficient subsistence. It is a well-documented selection process, which maintains the survival of the system and facilitates the processing of information within it, often, for example, articulating ecological variegations to the satisfaction of the whole community. If the chief gains controls over his economic role, rather than remaining the chairman – the man in the middle (as opposed to the top) – the system will gradually experience change, since this central person accumulates wealth sufficient to separate his position from the communities. Elman Service claimed that chiefdoms are the social expression of redistribution,[14] and it is therefore a key question whether the chief can gain authority over the revenue which is elicited for the community's benefit in the first place and expended in what Timothy Earle has called 'levelling processes', like assemblies, dowries, funerals, etc. (see Chapter 1).[15]

In circumstances where chiefs 'mobilise' this wealth to assert their status and create a ruling elite, there is a tendency to find the formation of what might be termed 'cyclical chiefdoms'. These establish exceptionally firm but temporary control over their own and adjacent territories. Yet their charisma alone is not sufficient to generate the feedback that will cause the morphogenesis of the system. Theirs is an unstable creation, achieved by aggression, though it is often the initial high-energy platform on which a subsequent state may be constructed.[16]

Finally, as power is accumulated centrally and an elite, and eventually a state leadership, emerges, the significance of the levelling processes – the fundamental rationale of chiefdomship – will diminish, and the community will be subsumed to the demands of reorganised high-energy processing structures: the market. In these circumstances the importance of long-distance trade, by which primitive valuables are acquired to sustain the levelling processes, will decline and will thereafter be confined, in the short term at least, to acquiring only utilitarian necessities. Trade will therefore assume a strictly regional pattern, and the distribution of wealth will gradually take a new spatial dimension which is more hierarchical and thus more predictable. This will be in contrast to the redistributive economic mode in which the levelling mechanism diffuses wealth and there are no concentrations – in theory at least. Gradually, long-distance trade will be re-established as nations function within continental and inter-continental commercial systems. This trade will be forged by entrepreneurs who become, with time, a new elite.

The primary state

In Chapter 1 we saw the conceptual difference between primary and secondary states, and this has been an inherent feature of our analysis throughout this book. The primary state comprised a number of complex territories which had earlier been core provinces of the Roman empire. Each of these territories possessed a level of socio-political complexity which was economically embodied in a redistributive system. By the early seventh century the mobilisation of goods and services for the benefit of an elite stratum is most evident. Craft-specialists were operating with a high level of production, while rural production was apparently injected with new labour acquired by trading manufactured goods under treaty to territories beyond the confines of Merovingia. Some periodic markets were permitted, though these were almost certainly directly regulated by kings or their agents and thus there were no signs of widespread urban growth before the later eighth or early ninth century. Until then the only urban communities consisted of the emporia, through which long-distance trade was conducted.

It is a classic evolution of a 'civilisation' with the cementing together of the kingdoms in a polity that stretched from the Pyrenees to Jutland under a charismatic leader, Charlemagne. This survived for scarcely thirty years, and during much of that time the elite were concerned with internal fission. The problems of distance made administration difficult, especially when the emperor had tried to stimulate a new economic trajectory. Charlemagne almost certainly intended to activate the rural potential and the industrial potential, but sought to do so by increasing trade to the territories beyond, as well as by introducing market-places under a strictly controlled monetary system. But this, as in the case of the Vorgebirge kilns, probably put the control of resources into the hands of a few, and the elite were further strengthened and further strained to create regional disharmony rather than the regional harmony Charlemagne was seeking.[17] This is demonstrated archaeologically by the emergence of fortified residences in Belgium during the ninth century, in the Rhineland, and early in the tenth century in France. These sites are witness to the origins of European feudalism.[18] Then there was the further factor of stress from beyond the system exacerbating divisions: penetrating raids on the wealth of the state by the Vikings in the north and by Arabs in the south. Stable territories were to emerge during the tenth century from the dissolution of Charlemagne's empire, with nearly a century and a half of slow agricultural and regional growth. From this platform came the urban expansion which Charlemagne had probably planned, with a speed and assurance he might have dreamed of. It occurred in a rigidly structured society with strong emphasis on stratification and corporation, a feature which was to mark the newly-fledged nations for almost another millennium.

Secondary states

The evolution of secondary states is rather more interesting, insofar as their pathways have usually been ignored in preference to 'civilisation'.[19] In this book we have concentrated on two case-studies, Anglo-Saxon England and Denmark, although reference has been made to other allied territories beyond Merovingia and Carolingia.

The evolution of Anglo-Saxon England, forming from the diverse tribes that migrated from the North Sea littoral, is now fairly clearly understood. These early tribal groupings are largely revealed in the document known as the Tribal Hidage, which was a taxation-survey prepared for Mercian kings. The most recent assessment of it attributes it to the late seventh-century king, Wulfhere.[20] In this assessment Davies and Vierck have also defined three sizes of territory as indicated by the survey. The smallest unit includes territories the size of the Isle of Wight and the medium unit territories the size of shires like Sussex, while the largest units are the kingdoms like Wessex or Mercia. The document was explicitly conceived for fiscal purposes, so the hidage in certain cases may have been inflated to the detriment of Wessex, for example, and the gain of the then king of kings – the bretwalda – king of the Mercians. Yet it is a most interesting analysis, because many of these kingdoms persisted until the ninth century, when they were all bonded into the unified kingdom of England. Ethnicity remained a feature until the post-Conquest period, as Sir Frank Stenton has shown in the case of the Isle of Wight.[21] Until the ninth century there is a certain fluidity in the polities, some of which temporarily contain the smallest units and even the medium units and some of which establish a permanent control over them.

The composition of the smallest units may have been only slightly hierarchical. At least that is one interpretation of the best known example, the territory of the Pecsaetan – the Peak District – where the rich burial at Benty Grange stands out from the other wealthy Peakland pioneer-farmers.[22] Bede tells us that 1,200 families were inhabiting the Isle of Wight, perhaps 6,000–10,000 persons, a number which, to judge by later Viking-period political structures in Iceland, could have been administered by a group of elders at a Folk Moot, the Anglo-Saxon equivalent of the 'thing', before the island was annexed by the West Saxons late in the seventh century. The medium-sized territories were subject to royal rule. These were founded by existing 'dynasties' and they exerted their authority by making continual progressions around their territories, being never more (in theory) than a day's ride from any boundary. These territories were almost certainly more densely occupied and sustained by their more structured hierarchy, although we doubt whether in true extent, because of uncultivated intervening land like woodland, they were initially much larger in terms of defined boundaries than the smallest units.

The scale of these territories seems to be defined by the area that might be efficiently administered and defended. In theory, from a central position, any point on the frontier could be quickly reached, and the native community could be adequately served by their leader, who regularly visited them, activating the institutional mechanisms which were a feature of his role. These administrative parameters correspond closely to what Renfrew has called the Early State Module (ESM).[23] This is an area which, he says, is approximately 1500 sq km in area, and has a central place which is nowhere more than 40–100 km (depending on the intervening parcels of land) from the next central place, in the adjoining ESM. Renfrew has illustrated the synchronic value of this model by drawing attention to its existence in Mycenean-Minoan Greece, Etruscan Italy, Iron Age England and Mesoamerica. It seems no coincidence then that a shire unit in Wessex was an administrative invention known then as a *regio*.[24]

As we have seen, however, the central place is not a feature of the Anglo-Saxon, Scandinavian, Irish or indeed Carolingian system of political control; it is an innovation dating from relatively recent centuries.[25] The central place is perhaps the result of a strongly centralised authority founded on a theocratic kingship which has attained a firm hold over the mobilisation of the economy and an advantage over any emergent elite. The peripatetic kingship still had to function as an integral part of the community, administering it directly. Only slowly, and in chosen circumstances, might the king accumulate wealth. The parallel roles of church and kingship in the community would have delimited the acquisition of great wealth. Whereas moveable objects had been interred with the dead in funerals that have a passing resemblance to the potlatch practised by the Kwakiutl Indians of north-west America, the church in the late seventh century ruled that the tradition was unacceptable. They were almost certainly the beneficiaries, building up powerful revenues and thus restraining the emergence of real power-blocks. Kings were pillars of the community,[26] but as one discovered, they could still be powerfully admonished and their prestige therefore tarnished by ecclesiastics.

The struggle to gain superiority over the church was undoubtedly fundamental to the formation of the state. The progression is charted by the laws of Ina, the late seventh- to eighth-century king of Wessex, and those of Alfred dating from the end of the ninth century. In the former, royal authority and ecclesiastical authority are the mutual pillars of the realm, the blood-price being the same for a king and a bishop. But by Alfred's reign the price of a king was still 120 shillings to be paid for his murder; for an archbishop it was 90 shillings and for a bishop 60. It is a telling devaluation, and an indication of the annexation of power by the secular arm of society.[27] The critical years lie around the end of the eighth century and early in the ninth century, when Offa and then Ceonwulf of Mercia tried to circumscribe the powers of the archbishop of Canterbury.[28] Here was a powerful restraint on kingship which, once removed, led to the evolution of a sacred status reflected in the anointing of king Edgar at Bath in 971 and the firm belief in the monarch as Christ's deputy among Christian people by Ethelred's reign.[29]

The creation of polities seems only to have been given a permanent value if the king could establish social autonomy over all including the church. Thus king Offa's cyclical chiefdomship, like many before, was an expression of that goal, but he could not achieve the feedback to alter the system. He could create a sufficiently powerful administration to cope with the scale of his achievement, and he could acquire a great deal of wealth through European contact to sustain the loyalty of his people. He may even have attempted to activate the regional properties of his kingdom by introducing a controlled scheme of markets rather in the image of his neighbour, Charlemagne. But Offa was forced to fight to maintain authority, and therefore it was to vanish with him. Instead he had probably extended the powers of kingship to a point that was to be the platform on which the West Saxons were successfully to build their nation, a phenomenon we examined in Chapter 8.[30]

The changes in the ninth century may have owed much to events in Carolingia, where civil disruption must have terminated the long-distance trade routes or at least have diminished their importance. It also owed much to the creation of a strong polity which (most significantly) was handed down from father to son, and from the injection of power given to these West Saxon kings under the stress conditions evoked by the Vikings. It owed much, too, to the evidently enlarged populace, to whom direct attention could no longer be administered. Positive feedback amplified change, and on this occasion the parameters of growth were overcome. At this point the ESMs disappeared and re-emerged as less significant sub-units – the shires of tenth-century England. A new form of government was created, administratively much more exacting, and the market was integral to its operation. Late Saxon England was as different structurally from Early to Middle Saxon England as those phases had been from the preceding Roman period. 'The formal institutional life of the kin was atrophied, if not stifled at birth, by the strength of territorial lordship and christian kingship', as one historian has asserted recently of Late Saxon England.[31] Increasingly in the place of kindred as a legal institution there was the tithing, the hundred and the shire providing hope of security.

It was the same, or very similar, systemic conditions that contrived to launch the Viking state in Denmark.[32] Indeed it was in a phase of economic recession, when the second period of Arabic trading to the Baltic was dying, that Harald Bluetooth began to extend his control. He was to raise a great runic inscription at his political base, Jellinge, which testified to this new political act. It reads: 'King Harald had this memorial made for Gorm his father and Thyric his mother: that Harald who won for himself all Denmark and Norway, and made the Danes Christian.' (Like the Anglo-Saxon Chronicle, an invention of the ninth-century kings of Wessex, the great Jellinge runestone attests the dynastic qualifications that stress Harald's right to this new status.) His authority, like that of the West Saxon kings, was usurped by his son Svein Forkbeard who largely completed the task of drawing eastern Denmark into the new realm. Integral to this success was the construction of a chain of royal forts, which probably housed the standing army that effected the new state. Important too was the innovation of the regional market, reinforced by silver stolen from Germany and England, which activated the ever-increasing rural population at a time of agricultural development, when the climate facilitated expansion.

The precise schedule of change is not so clear as the West Saxon one. How many territories were embraced in the new kingdom is not absolutely clear. But the preceding pattern of cyclical chiefdoms, growing to command a patchwork of small and large territorial units, is similar to that in England. Like Offa, king Godfred established an authority mighty enough to challenge Charlemagne, but not to pass the power on. Indeed where Godfred had led all the Danes against the Carolingians several Danish chiefs were to conclude the peace treaty in 811 after his death.

In Denmark there is only the impression of territorial size, and we are left to speculate whether the existence contemporaneously of Haithabu, and Ribe and *Reric* on either side of it, reflects the economic expression of three adjacent ESMs. *Reric* was certainly the trading-station of the Obodrits, as the Frankish Annals indicate, both when it was raided by Godfred in 808 and when it was refurbished with an encircling wall in 815.[33] Haithabu's initial size may owe much not only to its critical location, but also to Godfred's foundation when he had assumed the powers of a cyclical chiefdom. This may well have diminished when the territory was divided, and perhaps a rival king sought to intercede on the North Sea trade route, thus establishing Ribe. We shall probably never know for certain, although Louis' patronage of the Danish king Harald, formalised in 826, must have ensured a flow of Carolingian manufactured goods to these emporia.

The Danish ESMs may owe their origin to the migration period, when the Teutonic communities re-adjusted to their swift depopulation. For the most part growth seems to have been slow, possibly because the authority of kingship was limited. Paganism may have deterred the primary state from engaging consistently in long-distance trade with the north. This was changed by the end of the eighth century, when most of the Frisian coastline had been brought within the Christian orbit, and in any case the Baltic wealth must have been a vital element in the economic goal of Charlemagne's Carolingia. It was perhaps no coincidence that Carolingian missionaries went with merchants to the great emporia at Haithabu, Ribe and Birka, thus giving some countenance to the mercantile operation.

It was perhaps with astute awareness of this that in the tenth century Harold Bluetooth chose to become a Christian – a fact he associates with his new political status. It may well have been his means of asserting a new authority over his fellow countrymen and of evading the restraint that his pagan spiritualism had hitherto held over him. Clearly the new religion in Scandinavia, not only in Denmark, was moulded skilfully to new economic aspirations. Lund was given a great church by Canute; Oslo grew up around a church; Sigtuna, the town which replaced Birka, has the monumental remains of three great churches dominating the small lake-side centre. There too a runestone, surmounted with an incised cross, tells of the formation of a guild and is quite evidently witness,[34] like the West Saxon guilds of the early eleventh century, to a new age.

Ireland – 'an abortive civilisation'[35]

We have seen that two features were important in the creation of the secondary states: first, their reaction to long-distance trade and concepts offered by a more complex civilisation – the primary state; and secondly, their ability to use the wealth and concepts at a centralised point to draw apart from the inherent levelling mechanisms which were the fundamental rationale of Germanic leadership. The absence of sustained contact with either secondary states or a primary state was a severely limiting factor in the Early Christian period in Ireland. This was almost certainly a consequence of the restricted concept of kingship fostered in this Late Celtic outpost.

From the Iron Age, dating back to the first millennium B.C., until Strongbow led a mixture of Welsh and Anglo-Norman troops into south-eastern Ireland in 1169, it can justifiably be claimed that the society was 'tribal, rural, hierarchical and familiar'.[36] Irish kings seem only to have established some centralised authority in the brief periods that they were in contact with primary states. During the Roman period, for example, there are indications of accumulated wealth that suggest that the Celtic cultural regulators were overcome; and again during the phases of trading, first from the Mediterranean and then from Aquataine in the fifth, sixth and seventh centuries (see Chapter 2), there are marked concentrations of wealth at royal settlements. But these were spasmodic events and insufficient to reverse the delimiting nature of Celtic kingship.

It has been estimated that there were about 500 kings between about 500 and 1169 and a population of about half a million.[37] To paraphrase one historian, it was like a patchwork quilt of kingdoms with the traditional partible inheritance preventing the long-term creation of polities.[38] Moreover the traditional role of the king as – in effect – chairman over territorial councils, the *oenach*, further restricted the development of kingship and the accumulation of wealth through mobilisation.

This is not to suggest that Ireland was devoid of socio-economic development. There is clear evidence of regional trading indicated, for example, by the movements of both prestige goods like metalwork and utilitarian goods like quernstones (see Chapter 6). There were fairs and assemblies, where goods were evidently traded under controlled circumstances. Furthermore, it was a feature of the strongly organised Irish church which, like the secular arm of society, was divided and so equally competitive for the resources that did exist. Undoubtedly, however,the most significant socio-economic interaction was in the form of warfare and raids. These almost certainly acted as a means of maintaining a balanced economy in a country which was partly rich in agricultural resources and partly marginal. Warfare was perhaps the buffer against famine in the west, and the means by which kings were usually contained. Also, remarkably enough, it appears to have been a delimiting factor on the political aspirations of the church, with raids by the Irish on their own monasteries figuring more prominently in certain periods than those by the Vikings (contrary to popular belief).[39]

'Cyclical chiefdoms', however, occasionally emerged. Often these were the High Kings who were usually elected to their office and therefore rather weaker than the Anglo-Saxon *bretwalda*-ships. The most eminent king was Brian Boru, who established his road to success by sacking Limerick, a Viking emporium, in 967. He then created a great polity, the forces from which he lined up against the Viking settlers at the battle of Clontarf in 1014. This is said to have been a battle for the kingship of all Ireland, but that is a hollow claim. Brian Boru was then, by medieval standards, a remarkably old man, and the swift passing of his achievement after his death in the battle illustrates once again the difference between chiefdoms and the emergence of states. Brian was not the last of these powerful kings, and indeed one was to open the door to Ireland for the Anglo-Normans in the twelfth century. Brian, however, was keen to tackle the Vikings in 1014, and it is for this that he is remembered. Here we can find a small but interesting reflection of the socio-economic processes occurring elsewhere in north-east Europe at the time – events we have already alluded to in Chapter 9.

By the tenth century the Vikings had established *longports*, as the later chroniclers called them, at Dublin, Waterford, Wexford, Cork and Limerick. But these small trading-places set in territories the size of small ESMs were evidently dependent on their Scandinavian contacts in England and in the Baltic Sea countries. The dearth of early tenth-century evidence from the one major investigation of these emporia, at Dublin, suggests that their size was in fact rather more modest than we have hitherto appreciated and that while they were engaged in some trade it was also fairly modest.[40] This would appear to have changed in the last quarter of the tenth century, as a host of silver-hoards in eastern Ireland, for example, attests. It is feasible, perhaps, that the Scandinavian formation of the states was being felt in these faraway colonies. Certainly in the last years of the first millennium Sihtric of the Silken Beard at Dublin issued a coinage influenced greatly by the coinage of Ethelred the Unready.[41] He may have founded his new market on pirated English silver, but soon the trade-route from Dublin at least, to England was to develop slowly, whereas there is virtually no evidence of interaction between the Viking colonies isolated on the coastlines and the great heartland of Ireland with its dense population.[42] It was this goal that Brian almost certainly was after, and he began the road which led to Clontarf at a time that, as we have seen, was most critical to the Viking communities everywhere. The failure to capture these solar central places modelled on towns like Aarhus or Oslo was perhaps a reflection of the limited powers that even Brian Boru possessed and the ultimate indictment on Irish kingship.

The inability to centralise power, to generate sufficient control of scarce resources, meant that the Irish kings remained systemically restrained by the Celtic tradition of inheritance. Contact with the rest of

Europe was too infrequent or spasmodic for the negative feedback to be overcome. Instead they possessed:[43]

> Hounds, ale, horses and teams,
> Women, well-bred fosterlings.

This book began by quoting Marvin Harris, who proclaimed the power of cultures to the detriment, it could be said, of great men. There can be little doubt that the early history of western Europe reinforces this view, and yet this very appreciation puts the significance of its warrior kings in better perspective.

Archaeology may have over-emphasised this conclusion, and its value as a source may be inflated. Yet it can be fairly argued that the processes inherent in the creation of west European towns, the nub of the dilemma brilliantly aroused by Henri Pirenne, have been revealed with a growing precision that can only be enhanced, and indeed undoubtedly will be. It is a precision which is just beginning to enable us to give history a behavioural scale. But this book, as we have said, is no more than a rough set of notes on this central and pervading theme for our continent. Much more systematic research, devised on a regional level, is required to test the predictions and to equip these models with an historical accuracy which will enlarge our understanding of cultural phenomena generally.

In conclusion we can detect two inter-related origins of the European town. In Carolingia it was fostered by an elite for its own advantage, and was probably based to a large extent on the wealth generated from long-distance trade. This was the impetus to move from a highly complex and highly structured mobilisation economy to a system of competitive markets which had been extinct as a phenomenon since the fifth century. The economic platform in Anglo-Saxon England and Scandinavia appears to have been the cessation of long-distance trade. Its end in effect put the role of advanced chieftains in grave danger, and to this they responded, successfully, in systemic contexts which permitted morphogenesis. These secondary states were almost certainly aware of the economic concepts they were striving for. King Alfred probably learned of them from classical writers or from the capitularies issued by Charlemagne, while Harald Bluetooth and his son Svein Forkbeard – the two most eminent Scandinavians – may have learned from the market-founding which their powerful neighbour Otto the Great had undertaken in tenth-century Germany.

In all these contexts the urban process was being generated by massive injections of capital. In the primary state, however, it fell into the hands of a divided elite, who seem to have divisively restrained the process. Central authority, by contrast, is the mark of achievement of the West Saxon and Jellinge-based kings. The generalised stages of central organisation and their central places are outlined below. But we must note that while the significance of the elite becomes greater and greater in the emergence of a complex economy, the role of that central person becomes more distant. Kings figure most prominently in the directional down-the-line exchange outlined in Chapter 1, and in the sixth-century west-European long-distance trading system (Chapter 2). Long-distance trade is regulated at a fixed point, as kings achieve significant power and grasp the significance of wealth as a means to greater authority in a largely redistributive system. Their purpose is to restrict access to this wealth, though the trade may be directly controlled by the king's ministers. Type A emporia are founded near to royal residences. Type B must be the product of trade agreements with great economic potential. These sites, with populations at least ten times greater than villages or monasteries, are suddenly created. Their creation places greater emphasis on freelance traders, who are controlled at a distance by kings seeking to maximise the importation of specific prestige and utilitarian items. But, as we have seen, these sites stimulate regional (dendritic) exchange on a semi-commercial scale and necessitate the development of units of exchange. A regional (competitive) marketing economy based on a hierarchy of market-places requires less direct involvement by central authority if it is to function successfully. Yet the kings benefit from the taxing of activity, using media of exchange which they carefully monitor. Their power is increased by this taxation to maintain a standing army, while their capital in terms of landed wealth can be used to generate further wealth.

At each developmental stage the central person is gaining greater mastery over the traditional levelling mechanisms. The result is an evolving economy in which the direction of trade passes from royal control to merchants. The critical stage, as the Carolingians showed, is the point at which the economy is developing slowly and cannot be directly overseen by the king or his agents. Such decentralisation is divisive and indeed breeds anarchy. The organisational process is summarized in Table 6.

Table 6

Chiefdom	Redistribution	ESM	Type A Gateway community
Cyclical chiefdom	Mobilisation	Polity	Type B Gateway community
State formation	Incipient market economy	Polity	Solar central places
Nation	Market economy		Competitive markets

Of course, this model is strictly conditioned by the relationship between one system and another. The importance of contact, in the end, appears critical, as the Irish case seems to demonstrate. The inter-relationship between the articulate communities whose history is well known and those whose past lies at this time in prehistory seems to be clear. Moreover, the archaeology of trade has given a vivid and articulate character to the relationship. It also demonstrates the complexity that great men had to tackle, and therefore even when they were conditioned by the regularities of human action their intellect and imagination survives to be venerated. For ultimately, as Pirenne was perhaps the first modern historian to discern, the fascination of the past lies in its conflicts, and in the mastery with which certain individuals have attempted to solve these conflicts and altered their cultural circumstances to their own ends.

NOTES

INTRODUCTION

1. Harris 1978, 209–10
2. Latouche 1967, Duby 1968, and Duby 1974 are probably the most useful introductions to the overall problem, while the *Cambridge Medieval History of Europe* is a first-level source of historical detail. Ganshof 1971 provides a scholarly introduction to Charlemagne's empire and its institutions. Stenton's (1971) history of Anglo-Saxon England remains a classic, while Wilson (ed) 1976 is a valuable mine of archaeological data. Randsborg 1980 greatly illuminates the Scandinavian scene, as do Sawyer 1971, Jones 1968 and Foote and Wilson 1970. Christensen's reprinted essays 1976 and Smyth 1977 should be consulted. See also the vigorous debate on the later Viking raids in *Medieval Scandinavia* 2, 1969. Alcock 1971, Hughes 1972 and Ó'Córráin 1972 give lively introductions to the Celtic world embracing western Britain and Eire.
3. Boeles, P. C. J. A., 1951: *Friesland tot de elfe eeuw*, 2nd ed., 's-Gravenhage, with English summary should be consulted as a preliminary guide.
4. Levison 1946.
5. See Pirenne 1939.
6. Renfrew 1978b.

Chapter 1. THE SHADOW OF PIRENNE

1. Bridbury 1969, 527.
2. Lyon 1974; Pirenne 1925; 1939; Reynolds 1977, 17.
3. See Latouche 1967, 143ff. and Grierson 1959 for references, as well as Lyon 1974.
4. cf. Bridbury 1969.
5. Lyon 1974
6. Bolin 1953.
7. ibid., 8–9.
8. ibid., 25.
9. Morrison 1963, 405.
10. e.g. Metcalf 1965; 1967.
11. Metcalf 1965; 1967.
12. Bloch 1967; Grierson 1967; 1976.
13. Grierson 1959.
14. Mauss 1925; Malinowski 1922.
15. cf. Ennen 1979, 17.
16. Grierson 1959, 129.
17. Pirenne 1939, 240; Arbman 1940.
18. Arbman 1937.
19. Van Es et al. 1978, 196–200, 227–9.
20. Jankuhn 1976 (6th ed.)
21. Blindheim 1975a, esp. 130–8.
22. Addyman and Hill 1968.
23. Dunning 1956.
24. Dunning 1959.
25. Biddle 1976a, 102.
26. Biddle 1976a.
27. Finley 1971.
28. Trigger 1978, 19.
29. Clarke 1978; Trigger 1978, 19–36.
30. Binford 1972, 20; see also Binford 1977
31. Binford 1977, 2.

32. Renfrew 1975, 4.
33. Malinowski 1922.
34. Mauss 1925.
35. Sahlins 1974, xii.
36. Polanyi 1957; Sahlins 1974; Dalton 1975; 1977; Bohannan and Dalton 1962.
37. Polanyi 1957.
38. Sahlins 1974, 155–230.
39. Smelsner 1959.
40. Earle 1977.
41. Bohannan and Dalton 1962.
42. Skinner 1964–5.
43. e.g. Hodder 1965; Hodder and Lee 1974, 137ff., Hodder and Ukuru 1969.
44. Smith 1976.
45. Callmer 1977; Hardh 1977–8; Torrence in Hodges et al. 1978.
46. Earle 1977, 227.
47. Hodder and Lee 1974, 137.
48. Peebles and Kus 1977; Wright and Johnson 1975; Earle 1977.
49. Renfrew 1975, 1977.
50. Renfrew 1977, 72.
51. Renfrew 1972, 466. It should be pointed out that this model has been subject to considerable criticism recently, but it still serves a useful function.
52. Renfrew 1972, 466.
53. Renfrew 1975, 48–9.
54. Renfrew 1977, 88; Clark 1979.
55. Adams 1975, 457–8.
56. Hamond 1979, fig. 2; see also Renfrew 1977, 88.
57. Maitland 1897; Schledermann 1970–1.
58. Schnapp 1977.

59. Schledermann 1970–1 reviews Schlesinger's work; see Ennen 1979.
60. See Biddle 1976a, 100 for a discussion.
61. Quoted by Biddle 1976a, 99–100.
62. Biddle 1976a, 100.
63. Wheatley 1972, 623.
64. Childe 1950.
65. Friedman and Rowlands 1978; see Chapter 10.
66. Renfrew 1972, 7.
67. Redman 1978, 215.
68. Sjoberg 1967.
69. Hensel 1969–70.
70. Rathje and Sabloff 1973–4, 221.
71. Polanyi 1963.
72. Renfrew 1975, 43.
73. Rathje and Sabloff 1973–4, 222.
74. Hodges et al. 1978 discuss ports of trade. Much of my discussion is now superseded by this book; some of my discussion, moreover, is fallacious. However, Robin Torrence's points in reply to my article are valuable notes on the question of ports of trade.
75. Hirth 1978.
76. Hirth 1978, 36.
77. Hirth 1978, 37.
78. Sabloff et al. 1975, 396.
79. Southall 1967.
80. Carneiro 1968.
81. Trigger 1978, 54–74.
82. Service 1971; Fried 1967; Friedman and Rowlands 1978.
83. cf. Webb 1975.
84. Fried 1967, 226.
85. Wright and Johnson 1975; Redman 1978.
86. Rathje 1975.

Chapter 2.   TRADING SYSTEMS FROM THEODORIC TO CHARLEMAGNE

1. Pirenne 1939.
2. e.g. Hedeager 1978.
3. cf. Myhre 1978; van Es 1973 for recent appraisals.
4. Ammerman and Cavalli-Sforza 1973 provide an appropriate diffusion model for this.
5. e.g. James 1977, 243.
6. James 1977 discusses this at length.
7. Evidence of continued, fifth-century, occupation has been found in many Romano-British towns: Biddle 1976a.
8. See Warner 1976 and references cited there.

9. Alcock 1971; Pearce 1979, 53–7.
10. Vierck 1976 discusses the movement of East Anglian pottery.
11. e.g. Werner 1961.
12. Werner 1961; these tend to be found in seventh-century burials in England.
13. Latouche 1967, 121.
14. Dewing 1928, 267.
15. Decaens 1971.
16. See Vierck 1970.
17. O'Ríordáin 1942.
18. Pearce 1979, 158 publishes the most recent survey of finds.
19. Alcock 1971 for a useful appraisal.

20. See Werner 1961.
21. Himley 1955; see also Rigold 1975 and James 1977, 220ff.
22. Grierson 1952-4.
23. Kent 1975.
24. There is steadily growing evidence that international trade in Italy was entering a recession. This is largely based on Hayes's work (1972) on Late Roman pottery, but individual field-projects at Luni, in Etruria and in Molise substantiate it.
25. Sutherland 1948.
26. Stenton 1971, 59.
27. Rigold 1975.
28. e.g. Evison 1979.
29. Brent 1863.
30. Crowfoot and Hawkes 1967.
31. Sahlins 1974, 312.
32. Wade 1980.
33. It must be pointed out that some Dutch scholars believe that these imported pots are evidence of a Merovingian community linked to Merovingian control over the area. In view of the continued production of native hand-made pottery throughout the next two centuries, I consider these imports to be the result of commerce.
34. Ekholm 1958.
35. Bruce-Mitford 1975.
36. Clogher: I am indebted to Richard Warner of the Ulster Museum for information on this important site, though I have drawn my own conclusions; see also Peacock and Thomas 1967.
37. Liversage 1967.
38. See James 1977 for a review of this.
39. ibid.
40. ibid.
41. Latouche 1967, 123-4.
42. See Sawyer 1977.
43. Jellema 1955.
44. See Rigold 1975 and Evison 1979.
45. See Rigold 1975.
46. Eckstein, van Es and Hollstein 1975.
47. I have tried to reconstruct this chronology with the aid of Levison 1946.
48. Jankuhn 1976, Abb. 7. The absence of seventh- to eighth-century sceattas from Ipswich may suggest that only Kent (via (?)Sarre) was engaged in commerce with Dorestad at this time. It is possible that Ipswich was temporarily abandoned.
49. Bendixen 1974.
50. Jankuhn 1976, Abb. 9. Rigold (1960-1, 26) has drawn attention to disruptions caused by the Frisian insurrection in 732. This is usually ignored by modern historians, though Ermoldus Nigellus recalls it in his ninth-century history (Faral 1932, 164). These would have been more devastating if Dorestad's role was then focused on trade with Frisia. If this region was suffering a war, Dorestad's economic role would have been restricted.
51. Bendixen 1974.
52. Jankuhn 1976, 216.
53. Hougen 1969.
54. Holmqvist 1975.
55. Jankuhn 1976, Abb. 9.
56. e.g. van Es and Verwers 1975.
57. Andersen 1979.
58. Randsborg 1980, 85ff.
59. See Jankuhn 1976, 283-6 for a brief summary of the recent dendrochronological studies.
60. Randsborg 1980, 137 ff.
61. Andersen 1979.
62. cf. Weidemann 1970 and Steuer 1974.
63. Christensen 1976, 9-30.
64. Arbman 1940.
65. Callmer 1977.
66. Besteman 1974.
67. Dhondt 1962.
68. I am indebted to Geoff Watkin, a research student at Sheffield University, for providing me with details on this trade in advance of the completion of his thesis.
69. See Stenton 1971, 23.
70. Rigold 1975, phase IV.
71. Metcalf 1974 reviews this problem.
72. I am grateful to Mrs Leslie Webster for her written comments on this matter; the conclusions drawn, however, are my own.
73. Hodges 1979a, 192.
74. See Biddle 1976a, 114.
75. Cherry and Hodges 1978.
76. Dolley 1970; Hodges 1979a.
77. Metcalf 1972.
78. See Metcalf 1977.
79. Metcalf 1974; Cherry and Hodges 1978.
80. e.g. Metcalf 1974, 1977.

81. See Chapter 6.
82. Blunt 1961.
83. ibid.

84. Cherry and Hodges 1978.
85. Grierson 1941 pays attention to these details in an important essay.

Chapter 3.   THE EMPORIA

1. De Paor 1976, 29.
2. ibid.
3. Janssen 1976; Böhner 1977; 1978; Galinié 1978.
4. Hope-Taylor 1977, 161.
5. Levison 1946, 7.
6. Duby 1968, 361–3; Koch 1973; Hinz 1965; Hodges 1980.
7. Þorláksson in Hodges et al. 1978.
8. I am indebted to Hans J. Madsen for giving me access to the Aarhus pottery.
9. Torrence in Hodges et al. 1978.
10. Dalton 1975, 104.
11. Humphreys 1969 discusses this at length.
12. Whitelock 1955, 782.
13. Sawyer 1977, 150.
14. Discussed in Hodges et al. 1978; 1979a; Whitelock 1955, 366–7, 378.
15. Magnusson and Pálsson 1969, 90–1.
16. Sawyer 1977, 151.
17. Blindheim 1975b, 160ff; Hodges 1979a.
18. Both fortifications are usually considered as refuges, but there is no proof of this. A similar fort overlooks Helgö.
19. The monastic settlement at Armagh was raided three times in one month in 832: Ó'Córráin 1972, 89.
20. Dollinger-Leonard 1958, 210–14.
21. Besteman 1974, 47–8; it is interesting that no church is recorded at Quentovic (Dhondt 1962, 205) or Hamwih, although graveyards are known at the latter.
22. Cramp 1976.
23. O'Kelly 1973.
24. Hughes and Hamlin 1977, 52–3.

25. Blunt 1961.
26. This is discussed in Chapter 7, but it is apposite to indicate that fields have been identified within the Middle Saxon urban topography at Ipswich (K. Wade, personal communication) apart from other emporia.
27. See also Chapter 5.
28. Weidemann 1970; Steuer 1974.
29. Randsborg 1980, 87–8.
30. See Hougen 1969, who raised this point from her research on the Kaupang pottery.
31. Ellmers 1972, 298.
32. J. G. Hurst in Fenwick 1978.
33. Hodges 1980
34. Hinz 1965; Hodges 1980.
35. Winkelmann 1972; Hodges 1980.
36. Hodges 1980.
37. Cherry and Hodges 1978.
38. Rows of pits do, however, occur in Ipswich and Hamwih.
39. Van Es et al. 1978; Blindheim 1975a; Holdsworth 1976.
40. See Randsborg 1980, 87–8 for a general appraisal.
41. Ohlsson 1975–6.
42. Holdsworth 1976.
43. Foote and Wilson 1970, 211. Much of this discussion depends on the length of stay of the traders. Ganshof (1971, 175, 181) discusses the kinds of delays envoys to Carolingia had to endure. We may imagine that traders had more taxing experiences than these.
44. Sawyer 1971, 174.
45. Randsborg 1980, 80.
46. Jankuhn 1976, 137.
47. Renfrew 1978b.

Chapter 4.   A GAZETEER OF EMPORIA: IN OTTAR'S FOOTSTEPS

1. Pauli 1889, 253.
2. Ottar's journey is recorded in the introduction to king Alfred's version of 'the history of Paulus Orosius' (Pauli 1889, 248–53); see also Blindheim 1975a, 125–8. Of course, Ottar was a later ninth-century traveller

and therefore he would not have been able to visit many of the seventh- to early ninth-century sites listed in this chapter. Miguel 1966 gives an outline of Al-Tartushi's tour around northwest Europe. He, of course, was making his tour at a time when nearly all of these sites had been replaced by regional markets.

In this chapter I have omitted the monastic site of Dunwich, which may have been a trading station as well. Dunwich in Suffolk was certainly a major Late Saxon town, but whether it existed in competition with Ipswich in the Middle Saxon period remains unclear, because the sea has eroded almost the entire town away: Rigold 1961; Whitelock 1972, 4.

3. Liversage 1967.
4. Fox 1955; Pearce 1979, 46, 49; *Medieval Archaeology* 23, 1979, 235 notes the most recent investigations at Bantham.
5. Addyman and Hill 1968, 1969 are two excellent introductions, supplemented by Holdsworth 1976 and Hodges 1979a.
6. Brent 1863; Biddle 1976a, 115. I am indebted to Mrs Leslie Webster for correspondence on this site, and to Tim Tatton Brown for discussions about its location.
7. Wheeler 1935 provides the basic data, supplemented by Biddle and Hudson 1973, which reviews the documentation; similarly Hurst 1976b. Miller 1977 is an interim report on the Saxon wharfs; see also Brooke and Keir 1975, 58 – the most recent historical appraisal.
8. Layard 1907 is concerned with the Hadleigh Road cemetery; see also Ozanne 1961-3. West 1963; Dunmore, Gray, Loader and Wade 1975 and Wade 1980 discuss the urban excavations, while Hurst 1976a should also be consulted for the pottery.
9. Carter 1978 reviews the archaeology and history. I am indebted to Alan Carter for most stimulating discussions on Norwich's origins.
10. See Macgregor 1978 for an appraisal of the evidence for pre-Viking York.
11. Capelle 1976.
12. Capelle 1978.
13. Holwerda 1930, van Es 1969, van Es et al. 1978 review the excavations; Eckstein, van Es and Hollstein 1975 give details of the dendrochronology; van Es and Verwers 1975 discuss certain of the pottery, while Parkhouse

1976 lists the querns. I am most obliged to Professor van Es, Drs verwers and van Tent for discussing the archaeology with me on the site.
14. Bestemann 1974.
15. Lobbedey 1977, 134-6.
16. Lobbedey 1977, 130-4.
17. Jankuhn 1976 reviews the immense amount of research on this site; see also Randsborg 1980, 85-91. I am indebted to Dr Schietzel for discussing the site with me in 1974 and permitting me to examine the finds on that occasion.
18. Bencard 1973 reviews the recent excavations. I am grateful to Morgens Bencard for corresponding with me about the site, to Hans Madsen for discussing the pottery and to Dr Bendixen who replied to my queries on the coins.
19. Blindheim 1975a, 1975b, review the excavations and their history; see also Hougen, 1969 on the pottery. I am obliged to Drs Blindheim and Hougen for sparing time to discuss the site. Dr Blindheim has kindly corresponded over issues imported to this thesis.
20. Ohlsson 1975-6; see also Randsborg 1980, 95-6. I am indebted to Dr Ohlsson for his useful letters in response to my queries about this site.
21. For Västergarn see Floderus 1934; Per Lundström (1973) excavated Paviken, and I am grateful to him for sparing time to discuss the site in July 1977.
22. Holmqvist 1975, 1977 reviews this remarkable site; see also Holmqvist 1972 - one of the monographs on the site, containing details of the workshops. I am especially grateful to Agneta Lundström, now director of this project, for sparing me a number of days to discuss its complexity, and including a tour of the monuments in July 1977.
23. Arbman 1937, 1940; Ambrosiani and Arrhenius 1973; Odelberg 1974 all discuss the site. I am grateful to Agneta Lundström for guiding me through the finds both on display and in the reserves of the Statens Historiska Museum, Stockholm.

Chapter 5. DARK AGE ARGONAUTS AND THEIR CRAFT

1. Stenton 1971, 221.
2. Jellema 1955.
3. Ypey 1973 has published an interim report on the Rhenen cemetery. In 1978 I was fortunate in being able to study this material. As a result I am of the opinion that it is traded rather than the property of Merovingian immigrants (see Chapter 2).
4. See Levison 1946, 6.
5. Levison 1946, 64ff. The extent and significance of the Frisian uprising in 732 remains unclear (see Chapter 2 n. 50).
6. Jellema 1955.
7. ibid.
8. ibid.
9. Faral 1934, 210-11.
10. See Christensen 1976, 9-30.
11. Van Es 1969; van Es and Verwers 1975; see also Hodges 1980.
12. Hodges 1979a, 203-6 discusses this.
13. Skaare 1976, 46 gives a useful introduction and references to this problem.
14. See Bruce-Mitford 1975, figure 321(a), (b).
15. Whitelock 1955, 781.
16. Ganshof 1957.
17. ibid.; see also Ganshof 1971, 266.
18. Dhondt 1962 reviews these with regard to Quentovic.
19. Discussed by Stenton 1971, 221.
20. Discussed by Sawyer 1976, 1977; Metcalf 1974, 1977.
21. Sabbé 1950.
22. Whitelock 1955, 781.
23. Dollinger-Leonard 1958 discusses Verdun.
24. Latouche 1967, 163.
25. Christensen 1976, 9-30; 146-64.
26. Hodges 1979a, 203-6, 1980; it has, of course, to be emphasised that only pottery may have been traded and therefore it had a minimal value which in no way reflects any trading patterns. I do not adopt this view, as the reader will have judged.
27. Hodges 1980.
28. Hodges in Wade 1980.
29. Bradley 1970-1.
30. Hodder 1974.

31. In Hallam, Warren and Renfrew 1976.
32. Bradley 1970-1; Hodges 1979a.
33. Whitbread 1946.
34. Muckelroy 1978, 3.
35. Decaens 1971.
36. Brown 1971, 13.
37. Throckmorton 1972, 72.
38. Van Doornick 1972, 140.
39. Bruce-Mitford 1975.
40. Figures from Christensen 1976; Ellmers 1972; Fenwick 1978.
41. Sawyer 1971, Pl.IX.
42. On the Åskekärr boat: Ellmers 1972, 314-15; Crumlin-Pedersen 1972, Pl.2. On the graffito see Ohlsson 1975-6, 117-19.
43. Philipsen 1965.
44. Crumlin-Pedersen 1972, 186.
45. Skaare 1976, 46; Ellmers 1979, 11-12, figs. 1.8, 1.9.
46. cf. Severin 1978. Most of the journeys undertaken by the Frisians would have been along coasts or riverine; only the crossing to East Anglia (see below) posed them with an open-sea expedition and this might have been minimised by crossing the Channel opposite Dover.
47. ibid.
48. Garmonsway 1953, 90.
49. Miller 1977. Keel-less cogs occur in the Apocalypse ms. now in Trier that is probably the product of a Carolingian monastery in north-east France (Porcher 1970, fig. 169). See also the boat on the seventh-century Merovingian strap end (Bruce Mitford 1975, fig. 321(c), (d).
50. See Addyman and Hill 1968; Hodges 1979a.
51. Ellmers 1972, 195. Abb. 160. Schlesinger 1972 believes the bishop's seat was moved to Schleswig as early as the mid-tenth century, and that for a time Haithabu and this new settlement operated together.
52. Fenwick 1978.
53. Hurst in Fenwick 1978 with a note by Hodges.
54. Olsen and Crumlin-Pedersen 1967.

55. Ellmers 1972, 256–7; note also the tenth-century (or later) Pingsdorf boats found near Leiden demonstrating the continuity of the keel-less boats: Crumlin–Pedersen 1972, 186.
56. Lundström 1973 illustrates these splendid finds.
57. Levison 1946, 12.
58. Jones 1968, 109; Blindheim 1975a, 125–8.
59. Jones 1968, 110.
60. Green 1963.
61. Green 1963, 108–13.
62. Foote and Wilson 1970, 248.
63. Severin 1978.
64. ibid.

Chapter 6. THE OBJECTS OF TRADE

1. Quoted by Renfrew 1975, 4.
2. Renfrew 1975, 53.
3. Grierson 1959; 1978.
4. Polanyi 1957 reviews coinage at some length.
5. Collis 1971–2, esp. 71–3.
6. Collis 1971–2, esp.74–5.
7. Dalton 1977, esp. 198–9.
8. cf. Rathje 1975 discussed in Chapter 1.
9. These and other expectations are examined in a forthcoming essay by John F. Cherry and myself.
10. Vierck 1970.
11. There is an element of generalisation here, for there was probably much overlap in the two systems with down-the-line mechanisms obscuring directional trade. I have tried to clarify this picture in Chapter 2.
12. Rigold 1975.
13. Metcalf discusses these problems in a convenient form in Metcalf, Merrick and Hamblin 1968. This, however, is only an introduction from which to move to Lyon 1976.
14. Rigold 1960–1, 29; Rigold 1975; Rigold 1978, Rigold and Metcalf 1978.
15. Metcalf 1974, 1977.
16. Cherry and Hodges 1978.
17. Metcalf 1977.
18. Metcalf, Merrick and Hamblin 1968.
19. These and other points are considered in a forthcoming paper by John F. Cherry and myself.
20. Blunt 1961.
21. ibid.
22. See Grierson 1965 for a slightly different view of the chronology of events.
23. e.g. Metcalf 1965, 1967.
24. Metcalf 1965, 478.
25. Grierson 1967; 1976, 128ff.
26. See Chapter 9 for a discussion of Metcalf's figures for tenth-century early cash.
27. Bakka 1978; Skaare 1976, 9–11.
28. Warner 1975–6.
29. Hardh 1977–8.
30. Alexander 1966, 114–15.
31. I am indebted to J. W. Hedges for this information.
32. Blindheim 1975a, 149; on display in Oldsaksamling Museum, Oslo.
33. Metcalf 1977.
34. Hodges 1980.
35. Illustrated in Holmqvist 1975.
36. Ypey 1968; note also the celebrated Dorestad brooch from (?)south Germany: van Es 1978.
37. Vierck 1974; Lamm 1973; Müller-Wille 1977.
38. Arbman 1940 illustrates a selection of the Birka keys. They are a common find in Viking circumstances; cf. with the Hamwih keys: Addyman and Hill 1969, 65–6.
39. Illustrated by Capelle 1976; 1978.
40. Jankuhn 1952.
41. Ekholm 1958; Bakka 1971.
42. Crowfoot and Hawkes 1967.
43. Groenman-van Waateringe 1976 on the shoes from Dorestad.
44. Hinz 1965; Hodges 1980.
45. Discussed in Andersen, Crabb and Madsen 1971; Ohlsson 1975–6 and Jankuhn 1976.
46. Winkelmann 1972; Hodges 1980.
47. See Steinhausen 1939, Perin 1971, 37 on glass-houses; see also Harden 1956 and 1978.
48. Lundström 1976; Callmer 1977.
49. I am indebted to Professor R. Newton for discussions on this point.
50. Cramp 1970; Harden 1978.
51. Haevernick 1963.

52. See Sawyer 1977, 150 for a brief discussion.
53. See Werner 1961 for a review of these finds and further references.
54. Holmqvist 1975.
55. Parkhouse 1976; I am indebted to Jonathon Parkhouse for several useful conversations on querns.
56. To quote *Current Archaeology* 3, 1971, 167, these imported stones represent 'the marvels of salesmanship'!
57. Proudfoot 1961 for further references.
58. Blindheim 1973, 55.
59. Ellis 1969; see also Moore 1978.
60. Schietzel 1970; Blindheim 1975a, 147–8. Stone mortars were also traded in small numbers at this time as examples found in Dorestad testify: I am indebted to Professor van Es for this information. Other stone mortars are known from the monastic settlement at Jarrow, while at Hamwih pottery mortars imported from northern France were in use: Hodges 1980.

61. Whitelock 1955, 781–2.
62. Jellema 1955, 32.
63. See Wilson, 1976, 270–3 for a review of the Saxon textile industry generally.
64. Dhondt 1962, 88.
65. e.g. Groenman-van Waateringe 1976; Wilson 1976, 274–5.
66. Dhondt 1962, 88.
67. Grierson 1959, 139.
68. Note should also be taken of a goldsmith's die from a sunken hut of seventh-century date at Salmonby, Lincolnshire now on display in the City Museum, Lincoln.
69. Jellema 1955, 26.
70. cf. Dhondt 1962, 204, 217; Whitelock 1955, 375.
71. Bonser 1963, 353–4; Hodges 1980.
72. Useful discussion by Smyth 1977 on this; see also Wallace-Hadrill's essay on the Vikings in Francia, in Wallace-Hadrill 1975.
73. Sawyer 1977, 147–8.
74. Faral 1932, 210–11.

Chapter 7. SUBSISTENCE STRATEGIES

1. Price 1978, 165.
2. cf. Duby 1968; Ganshof 1949, 30.
3. cf. Jorns 1973; for Ingelheim: Rauch and Jacobi 1976. See Schlesinger 1976 on the forts; Brulet 1974, Mattys and Hossey 1973 on burgs in the Ardennes. the Ardennes.
4. Quoted from Duby 1968, 363–4.
5. Gladbach in Hussong 1938; Mayen in Ament 1974; Liebesheim in Schweitzer 1975–6; Brebières in Demolon 1972 and Wallace-Hadrill 1975, 2; Ensisheim in exhibition catalogue – *L'Habitat rural au Haut Môyen Age*, Mulhouse 1978.
6. Winkelmann 1954.
7. Randsborg 1980, 59–69 provides a most illuminating review of these sites.
8. ibid., 62.
9. Van Es 1973.
10. cf. Myhre 1978, 228 for a recent review.
11. Vierck in Davies and Vierck 1974, 264, n. 182; see also Myhre 1978, 228.
12. Randsborg 1980, 81.
13. See Rahtz 1976 and references therein.

14. Hume 1974: 'Bede attributes . . . a use of the hall as a positive existential metaphor; it represents to them the best that life has had to offer man . . .' (69).
15. Proudfoot 1961.
16. Hencken 1938.
17. Proudfoot 1961. A few nucleated sites without fortification are known at Knowth (possibly a royal site) and, on a small scale, at the 'Spectacles', overlooking Lough Gur, Co. Limerick.
18. Attenborough 1922, 57–9.
19. ibid., 59.
20. Sawyer 1976, 9.
21. See Graeme Barker and Derrick Webley in Branigan 1977, 198–200; I am indebted to both authors for the opportunity to discuss this point.
22. cf. Duby 1968, 14: 'The least insubstantial hypothesis would be that of overpopulated islands, where biological increase stimulated by agrarian prosperity pushed men to the verge of scarcity, contrasted with ocean-like stretches of country where farming was well-nigh impossible.' Duby 1974, 78–97; Harris 1978, 186.

23. Davies and Vierck 1974.
24. Duby 1974, 78ff.
25. Duby 1968, 67; Janssen 1976; also Duby 1974, 80.
26. White 1972; but see Duby 1974, 85.
27. Dansgaard et al. 1975.
28. Ganshof 1971, 133; Randsborg 1980, 26–44; Hardh 1977–8.
29. Herlihy 1961, 94–5; Wade-Martins 1975; Foard 1978; Taylor 1978.
30. Beresford 1977.
31. Beresford and Hurst 1976.
32. Rahtz 1976 and references therein.
33. Randsborg 1980, 66
34. ibid. 51–4; Myhre 1978 also states: 'Farm territories must have been larger in Viking times' (249); he also sees this as a phase of nucleation in Norway (265).
35. Platt 1978, 1.
36. Rahtz 1979 provides just a little insight into this vexing problem.
37. Randsborg 1980, 54–9.
38. ibid. 87.
39. I am grateful to Mrs Jennifer Boudillon for her comments on this; these, however, are strictly my views for which I am responsible.
40. Keith Wade, personal communication.
41. I have benefited from discussions with Mrs Boudillon and Keith Wade, but I have drawn my own conclusions.

Incidentally, 39 per cent of the Haithabu fish-bones were herring.
42. e.g. Pagham: Gregory 1976.
43. Holmqvist 1972 and 1975.
44. Hurst 1976a; Hodges 1980.
45. Hodges 1980.
46. Dunmore Gray, Loader and Wade 1975.
47. Keith Wade (personal communication), to whom I am most grateful for these points.
48. cf. Hodges 1980 for a full discussion of this.
49. Hodges 1980.
50. cf. Vierck 1976.
51. Hodges 1980.
52. cf. Duby 1968, 363.
53. Hodges 1980. It should be added that the close ties between this potting industry and the middle Rhineland wine industry are more than apparent as their surpluses passed through Dorestad (see Chapters 2, 3 and 4). The construction of the great imperial palace at Ingelheim near Mainz (Rauch and Jacobi 1976) in the heart of the wine-growing belt suggests the court's keen interest in this specialist agricultural production, and its involvement in the long-distance trade of the wine, and the concomitant pottery and wooden containers as well.
54. Metcalf 1977.

Chapter 8. SYSTEMIC CHANGE: THE NINTH CENTURY

1. Florus of Lyons, quoted from Poupardin 1922, 28.
2. Flannery 1972.
3. Athens 1977, esp. 357–60.
4. Renfrew 1972.
5. Renfrew 1972, 37.
6. Renfrew 1972, 36–8.
7. Ganshof 1971, 55–85.
8. Lobbedey 1977 on the towns; Hodges 1980 on the Rhenish pottery industries; Grierson 1965 on the coinage.
9. Bolin 1953.
10. What are we to make of the gold coins issued by king Offa of Mercia which clearly imitate arabic dinars? These purport to demonstrate some Christian contact with the Arabs.
11. Ganshof 1971, 240–55.

12. Coulson 1976, 29.
13. Ganshof 1971, 257.
14. Ganshof 1971, 205–39.
15. Hodges 1980.
16. Hodges 1980.
17. Vercauteren 1935–6.
18. Jankuhn 1976, 39; abb. 9.
19. Eckstein, van Es and Hollstein 1975.
20. ibid.
21. cf. Sawyer 1971, 140: the Annals of St. Bertin describe the sequence – in 834, 835, 836, 837, as well as three further raids before it was finally destroyed in 863.
22. Cherry and Hodges 1978.
23. It must be admitted that an earlier series of raids may have caused this as, for example, it caused the shift of a

monastic community on the coast to
the security of Canterbury's Roman-
period walls in about 811: Brooks
1971, 80. However, the remarkable
feature about Nithard's reference
(Lauer 1964, 124) is that it is the only
Viking raid he mentions in his history.
24. Randsborg 1980, 152–60.
25. See Sawyer 1971 for details.
26. Biddle 1976b, 450; Miller 1977. Note
should also be taken of the increasing importance of London as a mint
from king Ceonwulf's reign, around
800.
27. Biddle 1976a, 119.
28. Hodges 1978a discusses this; see

Pearce 1979, 170ff. for a discussion of
the fusion of Devon and Cornwall.
29. Dolley and Skaare, 1961 give an
authoritative account of the West
Saxon hoards of the 840s and 850s.
John 1966 also considers these points.
30. Smyth 1977 describes these events in
detail.
31. cf. Smyth 1977.
32. See, for example, Biddle 1976a, 124ff.
33. Biddle 1976a, 124ff.; Campbell 1975.
34. Sawyer 1971, 124–5.
35. Webb 1975, cited by Harris 1978, 94–
5 who amplifies the point.
36. Dansgaard et al. 1975; cf. Wailes 1972
on the demographic correlates of this.

Chapter 9.   MARKET PRINCIPLES AND PLACES

1. Whitelock 1955, 272.
2. Hodder and Lee 1974, 137ff.
3. Hinz 1965; Hodges 1980.
4. Renfrew 1978a, 115.
5. Trigger 1972, 584.
6. Hodder 1972.
7. I am indebted to Keith Branigan for
discussions on this point.
8. Biddle 1976a, 134.
9. Biddle 1976a.
10. Attenborough 1922, 135. See Blunt
1974 for an authoritative account of
the coins.
11. Attenborough 1922, 115.
12. Petersson 1969, 101; see also Metcalf
1978, 188, who rightly points out that
there is a regional as well as a
chronological dimension involved in
these weight variations.
13. Stenton 1971, 577–8.
14. Metcalf 1978, 166.
15. Hill 1978.
16. Contrast the significance given to
Canterbury in Athelstan's Laws and
then in Hill's (1978) list. The explanation must be that its role diminished as
the size of the kingdom increased, and
it remained primarily an archbishop's
seat.
17. Dolley and Metcalf 1961.
18. F. Neale in Rahtz 1979, 10–11.
19. Hill 1978, 217: here he suggests that
only two levels were recognised; this is
contested below.
20. Biddle 1976a; Miller 1977.
21. Biddle 1976b.

22. Biddle 1975, 129.
23. Hurst 1976a for a masterly review.
24. See Hodges 1979b. The date of the
Thetford ware tradition that succeeds
Ipswich ware, is very much in dispute.
Essentially the change-over to wheel-
thrown wares occurs some time in the
second half of the ninth century. I
favour a late date, but J. G. Hurst and
Keith Wade tend towards an earlier
one. I also favour a northern French
origin for some of these forms, and it
seems no coincidence that one of the
earliest Danelaw coinages, that in
York in the 890's, is modelled on coins
issued at Evreux (Dolley 1978, 26).
25. Hinton and Hodges 1977.
26. Hodges 1979a, 197; J. Williams 1979,
140–1.
27. Burpham: Sutermeister 1976; Axbridge: see Rahtz 1979 generally;
South Cadbury: Alcock 1972.
28. Randsborg 1980, 71ff.
29. I am indebted to Morgens Bencard
and Hans J. Madsen for permitting
me to study the Ribe material, and
for kindly dealing with my comments.
30. Andersen, Crabb and Madsen 1971.
31. Randsborg 1980, 73.
32. ibid. See also Olsen and Schmidt
1977, and Roesdahl 1977.
33. Bartolin, in Mårtensson 1976, 145–
69.
34. Randsborg 1980, 78–9.
35. ibid., 80–1.

36. Anders Andrén in Mårtensson 1976, figs. 16 and 17.
37. Ekman 1973.
38. H.-E. Liden in Herteig, Liden and Blindheim 1975.
39. e.g. Duby 1974, 134-5 for general comments.
40. I am indebted to the curator of Rouen Museum, Madame Chirol, for permitting me to see material and unpublished records from old excavations within the town.
41. Grierson 1941; see Sabbé 1950, 185-7 on the decline of Quentovic.
42. Trimpe Burger 1973.
43. Metcalf 1979, 10-11 reviews the numismatic evidence for tenth-century economic growth in Flanders.
44. Dumas-Dubourg 1971.
45. Duby 1974, 131-5; Janssen 1976; Lobbedey 1977; Böhner 1977; 1978; see also Al-Tartushi on Mainz (Miguel 1966, 1059).
46. Note Dean Arnold's essay in Hodder 1978 on the 'marginal' setting of pottery industries in Southern America.
47. Hodder 1965; Jackson 1971.
48. Blunt 1962; Dolley in Rahtz 1979, 292-3 for a note on later tenth-century half-pennies; Grierson 1965 and Dumas-Dubourg 1971, 63-4 on the Carolingian coins.
49. Lyon 1976, 183ff.
50. See Biddle 1976a and Hill 1978; also West 1963, 294 on Ipswich.
51. Sawyer 1965.
52. These are figures given in the Anglo-Saxon Chronicle and quoted by Richard Gem 1975, 42. There also survives a treaty probably attributable to 991 by which Ethelred bought peace for £22,000 in gold and silver: Whitelock 1955, 401-2.
53. From the people of east Kent only.
54. Gem 1975 and Hinton 1978 are useful reviews of Metcalf 1967 (and 1978) as well as of Sawyer 1965.
55. Hinton 1978, 142.
56. Sawyer 1965.
57. Hill 1978, 222; see also above the quotation from F. Neale in Rahtz 1979, 10-11.
58. Dolley 1971, 347.
59. Hinton 1978, 142-3.
60. Gem 1975; Rathje 1975.
61. Petersson 1969, 159.
62. Miller 1977.
63. Hodges 1979a, 195.
64. ibid.
65. Hodges in Wade 80; Carter 1978, 202, n.2.
66. I am indebted to Maureen Mellor of Oxford and Michael Rhodes of London for allowing me to handle the material from their respective units' excavations.
67. Parkhouse 1976.
68. Watson 1967, 2.
69. Jones 1968 paints a colourful picture of these events.
70. Randsborg 1980, 162-6.
71. Skaare 1976, 56-7.
72. Mårtensson 1976, 266-8.
73. Skaare 1976, 61ff.; Randsborg 1980.
74. Ellmers 1972, 195, Abb. 160.

Chapter 10. THE EVOLUTION OF STATES

1. Fried 1978, 35-6.
2. Pirenne's work tends to be the single early medieval history read by anthropologists and historians, who are often unaware of the controversy surrounding the thesis.
3. Renfrew 1972, 12-13 discusses the significance of writing.
4. Flannery 1972, 403.
5. Service 1971, 165; Flannery, 1972, 404.
6. Cohen 1978, 4.
7. Rappaport 1971, 41; cf. Cohen 1978, 16; Peebles and Kus 1977, 445.
8. Cohen 1978, 16.
9. Price 1978, 182.
10. Gall and Saxe 1977, 263.
11. Webb 1975; see also Chapter 1.
12. Hedeager 1978.
13. Chaney 1973, 223.
14. Service 1971; viz. Earle 1977, 216-17.
15. Earle 1977, 215.
16. Webb 1975.
17. Friedman and Rowlands 1978, 232; cf. Paul Wheatley (1975) for an Asian parallel to the Carolingian system.
18. e.g. Mattys and Hossey 1973; Brulet

1974; Debord 1975; Scapula 1975; Schlesinger 1976.

19. Friedman and Rowlands 1978, 271; Cohen 1978, 12; cf. Price 1978.
20. Davies and Vierck 1974, 227.
21. Stenton 1971, 23.
22. Ozanne 1962-3.
23. Renfrew 1975, 14.
24. Stenton 1971, 297.
25. An early medieval exception may well be Uppsala, a central place in Uppland. Otherwise sites like Cheddar (Rahtz 1979) and Yeavering (Hope-Taylor 1977) or Ingelheim (Rauch and Jacobi 1976) were each one of several residences. Brühl (1958) outlines the itineraries of the Carolingian kings.
26. See Chaney 1973 for a general introduction, and also Wallace-Hadrill 1971.
27. Hodges 1978, 443; Chaney 1973, 227.
28. Stenton 1971, 229.
29. Chaney 1973, 247; A. Williams 1979.
30. Wallace-Hadrill 1971, 120: 'Offa, notably was a king who spent much of his time fighting to establish his hold over central England and to hand on what he had won to his heir. . . (he) acted with a ruthlessness derived from

a sense of insecurity.' I have deliberated at length on Offa, in part, because there is a tendency among archaeologists to misinterpret his reign: cf. Hodges 1978, 441.
31. Loyn 1974, 9. On the significance of royal inheritance from the ninth century until the Conquest see A. Williams 1979, esp. 144-9.
32. Randsborg 1980, 167-9.
33. Andersen 1979; Randsborg 1980, 171.
34. Ellmers 1972, 195 and references therein.
35. Cited by Byrne 1973, 12.
36. A quote by D. A. Binchy cited by Byrne 1973, 28; see also Binchy 1970.
37. Byrne 1973, 7.
38. Ó'Córráin 1972, 42; cf. Binchy 1970.
39. See Hughes 1972 for a critique of this.
40. Ó'Ríordáin 1976, De Paor 1976, Loyn 1977, Smyth 1977, Graham 1979 all give some details. I have also benefited greatly from handling the material from the excavations in 1973 and 1975, thanks to Mr Ó'Ríordáin.
41. Dolley 1966.
42. cf. De Paor 1976 and Ó'Córráin 1972.
43. The Testament of Catháir: Hughes 1972, 54.

REFERENCES

Ber. R.O.B. is an abbreviation for *Berichten van de Rijksdienst voor het Oudheidkundig Bodemonderzoek.*

Adams, R. McC. 1974 Anthropological perspectives on ancient trade, *Current Anthropology* 15, 239-58.

Adams, R. McC. 1975 The emerging place of trade in civilisational studies, in J. Sabloff and C. C. Lamberg-Karlovsky (eds), *Ancient Civilisation and Trade*, 451-65, Albuquerque.

Addyman, P. V. 1964 A Dark-Age settlement at Maxey, Northants, *Medieval Archaeology* 8, 20-73.

Addyman, P. V. 1973 Saxon Southampton: a town and international port of the 8th to the 10th century, in H. Jankuhn et al. (eds), 218-28.

Addyman, P. V. and Hill, D. H. 1968 Saxon Southampton: a review of the evidence, part II, *Proceedings of the Hampshire Field Club* 24-5, 61-93.

Addyman, P. V. and Hill, D. H. 1969 Saxon Southampton: a review of the evidence, part II, *Proceedings of the Hampshire Field Club* 26, 61-96.

Alcock, L. 1971 *Arthur's Britain*, Harmondsworth.

Alcock, L. 1972 *'By South Cadbury is that Camelot. . .' Excavations at Cadbury Castle 1966-1970*, London.

Alexander, M. 1966 *The Earliest English Poems*, Harmondsworth.

Ambrosiani, B. 1972-3 Gravbegreppet i gravningsstatistiken, *Tor* 15, 122-36.

Ambrosiani, B. and Arrhenius, B. 1973 *Birka, Svarta Jordens hammområde*, Stockholm.

Ament, H. 1974 Eine fränkische Siedlung beim Künzerlof Gemeinde Mertloch, Kreis Mayen-Koblenz, *Germania* 52, 454-67.

Ammerman, A. and Cavalli-Sforza, L. L. 1973 A population model for the diffusion of early farming in Europe, in C. Renfrew (ed.) *The Explanation of Culture Change*, 343-58, London.

Andersen, H. 1979 Det bjerg der kalder Gamle Lybaek, *Skalk* 2, 9-13.

Andersen, H., Crabb, P. J. and Madsen, H. J. 1971 *Århus Søndervold*, Copenhagen.

Arbman, E. H. 1937 *Schweden und das karolingische Reich*, Stockholm.

Arbman, E. H. 1940 *Birka, Die Gräber*, Stockholm.

Athens, J. S. 1977 Theory building and the study of evolutionary process in complex societies, in L. R. Binford (ed.) *For Theory Building in Archaeology*, 353-84, London.

Attenborough, F. L. 1922 *The Laws of the Earliest English Kings*, Cambridge.

Bakka, E. 1971 Scandinavian trade relations with the Continent and the British Isles in pre-Viking times, *Early Medieval Studies* 3, 37-51.

Bakka, E. 1978 Two aurar of gold, *Antiquaries Journal* 58, 279–8.

Bencard, M. 1973 Ribes vikingetid, *Mark og Montre*, 28–48.

Bendixen, K. 1974 The first Merovingian coin-treasures from Denmark, *Medieval Scandinavia* 7, 85–101.

Beresford, G. 1977 The excavation of the deserted medieval village of Goltho, Lincolnshire, *Chateau Gailard* (Caen) 8, 46–68.

Beresford, M. W. and Hurst, J. G. 1976 Wharram Percy: a case study in microtopography, in P. Sawyer (ed.) *Medieval Settlement*, 114–44 London.

Besteman, J. C. 1974 Carolingian Medemblik, *Ber. R.O.B.* 24, 43–106.

Biddle, M. 1975 'Felix urbs Winthoniae': Winchester in the age of monastic reform, in D. Parsons (ed.) *Tenth-Century Studies*, 123–40, London.

Biddle, M. 1976a The towns, in D. M. Wilson (ed.) 1976, 99–150.

Biddle, M. (ed.) 1976b *Winchester in the Early Middle Ages* (Winchester Studies 1), Oxford.

Biddle, M. and Barclay, K. 1974 Winchester ware, in V. Evison et al. (eds.) *Medieval Pottery from Excavations*, 137–65, London.

Biddle, M. and Hill, D. H. 1971 Late Saxon planned towns *Antiquaries Journal* 51, 70–85

Biddle, M. and Hudson, D. 1973 *The Future of London's Past*, Worcester.

Binchy, D. A. 1970 *Celtic and Anglo-Saxon Kingship*, Oxford.

Binford, L. R. 1972 *An Archaeological Perspective*, London.

Binford, L. R. 1977 General introduction, in L. R. Binford (ed.) *For Theory Building in Archaeology*, 1–10, London.

Blindheim, C. 1973 Kaupang in Skiringssal in H. Jankuhn et al. (eds) 1973, 40–57.

Blindheim, C. 1975a Kaupang by Viks Fjord in Vestfold, in A. E. Herteig, H-E. Liden and C. Blindheim 1975, 125–53.

Blindheim, C. 1975b Kaupang by Viks Fjord, in A. E. Herteig, H-E. Liden, and C. Blindheim 1975, 154–74.

Bloch, M. 1967 Natural economy or money economy: a pseudo-dilemma, in J. E. Andersen (ed.) *Land and Work in Medieval Europe; Papers by Marc Bloch*, London, 230–43.

Blunt, C. E. 1961 The coinage of Offa, in R. H. M. Dolley (ed.) 1961, 39–62.

Blunt, C. E. 1962 Two Anglo-Saxon notes, *British Numismatic Journal* 31, 43–8.

Blunt, C. E. 1974 The coinage of Athelstan, 924–39: a survey *British Numismatic Journal*, 42.

Bohannan, P. and Dalton, G., 1962 *Markets in Africa*, Evanston.

Böhner, K. 1977 Urban and rural settlement in the Frankish kingdom, in M. W. Barley (ed.), *European Towns: their archaeology and early history*, 185–202, London.

Böhner, K. 1978 Bonn im frühen Mittelalter, *Bonner Jahrbücher* 178, 395–426.

Bolin, S. 1953 Mohammed, Charlemagne and Ruric, *Scandinavian Economic History Review* 1, 5–39.

Bonser, W. 1963 *The Medical Background of Anglo-Saxon England*, London.

Bradley, R. 1970–1 Trade competition and artifact distribution, *World Archaeology* 2, 347–52.

Branigan, K. 1977 *Gatcombe Roman Villa*, B.A.R.44, Oxford.

Brent, J. 1863 Account of the society s researches in the Saxon cemetery at Sarre, *Archaeologia Cantiana* 5, 305–22.

Bridbury, A. R. 1969 The Dark Ages, *Economic History Review* 22, 526–37.

Brooke, C., and Keir, G. 1975 *London, 800–1216: the Shaping of a City*, London.

Brooks, N. 1971 The development of military obligations in eighth- and ninth-century England, in P. Clemoes and K. Hughes (eds) *England Before the Conquest*, 69–84, Cambridge.

Brown, P. 1971 *The World of Late Antiquity*, London.

Bruce-Mitford, R. L. S. 1975 *The Sutton Hoo Ship Burial, 1*, London.

Brühl, C-R. 1958 Königspfalz und Bischofsstadt, *Rheinische Vierteljahresblätter* 23, 161–274.

Brulet, R. 1974 La roche à Lomme à Dourbes, *Archaeologica Belgica*, 160.

Burgess, L. 1964 *The Origins of Southampton*, Leicester.

Byrne, F. J. 1973 *Irish Kings and High Kings*, London.

Callmer, J. 1977 *Trade Beads and Bead Trade in Scandinavia*, Lund.

Campbell, J. 1975 Observations on English government from the tenth to the twelfth centuries, *Transactions of the Royal Historical Society* 25, 39–54.

Capelle, T. 1976 Die frühgeschichtlichen Metallfunde von Domburg 1/2, *R.O.B. Nederlandse Oudheden* 5.

Capelle, T. 1978 Die karolingische Funde von Schouwen, *R.O.B. Nederlandse Oudheden* 7.

Carneiro, R. 1968 Ascertaining, testing and interpreting sequences of cultural development, *Southwestern Journal of Anthropology* 24, 354–74.

Carter, A. 1978 The Anglo-Saxon origins of Norwich: the problems and approaches, *Anglo-Saxon England* 7, 175–208.

Chaney, W. 1973 *The Cult of Kingship in Anglo-Saxon England*, Manchester.

Cherry, J. F. and Hodges, R. 1978 The chronology of Hamwih, Saxon Southampton, reconsidered, *Antiquaries Journal* 58, 299–309.

Childe, V. G. 1950 The urban revolution, *The Town Planning Review* 21, 3–17.

Christensen, A. E. 1976 *Danmark, Norden og Ostersøen*, Copenhagen.

Clark, J. R. 1979 Measuring the flow of goods with archaeological data, *Economic Geography* 55, 1–17.

Clarke, D. L. 1978 *Analytical Archaeology*², London.

Cohen, R. 1978 Introduction, in R. Cohen and E. Service (eds) 1978, 1–20.

Cohen, R. and Service E. (eds) 1978 *The Origins of the State*, Philadelphia.

Collis, J. R. 1971–2 Functional and theoretical interpretations of British coinage, *World Archaeology* 3, 71–84.

Coulson, C. 1976 Fortresses and social responsibility in late Carolingian France, *Zeitschrift für Archäologie des Mittelalters* 4, 29–36.

Cramp, R. 1969 Excavations at the Saxon monastic sites of Wearmouth and Jarrow, Co. Durham, an interim report, *Medieval Archaeology* 13, 21–66.

Cramp, R. 1970 Decorated window-glass and millefiori from Monkwearmouth, *Antiquaries Journal* 50, 327–35.

Cramp, R. 1976 Monastic sites, in D. M. Wilson (ed.) 1976, 201–52.

Crowfoot, E. and Hawkes, S. C. 1967 Early Anglo-Saxon gold braids, *Medieval Archaeology* 11, 42–86.

Crumlin-Pedersen, O. 1972 The Vikings and the Hanseatic merchants, 900–1450, in G. Bass (ed.) *A History of Seafaring*, 182–204, London.

Dalton, G. 1975 Karl Polanyi's analysis of long-distance trade and his wider paradigm, in J. Sabloff and C. C. Lamberg-Karlovsky (eds) *Ancient Civilization and Trade*, 63–132, Albuquerque.

Dalton, G. 1977 Aboriginal economies in stateless societies, in T. K. Earle and J. Ericson (eds) *Exchange systems in prehistory*, 191–212, London.

Dansgaard, W., et al. 1975 Climatic changes, Norsemen and modern man, *Nature* 255, 24–8.

Davidson, H. R. E. and Webster, L. 1967 The Anglo-Saxon burial at Coombe, *Medieval Archaeology* 11, 1–41.

Davies, W. and Vierck, H. 1974 The contexts of Tribal Hidage: social aggregates and settlement patterns, *Frühmittelalterliche Studien* 8, 223–93.

Debord, A. 1975 Fouille du castrum d'Andonne à Villejoubert (Charente), *Chateau Gaillard* (Caen) 7, 35–48.

Decaens, J. 1971 Un nouveau cimitière du Haut Moyen Age en Normandie, Hérouvillete (Calvados), *Archéologie Médiévale* 1, 1–126.

Demolon, P. 1972 *Le Village mérovingien de Brebières* (VIe–VIIe siècles), Arras.

De Paor, L. 1976 The Viking towns of Ireland, in B. Almqvist and D. Greene (eds) *The Seventh Viking Congress*, 29–37, Dundalk.

Dewing, H. B. 1928 *Procopius*, V, London.

Dhondt, J. 1962 Les problèmes de Quentovic, *Studi in Onore di Amintore Fanfani*, 185-248, Milan.

Dolley, M. 1970 The location of the pre-Alfredian mints of Wessex, *Proceedings of the Hampshire Field Club* 27, 57-62.

Dolley, M. 1971 The nummular brooch from Sulgrave, in P. Clemoes and K. Hughes (eds) *England Before the Conquest*, 333-49, London.

Dolley, M. 1978 The Anglo-Norse coinages of York, in R. A. Hall (ed.) *Viking Age York and the North*, 26-31, London.

Dolley, R. H. M. (ed.) 1961 *Anglo-Saxon Coins*, London.

Dolley, R. H. M. 1966 *Hiberno-Norse Coins in the British Museum*, London.

Dolley, R. H. M. and Metcalf, D. M. 1961 The reform of the English coinage under Eadger, in R. H. M. Dolley (ed.) 1961, 136-68.

Dolley, R. H. M. and Skaare K. 1961 The coinage of Aethelwulf, king of the West Saxons, 839-58, in R. H. M. Dolley (ed.) 1961, 63-76.

Dollinger-Leonard, Y. 1958 De la cité à la ville médiévale dans la région de la Moselle et la Haute Meuse, *Studien zu den Anfangen des europäischen Städtewesens*, Constance, 195-226.

Duby, G. 1968 *Rural Economy and Country Life in the Medieval West*, London.

Duby, G. 1974 *The Early Growth of the European Economy*, London.

Dumas-Dubourg, F. 1971 *Le trésor de Fécamp et le monnayage en France occidentale pendant la seconde moitié du Xe siècle*, Paris.

Dunmore, S., Gray, V., Loader, T. and Wade, K. 1975 The origin and development of Ipswich: an interim report, *East Anglian Archaeology* 1, 57-67.

Dunning, G. C. 1956 Trade relations between England and the Continent in the Late Anglo-Saxon period, in D. B. Harden (ed.) *Dark-Age Britain*, 218-33, London.

Dunning, G. C. 1959 (in) Anglo-Saxon pottery: a symposium, *Medieval Archaeology* 3, 31-78.

Dunning, G. C. and Evison, V. I. 1961 The palace of Westminster sword, *Archaeologia* 98, 123-58.

Earle, T. K. 1977 A reappraisal of redistribution: complex Hawaiian chiefdoms, in T. K. Earle and J. Ericson (eds) *Exchange Systems in Prehistory*, 213-29, London.

Eckstein, D., van Es, W. A. and Hollstein, E. 1975 Beitrag zur Datierung der frühmittelalterlichen Dorestad, Holland, *Ber. R.O.B.* 25, 165-76.

Ekholm, G. 1958 Westeuropäischen Gläser in Skandinavien wahrend der spaten Kaiser- und frühen Merowingerzeit, *Acta Archaeologia* 29.

Ekman, J. 1973 Early medieval Lund - the fauna and the landscape, *Archaeologia Lundensia* 5.

Ellis, S. E. 1969 The petrography and provenance of Anglo-Saxon and Medieval English hones, *Bulletin of the British Museum (Natural History), Mineralogy* 2 (3).

Ellmers, D. 1972 *Frühmittelalterliche Handelsschiffahrt in Mittel- und Nordeuropa*, Neumünster.

Ellmers, D. 1979 The cog of Bremen, in S. McGrail (ed.) *Medieval Ships and Harbours*, 1-15, B.A.R. 66, Oxford.

Ennen, E. 1979 *The Medieval town* (English ed.), Amsterdam.

Evison, V. I. 1975 Pagan Saxon whetstones, *Antiquaries Journal* 55, 70-85.

Evison, V. I. 1979 *Wheel-thrown Pottery in Anglo-Saxon Graves*, London.

Faral, E. (ed.) 1934 *Ermold le Noir*, Paris.

Fenwick, V. 1978 *The Graveney Boat*, B.A.R. 53, Oxford.

Finley, M. I. 1971 Archaeology and history, *Daedalus* 100, 168-86.

Flannery, K. V. 1972 The cultural evolution of civilisations, *Annual Review of Ecology and Systematics* 3, 399-426.

Fletcher, J. (ed.) 1979 *Dendrochronology*, B.A.R. 51, Oxford.

Flicker, J. 1907 *Denkmäler der Elsässischen Altertumssammlung, Bd. 2, christliche Zeit*, Strasbourg.

Floderus, E. 1934 Vastergarn, *Fornvännen*, 65–83.

Foard, G. 1978 Systematic fieldwalking and investigation of Saxon settlement in Northamptonshire, *World Archaeology* 9, 357–74.

Foote, P. G. and Wilson, D. M. 1970 *The Viking Achievement*, London.

Fox, A. 1955 Some evidence of Dark-Age trading site at Bantham, near Thurlestone, south Devon, *Antiquaries Journal* 35, 55–67.

Fried, M. H. 1967 *The Evolution of Political Society*, New York.

Fried, M. H. 1978 The State: the chicken and the egg or what came first, in R. Cohen and E. Service (eds) *The Origins of the State*, 35–47, Philadelphia.

Friedman, J. and Rowlands, M. J. 1978 Notes towards an epigenetic model of the evolution of 'civilisation', in J. Friedman and M. J. Rowlands (eds) *The Evolution of Social Systems*, 201–76, London.

Galinié, H. 1978 Archéologie et topographie historique de Tours – IV ème – XI ème siècle, *Zeitschrift für Archäologie des Mittelalters* 6, 33–56.

Gall, P. L. and Saxe, A. A. 1977 The ecological evolution of cultures: the state as predator in succession theory, in T. K. Earle and J. Ericson (eds) *Exchange Systems in Prehistory*, 255–68, London.

Ganshof, F. 1949 Manorial organisation in the Low Countries in the seventh, eighth and ninth centuries, *Transactions of the Royal Historical Society* 31, 29–59.

Ganshof, F. L. 1957 Note sur le 'praeceptum negotiatorum' de Louis le Pieux, in *Studi in onore di A. Sapore*, 103–12, Milan.

Ganshof, F. 1971 *The Carolingians and the Frankish monarchy*, London.

Garmonsway, G. N. (ed.) 1953 *The Anglo-Saxon Chronicle*, London.

Gem, R. D. H. 1975 A recession in English architecture during the 11th century, *Journal of the British Archaeological Association* 38, 28–49.

Gough, J. W. 1930 *The Mines of Mendip*, Oxford.

Graham, B. 1979 The evolution of urbanisation in medieval Ireland, *Journal of Historical Geography* 5, 111–25.

Green, C. 1963 *Sutton Hoo: the Excavation of a Royal Ship-burial*, London.

Gregory, V. L. 1976 Excavations at Beckets Fm., Pagham, west Sussex, *Sussex Archaeological Collections* 114, 207–17.

Grierson, P. 1941 The relations between England and Flanders before the Norman Conquest, *Transactions of the Royal Historical Society* 23, 71–112.

Grierson, P. 1952–4 The Canterbury (St. Martin's) hoard of Frankish and Anglo-Saxon coin ornaments, *British Numismatic Journal* 27, 39–51.

Grierson, P. 1959 Commerce in the Dark Ages: a critique of the evidence, *Transactions of the Royal Historical Society* 9, 123–40.

Grierson, P. 1965 Money and coinage under Charlemagne, in *Karl der Grosse* 1, 501–36, Dusseldorf.

Grierson, P. 1967 The volume of Anglo-Saxon coinage, *Economic History Review* 20, 153–60.

Grierson, P. 1976 Numismatics, in J. M. Powell (ed.) *Medieval Studies: an introduction*, 103–50, Syracuse, New York.

Grierson, P. 1978 The origins of money, in *Research in Economic Anthropology* 1, 1–35.

Groenman-van Waateringe, W. 1976 Schuhe aus Wijk bij Duurstede, *Ber. R.O.B.* 26, 189–98.

Haevernick, T. E. 1963 Beitrage zur geschichte des antiken glases XII, *Jahrbuch Romisch-Germanischen Zentralmuseums Mainz* 10, 130–8.

Hall, R. A. 1978 The topography of Anglo-Scandinavian York, in R. A. Hall (ed.) *Viking Age York and the North*, 31–6, London.

Hallam, B. R., Warren, S. E. and Renfrew, C. 1976 Obsidian in the western Mediterranean: characterisation by neutron activation analysis and optical emission spectroscopy, *Proceedings of the Prehistoric Society*, 42, 85–110.

Hamond, F. W. 1978 The contribution of simulation to the study of archaeological processes, in I. Hodder (ed.), *Simulation Studies in Archaeology* 1–9, Cambridge.

Harden, D. B. 1956 Glass vessels in Britain and Ireland, A.D. 400-1000, in D. B. Harden (ed.) *Dark-Age Britain*, 132-67, London.

Harden, D. B. 1978 Anglo-Saxon and later medieval glass in Britain: some recent developments, *Medieval Archaeology* 22, 1-24.

Hardh B. 1976 *Wikingerzeitliche Depotfunde aus Südschweden*, Lund.

Hardh, B. 1977-8 Trade and money in Scandinavia in the Viking Age, *Papers of the Lund Institute* 2, 223-50.

Harris, M. 1977 *Cows, Pigs, Wars and Witches*, London.

Harris, M. 1978 *Cannibals and Kings*, London.

Hayes, J. 1972 *Late Roman Pottery*, London.

Hawkes, S. C. 1969 Early Anglo-Saxon Kent, *Archaeological Journal* 126, 186-92.

Hedeager, L. 1978 A quantitative analysis of Roman imports in Europe north of the Limes (0-400 A.D.), and the question of Romano-Germanic exchange, *New Directions in Scandinavian Archaeology* 1, 191-216.

Hencken, H. O'.N. 1938 *Cahercommaun: a Stone Fort in County Clare*, Dublin.

Hencken, H. O'.N. 1950 Lagore crannog: an Irish royal residence of the 7th to 10th centuries A.D., *Proceedings of the Royal Irish Academy* 53, section C, 1-248.

Hensel, W. 1969-70 The origins of western and eastern Slav towns, *World Archaeology* 1, 51-60.

Herlihy, D. 1961 Church property on the European Continent, 701-1200, *Speculum* 36, 81-105.

Herteig, A. E., Liden, H. E. and Blindheim, C. 1975 *Archaeological Contributions to the Early History of Urban Communities in Norway*, Oslo.

Hill, D. H. 1969 The Burghal Hidage: the establishment of a text, *Medieval Archaeology* 13, 84-92

Hill, D. H. 1978 Trends in the development of towns during the reign of Ethelred II, in D. Hill (ed.), 213-26.

Hill, D. (ed.) 1978 *Ethelred the Unready*, B.A.R. 59, Oxford.

Himley, F. J. 1955 Y-a-t-il emprise musulmane sur l'économie des états européens du VIIIe au Xe siècle, *Revue suisse d'histoire* 5, 35-48.

Hinton, D. A. 1978 Late Saxon treasure and bullion, in D. Hill (ed.) 1978, 135-58.

Hinton, D. A. and Hodges, R. 1977 Excavations at Wareham, Dorset, 1974, *Proceedings of the Dorset Archaeological and Natural History Society*, 99, 42-83.

Hinz, H. 1965 Die karolingische Keramik in Mitteleuropa, *Karl der Grosse* 3, 262-87, Dusseldorf.

Hirth, K. G. 1978 Inter-regional trade and the formation of prehistoric gateway communities, *American Antiquity* 43, 25-45.

Hodder, B. W. 1965 Some comments on the origins of traditional markets in Africa south of the Sahara, *Transactions of the Institute of British Geographers* 36, 97-105.

Hodder, B. W. and Lee, D. 1974 *Economic Geography*, London.

Hodder, B. W. and Ukwu, U. I. 1969 *Markets in Africa*, Ibadan.

Hodder, I. 1972 Locational models and the study of Romano-British settlement, in D. Clarke (ed.) *Models in Archaeology*, 887-909, London.

Hodder, I. 1974 Regression analysis of some trade and marketing patterns, *World Archaeology* 6, 172-89.

Hodder, I. (ed.) 1978 *The Spatial Pattern of Cultures*, London.

Hodges, R. 1977 Some early medieval French wares in the British Isles: an archaeological assessment of the early wine trade with Britain, in D. P. S. Peacock (ed.) *Pottery and Early Commerce*, 239-55, London.

Hodges, R. 1978 State formation and the role of trade in Middle Saxon England, in S. Green et al. (eds) *Social organisation and settlement*, 439-53, B.A.R. 47, Oxford.

Hodges, R. 1979a Trade and urban origins in Dark Age Britain and the Continent: an archaeological critique of the evidence, *Ber. R.O.B.* 27, (1977) 191-215.

Hodges, R. 1979b Pottery, potters and markets, A.D. 700-1000, *Sussex Archaeological Collections*, 118.

Hodges, R. 1980 *The Hamwih Pottery; the Local and Imported Wares from Thirty Years' Excavations and their European Context*, London.

Hodges, R. et al. 1978 Ports of trade in early medieval Europe, *Norwegian Archaeological Review* 11, 97-117.

Holdsworth, P. 1976 Saxon Southampton: a new review, *Medieval Archaelogy* 20, 26-61.

Holmqvist, W. 1972 *Excavations at Helgö IV, the Workshop, Part I*, Stockholm.

Holmqvist, W. 1975 Helgö, an early trading settlement in central Sweden, in R. L. S. Bruce-Mitford (ed.) *Recent Archaeological Excavations in Europe*, 111-32, London.

Holmqvist, W. 1977 Die Ergebnisse der Grabungen auf Helgö (1954-1974), *Praehistorisches Zeitschrift* 51, 127-77.

Holwerda, J. H. 1930 Opgravingen van Dorestad, *Oudheidkundige Mededelingen* 9, 32-93.

Hope-Taylor, B. 1977 *Yeavering: an Anglo-British Centre of Early Northumbria*, London.

Hougen, E-K 1969 Leirkar – materialet fra Kaupang, *Viking* 33, 97-118.

Hughes, K. 1966 *The Church in Early Irish Society*, London.

Hughes, K. 1972 *Early Christian Ireland: an Introduction to the Sources*, London.

Hughes, K. and Hamlin, A. 1977 *The Modern Traveller to the Early Irish Church*, London.

Hume, K. 1974 The concept of hall in Old English poetry, *Anglo-Saxon England* 3, 63-74.

Humphreys, S. C. 1969 History, economics and anthropology: the work of Karl Polanyi, *History and Theory* 8, 165-212.

Hurst, J. G. 1959 (in) Anglo-Saxon pottery: a symposium, *Medieval Archaeology* 3, 13-31.

Hurst, J. G. 1976a The pottery, in D. M. Wilson (ed.), 1976, 283-348.

Hurst, J. G. 1976b Anglo-Saxon and medieval, in *The Archaeology of the London Area: Current Knowledge and Problems*, (London and Middlesex Archaeological Society), 60-7.

Hussong, L. 1938 Fränkische Siedlung bei Gladbach, Kr. Neuwied, *Germania* 22, 180-90.

Hvass, S. 1977 Vikingebebyggeben i Vorbasse, *Mark og Montre*, 18-29.

Jackson, R. T. 1971 Periodic markets in southern Ethiopia, *Transactions of the Institute of British Geographers* 53, 31-42.

James, E. 1977 *The Merovingian Archaeology of South-West Gaul*, B.A.R. SS 25, Oxford.

Jankuhn, H. 1952 Ein Ulfberht-Schwert aus der Elbe bei Hamburg, *Festschrift für Gustav Schwantes*, Neumünster, 212-29.

Jankuhn, H. 1976 *Haithabu, ein Handelsplatz der Wikingerzeit*,[6] Neumünster.

Jankuhn, H. et al. (eds) 1973 *Vor- und Frühformen der europäischen Städt im Mittelalter*, Göttingen.

Janssen, W. 1970 Der karolingische Töpferbezirk von Brühl-Eckdorf, *Neue Ausgrabungen und Forschungen in Niedersachsen* 6, 224-39.

Janssen, W. 1976 Some major aspects of Frankish trade and medieval settlement in the Rhineland, in P. Sawyer (ed.) *Medieval Settlement*, 41-60, London.

Jellema, D. 1955 Frisian trade in the Dark Ages, *Speculum* 30, 15-36.

John, E. 1966 *Orbis Britanniae and other studies*, Leicester.

Jones, G. 1968 *A History of the Vikings*, Oxford.

Jorns, W. 1973 Der spatrömische Burgus mit Schiffslände und die karolingische Villa Zullestein, *Archäologisches Korrespondenzblatt* 3, 75-80.

Kent, J. P. C. 1975 The date of the Sutton Hoo hoard, in R. L. S. Bruce-Mitford, *The Sutton Hoo Ship Burial* 1, 578-607, London.

Koch, R. 1973 Absatzgebiete merowingerzeitlicher Töpferewen des nördlichen Nechagelsieter, *Jahrbuch für Schwabisch-Frankische Geschichte* 27, 31-43.

Laing, L. 1975 *The archaeology of Late Celtic Britain and Ireland, c.* A.D. 400-1200, London.

Lamm, C. 1973 The manufacture of jewellery during the Migration period at Helgö in Sweden, *Bulletin of the Historical Metallurgy Group* 7, 1-7.

Larson, L. M. 1904 *The King's Household in England before the Norman Conquest*, Wisconsin.

Latouche, R. 1967 *The Birth of Western Economy*[2], London.

Lauer, P. (ed.) 1964 *Nithard: histoire des fils de Louis le Pieux*, Paris.

Layard, N. F. 1907 An Anglo-Saxon cemetery in Ipswich, *Archaeologia* 60, 325–52.
Levison, W. 1946 *England and the Continent in the Eighth Century*, Oxford.
Liversage, G. D. 1967 Excavations at Dalkey Island, Co. Dublin, *Proceedings of the Royal Irish Academy* 66, section C, 53–235.
Lobbedey, U. 1977 Northern Germany, in M. W. Barley (ed.), *European Towns: their archaeology and history*, London, 127–57.
Loyn, H. R. 1962 *Anglo-Saxon England and the Norman Conquest*, London.
Loyn, H. R. 1974 Kinship in Anglo-Saxon England, *Anglo-Saxon England* 3, 197–209.
Loyn, H. R. 1977 *The Vikings in Britain*, London.
Lunden, K. 1972 *Okonomi og samfunn*, Oslo.
Lundström, A. 1976 *Bead-making in Scandinavia in the Early Middle Ages*, Stockholm.
Lundström, P. 1973 Paviken 1 bei Västergarn – Hafen, Handelsplatz und Werft, in H. Jankuhn et al. (eds) 1973, vol. 2, 82–93.
Lyon, B. 1974 *Henri Pirenne: a Biographical and Intellectual Study*, Ghent.
Lyon, S. 1976 Some problems in interpreting Anglo-Saxon coinage, *Anglo-Saxon England*, 5, 173–224.
MacGregor, A. 1978 Industry and commerce in Anglo-Scandinavian York, in R. A. Hall (ed.) *Viking-Age York and the North*, 37–57, London.
Magnusson, M. and Pálsson, H. 1969 *Laxdaela Saga*, Harmondsworth.
Maitland, F. W. 1897 *Domesday Book and Beyond*, London.
Malinowski, B. 1922 *Argonauts of the Western Pacific*, London.
Mårtensson, A. W. 1976 *Uppgrävt förflutet för PKbanken i Lund*, Lund.
Mattys, A. and Hossey, G. 1973 Le château des Fées à Bertaux, *Archaeologica Belgica* 146.
Mauss, M. 1925 *Essai sur le don*, Paris.
Metcalf, D. M. 1965 How large was the Anglo-Saxon currency? *English History Review* 18, 475–82.
Metcalf, D. M. 1967 The prosperity of north-western Europe in the eighth and ninth centuries, *English History Review* 20, 344–57.
Metcalf, D. M. 1972 The 'bird and branch' sceattas in the light of a find from Abingdon, *Oxoniensia* 37, 51–65.
Metcalf, D. M. 1974 Monetary expansion and recession: interpreting the distribution and patterns of seventh and eighth-century coins, in J. Casey and R. Reece (eds) *Coins and the Archaeologist*, B.A.R. 4, Oxford, 206–23.
Metcalf, D. M. 1977 Monetary affairs in Mercia in the time of Aethelbald, in A. Dornier (ed.) *Mercian Studies* 87–106, Leicester.
Metcalf, D. M. 1978 The ranking of the boroughs: numismatic evidence from the reign of Aethelred II, in D. Hill (ed.) 1978, 159–212.
Metcalf, D. M. 1979 Coinage and the rise of the Flemish towns, in N. J. Mayhew (ed.) *Coinage in the Low Countries*, B.A.R. 54, Oxford, 1–23.
Metcalf, D. M., Merrick, J. M. and Hamblin, L. K., 1968 *Studies in the Composition of Early Medieval Coins*, Newcastle.
Miller, L. 1977 New Fresh Wharf 2, the Saxon and early medieval waterfronts, *The London Archaeologist* 3(2), 47–53.
Miguel, A. 1966 L'Europe occidentale dans la relation arabe d'Ibrâhîm b Ya'qûb, *Annales, Economie, Sociétés, Civilisations* 21, 1048–64.
Moore, D. T. 1978 The petrography and archaeology of English honestones, *Journal of Archaeological Science* 5, 61–73.
Morrison, K. F. 1963 Numismatics and Carolingian trade: a crititque of the evidence, *Specutum* 38, 403–32.
Morrison, K. F. 1964 *The Two Kingdoms: Ecclesiology in Carolingian Political Thought*, Princeton.
Muckelroy, K. 1978 *Maritime Archaeology*, Cambridge.
Müller-Wille, M. 1974 Boat graves in northern Europe, *International Journal of Nautical Archaeology* 3, 187–204.

Müller-Wille, M. 1977 Der frühmittelalterliche Schmied im Spiegel skandinavischer Grabfunde, *Frühmittelalterliche Studien* 11, 127-201.

Myhre, B. 1978 Agrarian development, settlement history and social organisation in south-west Norway in the Iron Age, *New Directions in Scandinavian Archaeology* 1, 224-71.

Ó Corráin, D. 1972 *Ireland before the Normans*, Dublin.

O'Kelly, M. J. 1973 Monastic sites in the west of Ireland, *Scottish Archaeological Forum* 5, 1-16.

O'Rain, P. 1972 Boundary association in early Irish society, *Studia Celtica* 7, 12-29.

Ó'Riórdáin, A. B. 1976 The High Street excavations, in B. Almqvist and D. Green (eds) *Proceedings of the Seventh Viking Congress* 135-40, Dundalk.

Ó'Riórdáin, S. P. 1942 The excavation of a large earthen ringfort at Garranes, Co. Cork, *Proceedings of the Royal Irish Academy* 47, section C, 77-150.

Odelberg, M. 1974 *Birka*, Stockholm.

Odner, K. 1972 Ethno-historic and ecological settings for economic and social models of an Iron Age society: Valldalen, Norway, in D. L. Clarke (ed.) *Models in Archaeology*, 623-51, London.

Ohlsson, T. 1975-6 The Löddeköpinge investigation 1. The settlements at Vikhögsvägen, *Papers of the Lund Institute* 1, 59-161.

Olsen, O. and Crumlin-Pedersen, O. 1967 The Skuldelev ships, *Acta Archaeologica* 38, 73-174.

Olsen, O. and Schmidt, H. 1977 *Fyrkat, en jysk Vikingeborg*, Copenhagen.

Ozanne, A. 1961-3 The context and date of the Anglian cemetery at Ipswich, *Proceedings of the Suffolk Institute of Archaeology* 29, 208-12.

Ozanne, A. 1962-3 The Peak dwellers, *Medieval Archaeology*, 6-7, 15-52.

Pagán, H. E. 1968 A new type for Beonna, *British Numismatic Journal* 37, 10-15.

Parkhouse, J. 1976 The Dorestad quernstones, *Ber. R.O.B.* 26, 181-6.

Pauli, R. 1889 *The Life of Alfred the Great to which is appended Alfred's Anglo-Saxon version of Orosius* (translated from the German by B. Thorpe), London.

Peacock, D. P. S. and Thomas, C. 1967 Class 'E' imported post-Roman pottery: a suggested origin, *Cornish Archaeology* 6, 35-46.

Pearce, S. M. 1979 *The Kingdom of Dumnonia*, Padstow.

Peebles, C. and Kus, S. 1977 Some archaeological correlates of ranked societies, *American Antiquity* 42, 421-48.

Perin, P. 1971 Typologie et chronologie des verrèries provenant des sépultures mérovingiennes de la region ardennaise, *IX Congrès International du Verre*, 11-50.

Petersson, H. B. A. 1969 *Anglo-Saxon Currency*, Lund.

Philipsen, J. P. W. 1965 The Utrecht ship, *Mariner's Mirror* 51, 35-46.

Pirenne, H. 1925 *Medieval Cities: their origin and the revival of trade*, Princeton.

Pirenne, H. 1939 *Mohammed and Charlemagne*, London.

Platt, C. 1978 *Medieval England*, London.

Platt, C. and Coleman-Smith, R. 1975 *Excavations in Medieval Southampton, 1953-1969*, Leicester.

Polanyi, K. 1957 The economy as instituted process, in K. Polanyi, C. Arensburg and H. W. Pearson (eds) *Trade and Markets in the Early Empires*, 243-70, Glencoe.

Polanyi, K. 1963 Ports of trade in early societies, *Journal of Economic History* 23, 30-45.

Porcher, J. 1970 Book painting, in J. Hubert, J. Porcher and W. F. Volbach, *Carolingian Art*, 71-206, London.

Poupardin, R. 1922 The Carolingian kingdoms, in *The Cambridge Medieval History*, vol. 3, Cambridge, 23-54.

Price, B. J. 1978 Secondary state formation: an explanatory model, in R. Cohen and E. Service (eds) *The Origins of the State*, 161-86, Philadelphia.

Proudfoot, V. B. 1961 The economy of the Irish rath, *Medieval Archaeology* 5, 94-122.

Rahtz, P. 1976 The buildings and rural settlement, in D. M. Wilson (ed.) 1976, 49-98.

Rahtz, P. 1979 *The Palaces at Cheddar*, B.A.R.65, Oxford.
Rahtz, P. and Fowler, P. J. 1972 Somerset A.D. 400–700, in P. Fowler (ed.) *Archaeology and the Landscape*, 187–221, London.
Raleigh Radford, C. A. 1972 Excavations at Cricklade: 1948–63, *Wiltshire Archaeological Magazine* 67, 61–111.
Ramskou, T. 1953 Lindholm Høje, *Acta Archaeologica* 24, 186–96.
Randsborg, K. 1980 *The Viking Age in Denmark: the Formation of a State*, London.
Rappaport, R. 1971 The sacred in human evolution, *Annual Review of Ecology and Systematics* 2, 23–44.
Rathje, W. L. 1975 The last tango in Mayapán; a tentative trajectory of production-distribution systems, in J. Sabloff and C. C. Lamberg-Karlovsky, *Ancient Civilisation and Trade*, 409–48, Albuquerque.
Rathje, W. L. and Sabloff, J. A. 1973–4 Ancient Maya commercial systems: a research design for the island of Cozumel, Mexico, *World Archaeology* 5, 221–31.
Rauch, C. H. R. and Jacobi, H. J. 1976 *Die Ausgrabungen in der Königspfalz Ingelheim, 1909–1914*, Mainz.
Redman, C. L. 1978 *The Rise of Civilisation*, San Francisco.
Renfrew, C. 1972 *The Emergence of Civilisation: the Cyclades and the Aegean in the Third Millennium B.C.*, London.
Renfrew, C. 1975 Trade as action at distance: questions of integration and communication, in J. Sabloff and C. C. Lamberg-Karlovsky (eds) *Ancient Civilisation and Trade*, 3–59, Albuquerque.
Renfrew, C. 1977 Alternative models for exchange and and spatial distribution, in T. Earle and J. Ericson (eds) *Exchange Systems in Prehistory*, 71–90, London.
Renfrew, C. 1978a. The anatomy of innovation, in D. Green et al. (eds) *Social Organisation and Settlement*, 89–117, B.A.R. 47, Oxford.
Renfrew, C. 1978b. Trajectory discontinuity and morphogenesis, *American Antiquity*, 43, 203–22.
Renfrew, C. and Dixon, J. 1976 Obsidian in western Asia: a review, in G. de G. Sieveking et al. (eds) *Problems in Economic and Social Archaeology*, 138–50, London.
Reynolds, S. 1977 *An Introduction to the History of English Medieval Towns*, Oxford.
Rigold, S. E. 1960–1 The two primary series of sceattas, *British Numismatic Journal* 30, 6–53.
Rigold, S. E. 1961 The supposed see of Dunwich, *Journal of the British Archaeological Association* 14, 55–9.
Rigold, S. E. 1966 Two primary series of sceattas: addenda and corrigenda, *British Numismatic Journal* 35, 1–6.
Rigold, S. E. 1975 The Sutton Hoo coins in the light of the contemporary background of coinage in England, in R. L. S. Buce-Mitford, *The Sutton Hoo Ship Burial* 1, London, 653–77.
Rigold, S. E. 1978 The principal series of English sceattas, *British Numismatic Journal* 47, 21–30.
Rigold, S. E. and Metcalf, D. M. 1978 A check-list of English finds of sceattas, *British Numismatic Journal*, 47, 31–52.
Rigoir, J. 1968 Les sigillées paléochrétiennes grises et orangées, *Gallia* 26, 177–244.
Roberts, B. K. 1977 *Rural Settlement in Britain*, London.
Roesdahl, E. 1977 Aggersborg: the Viking settlement and fortress, *Château Gaillard* (Caen) 8, 269–78.
Rousseau, E. 1930 La Meuse et les pays mosan: leur importance historique avant le XIIIe siècle, *Annales de la Société archéologique de Namur* 39, 1–248.
Sabbé, E. 1950 Les relations économique entre l'Angleterre et le Continent au Haut Moyen Age, *Le Moyen Age* 56, 169–93.
Sabloff, J. et al. 1975 Trade and power in Postclassic Yucatan: initial observations, in N. Hammond (ed.) *Mesoamerican Archaeology: New Approaches*, 397–416, Cambridge.
Sahlins, M. 1974 *Stone Age Economics*, London.

Sawyer, P. 1965 'The wealth of England in the eleventh century, *Transactions of the Royal Historical Society* 15, 145-64.

Sawyer, P. 1971 *The Age of the Vikings*², London.

Sawyer, P. 1976 Introduction: early medieval English settlement, in P. Sawyer (ed.) *Medieval Settlement* 1-7; London.

Sawyer, P. 1977 Kings and merchants, in P. Sawyer and I. N. Wood (eds) *Early Medieval Kingship*, 139-58, Leeds.

Scapula, J. 1975 *Les fouilles d'Isle-Aumont*, Troyes.

Schietzel, K. (ed.) 1970 *Das archäologische Fundmaterial I der Ausgrabung Haithabu, 1963-4*, 4, Neumünster

Schledermann, H. 1970-1 The idea of the town: typology, definitions and approaches to the study of the medieval town in northern Europe, *World Archaeology* 2, 115-27.

Schlesinger, W. 1972 Vorstufen des Städtewesens im ottonischen Sachsen, *Die Städt in der europäischen Geschichte* (Festschrift Edith Ennen), Bonn, 234-58.

Schlesinger, W. 1976 Early medieval fortification in Hesse: a general historical report, *World Archaeology* 7, 243-70.

Schnapp, A. 1977 Archéologie et nazisme, *Quaderni di Storia* 5, 1-26.

Schweitzer, J. 1975-6 Leibersheim, *Bulletin du Musée historique de Mulhouse* 83, 68-128.

Service, E. R. 1971 *Primitive Social Organisation*², New York.

Severin, T. 1978 *The Breandan Voyage*, London.

Sjoberg, G. 1967 *The Pre-Industrial City*, Glencoe.

Skaare, K. 1976 *Coins and Coinage in Viking-age Norway*, Oslo.

Skinner, G. W. 1964-5 Marketing and social structure in rural China, *Journal of Asian Studies* 24, 3-43; 195-228; 363-99.

Smedley, N. and Owles, E. 1967 A sherd of Ipswich ware with face-mask decoration, *Proceedings of the Suffolk Institute of Archaeology* 31, 84-7.

Smelsner, N. 1959 A comparative view of exchange systems, *Economic Development and Cultural Change* 7, 173-82.

Smith, C. A. 1976 Exchange systems and the spatial distribution of elites: the organisation of stratification in agrarian societies, in C. A. Smith (ed.) *Regional Analysis* 2, 309-74, London.

Smyth, A. P. 1977 *Scandinavian Kings in the British Isles, 850-880*, Oxford.

Southall, A. W. 1967 A note on State organisation: segmentary states in Africa and in medieval Europe, in S. L. Thrupp (ed.) *Early Medieval Society*, 147-59, New York.

Steinhausen, J. 1939 Frühmittelalterliche Gläshutten im Trierland, *Trierer Zeitschrift* 14, 29-57.

Stenton, F. M. 1971 *Anglo-Saxon England*³, Oxford.

Steuer, H. 1974 *Die Südsiedlung von Haithabu*, Neumünster.

Sutermeister, H. 1976 Burpham: a settlement site within the Saxon defences, *Sussex Archaeological Collections* 114, 194-206.

Sutherland, C. H. V. 1948 *Anglo-Saxon Gold Coinage in the Light of the Crondall Hoard*, Oxford.

Taylor, C. C. 1978 Aspects of village mobility in medieval and later times, in S. Limbrey and J. G. Evans (eds) *The Effect of Man on the Landscape: the Lowland Zone*, 126-34, London.

Terray, E. 1974 Long-distance exchange and the formation of the State: the case of the Abron kingdom, *Economy and Society* 3, 315-45.

Thomas, C. 1959 Imported pottery in Dark-Age western Britain, *Medieval Archaeology* 3, 89-111

Thomas, C. 1976 Imported Late-Roman Mediterranean pottery in Ireland and western Britain: chronologies and implications, *Proceedings of the Royal Irish Academy* 76, 245-55.

Throckmorton, P. 1972 Romans on the sea, in G. Bass (ed.) *A History of Seafaring*, 66-86, London.

Tischler, F. 1952 Zür Datierung der frühmittelalterlichen Tönwaren von Badorf, *Germania* 30, 194–200.

Trigger, B. 1972 Determinants of urban growth in pre-industrial societies, in P. Ucko et al. (eds) *Man, Settlement and Urbanism*, 575–99, London.

Trigger, B. 1978 *Time and Traditions*, Edinburgh.

Trimpe Burger, J. A. 1973 Oost-Souburg, Province of Zeeland: a preliminary report on the excavation of the site of an ancient fortress (1969–1971), *Ber.R.O.B.* 23, 355–65.

Van Doornick, F. 1972 Byzantium, mistress of the sea 330–641, in G. Bass (ed.) *A History of Seafaring*, 134–58, London.

Van Es, W. A. 1969 Excavations at Dorestad: a pre-preliminary report: 1967–68, *Ber. R.O.B.* 19, 183–207.

Van Es, W. A. 1973 Roman-period settlement on the 'Free Germanic' sandy soil of Drenthe, Overijssel and Gelderland, *Ber. R.O.B.* 23, 273–80.

Van Es, W. A. 1978 La grande fibule de Dorestad, in E. Chirol (ed.) *Centenaire de L'Abbé Cochet 1975: actes du colloque international d'archéologie*, 489–510, Rouen.

Van Es, W. A. and Verwers, W. J. H. 1975 Céramique peinte d'époque carolingienne trouvées à Dorestad, *Ber. R.O.B.* 25, 133–64.

Van Es, W. A. et al. 1978 Dorestad, *R.O.B.; Overdrukken*, 105.

Vercauteren, F. 1935–6 Comment s'est-on défendu, au IXe siècle dans l'empire Franc contre les invasions normandes?, *Annales du XXXe Congrès de la Fédération Archéologique et Historique de Belgique*, 117–32.

Vercauteren, F. 1967 The circulation of merchants in western Europe from the 6th to the 10th centuries: economic and cultural aspects, in S. L. Thrupp (ed.) *Early Medieval Society*, 185–95, New York.

Vierck, H. 1970 Zum fernverkeher über 5 um 6 Jahrhundert angesichts angelsächsischer Fibelsätze in Thuringen eine Problemskizze, in K. Hauck (ed.), *Goldbrakteaten aus Sievern*, 355–95, Munich.

Vierck, H. 1974 Werke des Eligius, *Studien zur Vor- und Frühgeschichtlichen Ärchaologie*, Munich, 309–80.

Vierck, H. 1976 Noel Myres und die Besiedlung Englands, *Praehistorisches Zeitschrift* 51, 43–55.

Wade, K. 1980 Excavations in Ipswich, 1974–1977, *East Anglian Archaeology*, forthcoming.

Wade-Martins, P. 1975 The origins of rural settlement in East Anglia, in P. J. Fowler (ed.) *Recent Work in Rural Archaeology*, 137–57, Bradford-on-Avon.

Wailes, B. 1972 Plow and population in temperate Europe, in B. Spooner (ed.) *Population Growth: Anthropological Implications*, 154–80, Cambridge, Mass.

Walker, J. 1978 Anglo-Saxon traded pottery, appendix to D. F. Mackreth, in M. Todd (ed.) *Studies in the Romano-British Villa*, 224–8, Leicester.

Wallace-Hadrill, J. M. 1971 *Early Germanic Kingship in England and on the Continent*, Oxford.

Wallace-Hadrill, J. M. 1975 *Early Medieval History*, Oxford.

Warner, R. 1975–6 'Ring-money': plain penannular arm-rings, *Proceedings of the Society of Antiquaries of Scotland* 107, 136–43.

Warner, R. 1976 Some observations on the context and importation of exotic material in Ireland from the first century B.C. to the second century A.D., *Proceedings of the Royal Irish Academy* 76, 267–92.

Watson, A. M. 1967 Back to gold – and silver, *Economic History Review* 20, 1–34.

Webb, M. C. 1975 The flag follows trade: an essay on the necessary interaction of military and commercial factors in state formation, in J. Sabloff and C. C. Lamberg-Karlovsky (eds) *Ancient Civilisation and Trade*, 155–209, Albuquerque.

Weidemann, K. 1970 Importkeramik aus Haithabu (Ausgrabungen 1963–1964), *Das archäologische Fundmaterial 1 der Ausgrabung Haithabu 1963–64* 4, 46–52, Neumünster.

Werner, J. 1961 Fernhandel und Naturalwirtschaft im östlichen Merowingerreich nach archäologischen und numismatischen Zeugnissen, *Bericht der Römisch-Germanisch Kommission* 42, 307–46.

West, S. E. 1963 Excavations at Cox Lane and at the town defences, Shire Hall Yard, Ipswich, *Proceedings of the Suffolk Institute of Archaeology* 29, 233–303.

West, S. E. 1969 The Anglo-Saxon village of West Stow: an interim report of the excavations 1965–8, *Medieval Archaeology* 13, 1–20.

Wheatley, P. 1972 The concept of urbanism, in P. Ucko et al. (eds) *Man, Settlement and Urbanism*, 601–37, London.

Wheatley, P. 1975 Satyanrta in Suvarnadvipa: from reciprocity to redistribution in Ancient south-east Asia, in J. Sabloff and C. C. Lamberg-Karlovsky (eds), *Ancient Civilisation and Trade*, 227–83, Albuquerque.

Wheeler, R. E. M. 1935 *London and the Saxons*, London.

Wheeler, R. E. M. 1954 *Rome beyond the Imperial Frontiers*, London.

Whitbread, L. S. 1946 The 'Frisian sailor' passage in the Old English Gnomic verses, *Review of English Studies* 22, 215–19.

White, L. jr. 1972 The expansion of technology, 500–1500 in C. M. Cipolla (ed.) *The Fontana Economic History of Europe: the Middle Ages*, 143–74, London.

Whitelock, D. 1955 *English Historical Documents* 1, London.

Whitelock, D. 1972 The pre-Viking age church in East Anglia, *Anglo-Saxon England* 1, 1–22.

Williams, A. 1979 Some notes and considerations on problems connected with the English royal succession, 860–1066, in R. A. Brown (ed.), *Proceedings of the Battle Conference on Anglo-Norman Studies* 1, Ipswich, 144–67.

Williams, J. 1979 *St. Peter's Street, Northampton; excavations 1973–76*, Northampton.

Wilson, D. M. (ed.) 1976 *The Archaeology of Anglo-Saxon England*, London.

Wilson, D. M. 1976 Crafts and industry, in D. M. Wilson (ed.) 1976, 253–82.

Winkelmann, W. 1954 Eine westfälische Siedlung des 8 Jahrhunderts bei Warendorf, Kr. Warendorf, *Germania* 32, 189–213.

Winkelmann, W. 1972 Litürgisches Gefäss der Missionszeit aus Paderborn, in P-W. Scheele (ed.) *Paderbornensis Ecclesia*, 37–47, Paderborn.

Wright, H. and Johnson, G. 1975 Population, exchange and early state formation in southwestern Iran, *American Anthropologist* 77, 267–89.

Ypey, J. 1968 Fundstucke mit anglo-karolingische Tierornamentik in niederlandischen Sammlungen, *Ber. R.O.B.* 18, 175–91.

Ypey, J. 1973 Das fränkische Gräberfeld zu Rhenen, Prov. Utrecht, *Ber. R.O.B.* 23, 289–312.

INDEX

Aachen (royal palace), 139, 155, 176
Aarhus, 52, 64, 148, 171, 173, 183, 195
Aardenburg, 175
Adam of Bremen, 86, 171, 172
Aethelbald, king of Mercia, 4, 44, 45, 112, 113, 157
Aethelweald, 54
Aethelwulf, king of Wessex, 126, 158
African Red Slip ware, 33, 37
Aggersborg, 172
Agobard, bishop of Lyons, 91
agriculture and farming, 40, 130–44, 149–50, 155, 164
Alborg, 172
Alcock, Leslie, 178, 199, 200, 208
Alcuin, 73, 88, 127, 128
Aldgisl, king of the Frisians, 40, 88
Alfred, king of Wessex, 4, 5, 10, 54, 66, 78, 81, 100, 101, 114, 151, 158–65, 170, 177, 178, 191, 196; navy, 98
Alsace, 34, 45, 132, 155
Altfrid, biographer of St Luidger, 73
Alt-Ladoga, 66
Al-Tartushi, 67, 78, 202, 209
Alt-Lübeck, 42
Alur (African state), 26
amber/amber trade, 122
Ambrosiani, B., 85
Amiens, 45
amphorae, 33, 57, 80, 95; Bi and Bii; 67; from Yassi Ada wreck, 129
Annapes, 131, 132, 138, 149
Anastasius, Emperor of Byzantium, 32
Anglo-Saxon Chronicle, 4, 159, 160, 168, 179
Anglo-Saxon England, 3–5, 10, 11, 21, 26, 30–48, 53–6, 60, 65–73, 87, 101, 102, 111–19, 122, 125–9, 134–51, 157–72, 178–84, 189–92
Ansgar, Bishop of Hamburg, 5, 78, 80, 85, 86; see also Rimbert
Arabs/Arab civilization, 29, 34, 38, 39, 91, 122, 128, 160, 182, 189, 192, coins, 154; silver, 157
Arbman, Holger, 10, 199, 201, 203
Argonauts of the Western Pacific by Bronislaw Malinowski, 9, 13
Aristotle, 20
Arthur, King, 3
Arup, Erik, 42, 89
Asia Minor, 5, 163, 182
Askekärr ship, 96, 106, 204
Asser, biographer of king Alfred, 159

Aston Rowant, Oxfordshire (coin-hoard), 40
Athelstan, king of Wessex, 4, 165, 168, 182; mints, 166
St Aubin, France (coin-hoard), 34
St Augustine, 3, 4
Austrasia, 32, 34, 36, 39, 41, 74, 87, 88
Axbridge, 171, 208
Axbridge Chronicle, 168

Badorf ware/kilns, 41, 58, 80, 84, 89, 93; Badorf/ Pingsdorf, 176
Baghdad, 182
Bakka, E., 116, 205
Bantham, Devon, 33, 51, 67, 203
Bantry pillar stone, 102, 105
Barker, Graeme, 136, 137, 206
Bårset boats, 96, 100
Basle, 132
Bath, 191
battle of Etheldun (A.D. 878), 159
battle of Clontarf (A.D. 1014), 195
battle of Maldon (poem), 116
battle of Svold, 182
bead trade, see glass beads
Beaduheard, 54
Beauvais, kilns/pot industry, 155
Bede, 4, 44, 55, 69, 88, 90, 100, 122; A History of the English Church and People, 127; on population, 190
Benty Grange burial, 190
Beresford, M. W., 21, 207
Bertha, queen of Kent, 35
Biddle, Martin, 11, 158, 165, 170, 199, 200, 203, 208
Binford, Lewis, 12, 152, 198
Birka, 10, 43, 52–5, 59, 60, 63, 64 fig. 13, 80–6, 89, 91, 98, 118, 142, 173, 183, 193, 203; cemetery, 120; textiles, 119
Bishopstone, 135
Bitterne, 44, 68
Bjorn, king of Uppland, 85
Black Hrocbert, 88
Black ware, 92
Blindheim, C., 10, 55, 200, 202, 203, 206
Bloch, M., 9
Blunt, C. E., 56, 114, 115
boats/ships/shipping, 53, 62, 72, 75, 78, 79, 85, 90, 94–103, 124, 126, 129, 180; wrecks, 57
boat builders, 33, 34, 70, 77, 81, 82, 95, 99, 100; grave of, 94

boat-shaped buildings, 62; Hamwih, 68
Bohannan, P., 15, 25, 30, 200
Bolin, Sture, 7-9, 154, 157, 165
boneworking, 68, 73, 74, 77; skates, 86
Bonn, 120, 176
bracteates (Danish), 33
Bradley, Richard, 92, 204
St Breandan (voyages of), 103
Brebières village, France, 132
Brent, John, 69
Bretwalda, 195
Brian Boru, 195
Bridbury, A. R., 6, 199
St Brigid, 47
Brittany, 122, 124
brooches, 41, 75, 144; Lombardic and Allemanic, 32; radiate, 118
Bruce-Mitford, R. L. S., 37, 201, 204
Brühl-Eckdorf kilns, 119
Bryhtnolt, Earl, 116
bullion, 35, 37, 104, 105, 108, 109, 116, 117, 166, 179, 181
Büraberg, West Germany, 131
Burgh Castle, Suffolk, 55; glass furnaces, 122
burhs, 131, 158, 165, 166-9, 170, 171, 174, 178-81; Dutch, 175
Burpham, Sussex, 171
B-ware amphora, 33, 37, 67
Byzantine/Byzantium, 2, 5, 32-5, 38, 66; coins, 108-11; merchants, 129; ships, 94; spoons, 122

Cahercommaun, Co. Clare, Ireland, 135
Cambridge, 181
Canterbury, 36, 56, 69, 158, 159, 165, 166; archbishop, 191; St Martins, 34; St Martins coin-hoard, 35
Canute, king of England and Denmark, 172, 181, 183, 193
Capelle, Torsten, 74, 203, 205
Capitulare de Villis vel Curtis Imperialibus, 49
Carneiro, Robert, 26
Carolingia, 3-8, 21, 39, 42, 43, 49, 52-6, 65, 68, 77, 87-91, 107, 113, 120, 124, 126, 131, 139, 141, 151-7, 161-3, 191
cashels, 135
catastrophe theory, 65
Catholme, Staffordshire, 135
cemeteries/cemetery evidence, 32, 62, 67, 69, 70, 81, 84, 85, 88, 109, 118, 120, 135, 145
Ceolfrid, abbot of Monkwearmouth and Jarrow, 90, 100
Ceonwulf, king of Mercia, 158, 191, 208
Chalton, Hampshire, 134, 135
Chapelot, Jean, 119
Charibert I, king of Paris, 35
Charlemagne, 2-4, 7, 8, 29, 39, 41-3, 54, 55, 73, 78, 86, 116, 119, 128, 129, 149, 153, 155, 158, 177, 188, 189, 191, 196; letter, 126; letter to Offa, 124; reforms of, 144
Charles, son of Charlemagne, 154
Charles the Bald, 156, 157, 158
Charles Martel, 2, 40, 45, 88
Cheddar, Somerset (Saxon palace), 168
Cherry, John F., 205
Chester, 168, 181
Chichester, Sussex, 168, 170, 178; burh, 165
chiefdoms, 15, 27, 187, 188, 191, 193, 195, 197
Childe, V. Gordon, 9, 21, 22, 26, 104

China, 16, 85, 164
Chissey-en-Morvan, France (coin-hoard), 34
Christensen, A. E., 89, 201, 204
Christianity, 55, 193, 194
Christian missions/missionaries, 4, 35, 88, 90, 103, 193
Church/churches, 55, 56, 66, 173, 180, 183, 192-4
civil war in Carolingia, 154, 157
Clarke, David, L., 12, 199
Climate, 135, 139, 183
clinker-built vessels, 95, 97, 98
Clogher, Co. Tyrone, N. Ireland, 37, 201
Clonmacnoise, Co. Offaly, Ireland, 48
Clovis, 2, 32, 38
cnicht's guild, Canterbury, 158
Coblenz, 57
Cogitosus, biographer of St Brigid, 47, 49, 50, 56
coinage, 8-10, 32-45, 55, 60, 67-75, 81, 84, 85, 88, 90, 96, 97, 104-118, 149-58, 163-70, 176-83
coin hoards, 34, 35, 38, 40, 41, 82, 110, 116, 157, 176, 180
Collis, John, 105-7, 111, 117, 205
Cologne, 48, 49, 75, 119, 176
Constantinople, 2; ships from, 94
Cordoba, 67, 91, 128
Cork, 195
Coslany (Norwich), 73
cowrie shells, 32, 35, 108, 122
Crannogs, 126, 135
Crawford, O. G. S., 10, 67
Crondall hoard, 35, 110
Crusades, 183
curraghs, 97, 100, 103
currency bars, 117, 124, 145
cybernetics, 12, 152

Dagobert, king of Neustria, 2, 34, 127
Dalkey Island, 38, 51, 63, 67
Dal n'Araide, 124
Dal Riata, 124
Dalton, George, 14, 15, 25, 30, 53, 107, 108, 200, 205
Danegeld tribute, 166, 168, 182
Danelaw, 4, 159, 168, 170, 172, 178
Danevirke, 78, 79
Dankirke, Denmark, 40, 41
Darwin, Charles, 26
Deira, kingdom of, 43
denarius/denier, 8, 43, 176
dendrochronology, 70, 88, 156, 172, 180
Denmark, 4, 5, 29, 33, 40, 52-5, 58-66, 74, 78, 80, 82, 89, 95, 98, 103, 116-21, 125, 127, 133, 139-43, 171, 172, 183, 192-6
St Denys fair, Paris, 43, 49, 55, 88, 90, 127
St Denys monastery, 90
De Paor, Liam, 47, 202, 210
dies, 9, 115, 166
Dinas Powys, Wales, 33
dogs, 38, 127, 196
Dolley, Michael, 178-80, 208, 209
Domburg, 40, 43, 53, 73, 89, 101, 118
Domesday Book, 140, 141, 179
Dopsch, Alphons, 6
Dorchester, Dorset, 167, 178
Dronrijp, coins, 40
Dorestad, 10, 39-45, 51, 55, 57, 60-2, 73-7, 86, 88-93, 102, 103, 111, 117, 118, 120, 122-5, 129, 141, 143, 158, 174, 201, 206; coins, 156; mint, 36
Dublin, 38, 51, 53, 66, 67, 126, 181, 195
Dunning, Gerald, 10, 179, 181, 199

Dunwich, 181, 203

Eadbert, king of Kent, 69
Eadberht, king of Northumbria (coins), 112
Eanbald, archbishop of York, 127, 128
Earle, Timothy, 14, 15, 26, 187, 200
Early State Module (ESM), 192, 193
East Anglia, 4, 36, 39, 70-3, 101, 146, 204
Eckman, Jan, 173
economic anthropology, 6, 9, 13-17, 104, 107, 186
Edgar, king of England, 165, 168, 178-80, 191
Edict of Pitres, 156
Edmund, king of England, 168
Edred, king of England, 168
Edward the Elder, king of Wessex, 4, 165
Edward the Confessor, king of England, 180, 182, 183
Edward the Martyr, king of England (coins), 165
Egbert, king of Wessex, 4, 45, 158
Elegius, bishop of Noyon, 118, 127
Emden, West Germany, 43, 77
emporia, 10, 21, 23, 25, 28, 36, 40-86, 88, 89, 92, 93,
    100, 117, 122-5, 138, 141-9, 163, 171-5, 193-7;
    Dutch, 174-5
Ennen, Edith, 21, 199
Ensisheim, France, 132, 206
Eric Bloodaxe, king of Jorvik, 4
Ermoldus Nigellus, 89, 129, 201
Esbjerg, 80, 101
Escharen, the Netherlands (coin-hoard), 34
Escomb, Co. Durham (glass), 122
Ethelbert, king of Kent, 35
Ethelred the Unready, king of England, 4, 169, 178-
    80, 191, 195, 209; coins, 166
Etruria, 201
E-wares, 37, 38, 67
Exeter, 165, 168, 181
Exeter Book, 94, 127

fairs, 16, 23, 30, 47, 49, 51, 53, 112, 149, 150
farms, 47, 69, 75, 88, 130-43, 158; Viking, 81
faunal assemblages, 68, 75, 131, 132, 135, 141-3, 173
Fécamp hoard, France, 176
Feddersen Wierde, West Germany, 29, 133
Ferrières abbey, France, 127
feudalism, 138, 139, 176, 189
Finley, Moses, ix, 11, 199
fishing/marine resources, 68, 75, 138, 142, 143
Flannery, Kent, 152, 186, 187, 207, 209
fluctburghs, 166, 178
folk moot, 190
Foote, P., 62, 199, 202, 205
Fordwich, 44, 69
formalists (economic anthropologists), 14
France/Franks, 3, 7, 30-45, 49, 55, 66, 70, 75, 87-94,
    100, 109, 118-20, 122-5, 127-9, 131, 132, 156, 157,
    176
Frankfurt, 176
Frankish Royal Annals, 78, 193
Fried, Morton, 26, 27, 185, 200, 209
Friedman, Jonathon, 22, 26, 200, 209, 210
Frisia/Frisians, 3, 4, 29, 32-4, 37, 39, 40, 42, 73-5, 87-
    94, 97, 100, 111, 116, 124-7, 143
Frisian pottery, 40, 81; guild, 89
Fyrkat, Denmark, 172

Gall, P. L., 186, 209; *see also* Saxe
St Gall, monastery of, 140
Ganshof, F., 139, 198, 202, 204, 207

Garranes, Co. Cork, Ireland, 33, 126
gateway communities, 24, 25
Gem, Richard, 179, 180, 209
Germany/Rhineland, 10, 11, 13, 21, 29-43, 48-52,
    56-66, 72-5, 78-84, 88-93, 96-103, 118-20, 124-8,
    131, 132, 139-41, 155, 157, 163, 171-6, 183
Gervold, abbot of St Riquier, 90
Gibbon, Edward, 6
gift exchange, 9
Gladbach, West Germany, 132
glass beads/bead trade, 41, 68, 80-2, 85, 120
glass industry, 120, 122
glass, stained (Anglo-Saxon), 122
glassware, 37, 43, 67, 68, 72, 75, 79, 85, 105, 120, 122
Glastonbury, Somerset, 56; glass furnaces, 122
Gloucester, 168, 171
Gnupa, Swedish king, 78
Godfred, king of the Danes, 4, 42, 43, 55, 56, 78, 79,
    192, 193; founder of Haithabu, 154
Gokstad ship, 94, 95
Goltho, Lincolnshire, 140, 183
Gorm, king of the west Danes, 192
Granges, 131
Grately Laws (of king Athelstan), 165, 166, 168
Graveney boat, 57, 98, 100
Green, Charles, 101, 103, 205
Greenland, 99, 126, 139
Gregory, pope, 32
Grierson, Philip, 9-11, 111, 127, 199, 201, 205; debate
    with Metcalf, 115
Grobin, Poland, 66
guilds, 89 (of Frisians), 193
Guthram, king of the Danes, 178

hack silver, 108, 116, 182
Hadleigh, Suffolk, Early Saxon cemetery, 70, 71, 203
Hadorph, Joseph (1630-1693), 85
Haithabu/Hedeby, 10, 11, 41, 43, 51-66, 78-80, 84,
    89-91, 98, 100-2, 118, 120, 124-6, 141, 142, 171-3,
    193, 207; coins, 96
Hamburg/*Hammaburg*, 43, 77, 78, 103; Viking raid,
    157
Hamwih, Saxon Southampton, 41-5, 52, 53, 55, 56,
    58, 60-3, 67, 68, 90-4, 101, 111-13, 118, 122-6,
    141-3, 147, 148, 156, 158, 181
Hanseatic League/Hanse, 100, 128, 183
Harald Bluetooth, king of the Danes, 5, 172, 182, 192,
    193, 196
Harald Haldrada, king of Norway, 78, 173, 180
Hardh, Birgitta, 116, 205, 207
St Harlinde monastery, 126
Harris, Marvin, 1, 12, 138, 196, 199, 206, 208
Hastings (burh), 165
Hausa trade, 53
Hedeager, Lotte, 187, 200
Helgö, 11, 41, 43, 53, 56, 61, 63, 83-5, 118, 120, 141,
    144-6; buddha from, 85, 121, 122; Coptic ladle
    from, 84
Henry I of Germany, 78
Hensel, Witold, 23, 200
Hergeir, town captain of Birka, 85
Hérouvillette, France (cemetery), 33; Merovingian
    chieftain's grave, 94
Herpes, France, 33
Hill, David, 166-9, 179, 208, 209
Himley, F. J., 34, 38
Hinton, David, 179, 180, 208, 209
Hirth, K. G., 24, 50, 200

Hisperica Famina, 56
Hlothere, king of Kent, 111
hochburg, 55, 78
Hodder, B. W., 16, 17, 163, 200, 208
Hodder, Ian, 92, 164, 165, 208
Holland and Belgium, 1, 10, 29, 36, 40-5, 53, 55, 58, 60-6, 73-7, 86-91, 96-8, 101-3, 111, 118, 122-6, 129-33, 139-43, 155, 156, 158, 174, 175
Holwerda, J. H., 10, 74, 203
honestones, 105, 124-6; with graffito, 82
householding, 15
Hughes, Kathleen, 56, 199, 202, 210

Iaenbert, archbishop of Canterbury, 56
Ibbo, Frisian trader, 89
Iceland, 99, 190; fairs, 51; sagas, 118
Ilchester, Somerset, 168; Cissbury, nearby fort, 178
Imma, a slave, 69
Ina, king of Wessex, 44, 136-8; laws of, 127
industries and crafts, 61, 68, 76-85, 118-27, 132, 135, 136, 153, 155, 163, 170, 173, 179-84
Ingelheim palace, 131, 155, 207
Ipswich, 36, 40, 53, 55-7, 60, 62-4, 70-3, 91-3, 86, 102, 120, 124, 125, 141, 142, 146, 158, 170, 178, 181
Ipswich ware, 41, 70, 71, 73, 91, 142, 146-8, 148, 208
Ireland, 1, 5, 30, 33, 37, 38, 47-52, 54, 66, 67, 103, 116, 124, 126-8, 135, 137, 156, 185, 194, 195, 198
Italy, 6, 30, 35, 190, 201; pottery, 155

James, Edward, 34, 201
Jankuhn, H., 10, 40, 63, 79, 120, 199, 201, 202, 203
Janssen, L. D. F., 74
Jarrow, monastery, 55, 93, 206; glaziers, 122
Jelling/Jellinge stones, 120, 196; runestones, 192
jewellery, 56, 84, 85, 122, 146
Jews/Jewish traders, 32
Justinian, Emperor of Byzantium, 2, 32, 34

Kaupang (Skiringssal), 10, 11, 53, 55, 61-3, 81, 98, 101, 117, 120, 141, 142, 173; boat from, 126
Kent, 4, 33-7, 43, 44, 55, 66, 69, 108-11, 114
Kent, J. P. C., 35, 201
Kildare, Ireland (monastery of), 47-9
kilns, pottery, 55-8, 71, 93, 119, 146, 155, 189
Kiltiernan Monastery, Co. Galway, Ireland, 48
kingship, 25, 189-98
Kluckholm, Clyde, 22
knarr, 99
Knowth, Co. Meath, Ireland, 126, 206
Kula Ring, 9, 13, 49
Kvalsund Boat, 95, 96, 100
Kwakiutl Indians, 191

Ladby boat, 94, 95
Lagore Crannog, Co. Meath, Ireland, 126
Layard, N. L., 70, 203
Laxdaela Saga, 54
lead, 117, 127
leather, 38, 120, 127; shoes, 164; trade, 33
Lebor Gabala (The Book of Conquests), 67
Leeds, E. T., 11
Lewes, Sussex, 165, 168, 170, 171
Liffey, river, 67
Limerick, Ireland (Viking emporia), 195
limes (Roman frontier), 29, 75, 133, 187
Lincoln, 168, 170, 178, 181; Petergate excavations, 183
Lindholme Høje, Denmark, 140, 183

literacy, 186
Löddeköpinge, 51-3, 56, 62-4, 81, 82, 141, 142, 149
London, 10, 44, 53, 55, 69, 70, 88, 90, 98, 128, 158, 159, 165, 166, 168, 179, 180, 181, 208; Ipswich ware from, 147
long houses, 133-5, 142
longports, 195
Lothar, Emperor of Carolingia, 154, 156, 157
Louis the Pious, Emperor of Carolingia, 3, 90, 91, 154, 156, 157, 160, 193
Lund, 81, 172, 173, 183, 193
Luni, Italy, 201

Macqenoise, France (glass-houses), 120
Mainz, 75, 88, 127, 163, 176, 209
Maitland, F. W., 20
Mälaren, lake, 41, 53, 173, 183
Malinowski, Bronislaw, 6, 9, 13, 18, 104, 199
Malta (temples), 22
manor, 140
markets/market places, 6, 15-17, 20, 21, 25, 48, 49, 86, 92, 108, 112, 117, 149, 153, 160, 163-88
market exchange, 1, 3, 4, 15, 17, 30, 98, 105, 108, 153
Markets in Africa by P. Bohannan & G. Dalton, 15
Marxism/Marxist theory, 22, 26
Mauss, Marcel, 9, 13, 198, 200
Mayen, 181
Mayen ware/potteries, 41, 57, 75, 80, 89, 120, 124
Maxey, Northamptonshire, 135
Mecklenburg, Poland, 120
Medemblik (*Medemelacha*), 43, 55, 77, 89, 103, 125
merchants and traders, 85-101, 127, 157, 179, 181, 183
Mercia, 4, 44, 111, 112, 114, 125, 138, 157
Merovingia, 3-5, 7, 30 32-6, 38-41, 43, 45, 48, 49, 52, 55, 56, 88, 107-11, 120, 122, 124, 131, 155
metalwork, 30, 68, 72, 74, 75, 79, 105, 117, 118, 144, 145, 180; moulds, 84
Metcalf, D. M., 9, 44, 112, 115, 166, 179, 200, 201, 205, 208, 209; fairs, 149
Meuse valley, 118; swords and smiths, 119
Middleburg, the Netherlands, 175
migrations, 2, 3, 7, 100, 101, 151, 157, 187
Millfield, Northumberland, 135
mints/minting, 9, 21, 34-6, 38, 39, 55, 70-3, 79, 105-16, 166-72, 176, 177, 181
mobilisation (economy), 14, 15
Mohammed, 7, 8
Mohammed and Charlemagne by Henri Pirenne, 7
Molise, Italy, 207
monasteries and abbeys, 23, 47-9, 55-7, 69, 77, 89, 90, 122, 125, 126, 131, 138, 194, 197
Monkwearmouth Monastery, Co. Durham (glass industry), 122
moot courts, 150,
Morgan, L. H., 22
Morrison, Karl, 8, 9, 199
mortars, 75, 206

Neale, F., 168, 208
Needham, Norwich, 73
Nendrum monastery, Co. Down, Ireland, 56
St Neots, Cambridgeshire, 122
Neustria, 32, 34, 35-7, 39, 41-5
Niedermendig lava querns, 75, 79, 123
Nijmegen palace, 155
Nithard, 156, 208
Noirmoutier, France, 128

Normans, 5
Northampton, 171
Northumbria, 4, 111, 112
Norway, 5, 10, 11, 41, 43, 55, 60-4, 81, 95. 98-103, 116-20, 124-6, 173, 180, 195
Norwich, 73, 168, 170, 203
Novgorod, 11
numismatics, 7-9, 34, 38, 105, 166-83
Nydam boat, 95, 101, 103

Obodrits (tribe), 193
obol (half denier), 177
obsidian trade, 18, 92
Odense, 172
oenach, 194
Offa, king of Mercia, 53, 56, 87, 90, 112, 114-16, 124, 126, 129, 157, 158, 191, 192, 210; coins, 45; letter to Charlemagne, 4
Ohlsson, T., 51, 52, 62, 202, 203, 204
Olaf Tryggvason, king of Norway, 5, 54
Old Windsor, Berkshire, 70; glass, 122
Oost-Souberg, the Netherlands, 175
Ørbaek, Denmark, 172
O'Riordáin, S. P., 33, 200
Orléans, France, 119, 176
Orn, 54
Orosius, 66, 81; his history, 162
Oseberg boat, 94, 95, 103; tapestry from, 126
Oslo, Norway, 173, 183, 193, 195
Ottar (Othere), 5, 10, 66, 78, 81, 101, 178, 202
Otto the Great, Emperor of Germany, 3, 172, 182, 196
Ottonians, 172, 176
Oxford, 168, 170, 177, 179, 181

Panopeus, 21
Paris, 34-7, 48, 93, 176
Parker Chronicle, 97
pattern welding, 118
Pausanias, 21, 22
Paviken, Gotland, 43, 82, 100, 120, 141
Pecsaetan (Peak District territory of), 190
pennies, 45, 60, 68, 72, 109, 114, 115, 179, 180, 183, 190; Peter's pence, 56
Pepin II, 39, 110, 113; coin reforms, 88
Pepin III, 2, 39, 43, 75, 77, 111, 113, 114; coin reforms, 41
Petersson, H. B. A., 165, 166, 208, 209
petrological analysis, 124
St Philibert, 128
Phocians, 21
Pingsdorf ware, 183; pottery boats, 205; *see also* Badorf ware
Pippin, king of Italy, 154
Pirenne, H., 6-10, 13, 20, 22, 29, 30, 34, 35, 39, 196, 198-200, 209
place names, 73
planned streets, 21, 52, 55, 60, 68, 170, 173
Plassac, France (coin-hoard), 38
Poland, 41, 66, 77
Polanyi, K., 14, 15, 23, 24, 50, 105, 200, 205
population/demography, 56, 135, 140, 164, 173, 181, 183, 194; Bede, 190
Portchester Castle, Hampshire, 140
ports of trade, 23-5, 50, 200
potlatch, 15
pottery, 11, 30, 36, 37, 56-60, 67-92, 120, 124, 129, 149, 155, 156, 164, 183
pottery industries and trade, 49, 57, 58, 70, 71, 75, 119,

120, 147, 149, 155, 160, 169, 170, 176, 177, 181-3
Price, B. J., 130, 206, 209
Procopius, 32, 33
Prou, Marcel, 7

Quentovic (near Étaples), 36, 43, 45, 55, 90, 93, 98, 127, 156, 174, 202, 209
Quernstones, 79, 98, 105, 123-6, 129, 181, 194, 206

Radbod, king of the Frisians, 40, 88
Rahtz, Philip, 168
Randsborg, Klavs, 63, 82, 133, 135, 140, 142, 157, 171, 172, 202, 203, 206-10
Rathje, William, L., (cost-control model), 24, 27, 180
raths, 135, 137
Ravenna, Italy, 32
reciprocity (exchange), 14, 18, 27, 36
Reculver, Kent, 69, 114
redistribution, 15, 18, 19, 26, 27, 30, 36, 105, 182, 184, 197
Redman, Charles L., 23, 200
Redwald, king of the East Anglians, 36, 37
relief-band amphorae, 58, 80; *see also* Badorf ware
St Relinde Monastery, 126
Renfrew, Colin, 18, 19, 22-4, 32, 36, 104, 153, 200, 207, 209, 210; Early State Module, 190; gavity model, 92
Renovatio Imperii, 3
Repton, Derbyshire (glass), 122
Reric, 42, 43, 78, 193
Rheims, 129, 163
Rhenen cemetery, the Netherlands, 88, 204
Rhine, river, 4, 29, 34, 39, 74, 75, 111, valley, 57
Rhone, river, 34
Ribe, Denmark, 40, 53, 54, 58, 60, 80, 81, 89, 118, 120, 125, 141, 142, 148, 171, 172, 193, 208; amber working, 122
Richborough, Kent, 69, 114
Rigold, S., 34, 35, 37, 38, 40, 109-11, 201, 203, 205
Rimbert (biographer of Ansgar), 5, 77, 78, 85
Romans/Roman Empire, 5, 6, 22, 28-30, 39, 69, 70, 75, 129, 168, 194; glass, 122; shipping, 94; towns, 164-5
Romania, 22
Rome, 32, 56, 88, 90
Ringstead, Denmark, 172
Roskilde, Denmark (boats), 98-100, 172, 173, 180
Rouen, France, 45, 174, 181, 209; pots, 56, 98
'rounds', 135
Rowlands, M. J., 22, 26, 200, 209, 210
royal sites and settlements, 23, 45, 55, 125, 131, 138, 139, 149, 155, 168, 171, 172, 181, 189, 192, 194, 207, 210
runestones, 78, 89, 140, 192, 193
Russia, 11, 60, 66, 82, 120, 182

Sabloff, J., 24, 25, 200
sagas, 54, 118
Sahlins, M., 14, 15, 200
Salmonby, Lincolnshire, 206
Sandwich, Kent, 69
Saran pottery kilns, France, 93, 119
Sarre, Kent, 36, 44, 53, 66, 201
Sawyer, Peter, 53, 136, 157, 179, 180, 202, 209
Saxe, A. A., 186, 209
sceattas, 40, 41, 44, 45, 60, 68, 72, 74, 80, 88, 90, 91, 109-17, 149, 156
Schindler, Reinhard, 77, 78

Schlei, river, 78
Schleswig, 79, 98, 171, 173, 183, 204
Schouwen, island of, the Netherlands, 74
Schweden und Das Karolingische Reich, 10
Sciringes Heal, 66; *see also* Skiringssal
Scotland/Scots, 30, 116; migrations, 156
seafaring, 116
Sedgeford, Norfolk, 147
Service, Elman, 26, 27, 186, 187, 200, 209
Setga (Dalkey Island, Co. Dublin, Ireland), 67
Seton, Alexander, 85
Severin, Tim, 100, 103, 204
Shaftesbury, Dorset, 178; burh, 165
Shannon, river, 48
ship and boat burial, 36, 37, 94-7, 103, 110
Sigtrygg, king of the Swedes, 78
Sigtuna, 86, 89, 98, 173, 183, 193
Sihtric of the Silken Beard, 181, 195
silver, 7, 110-17, 157, 166, 172, 176, 177, 179, 180, 192; hoards, 195; Kufic, 171; mines, 182
Sjoberg, Gideon, 23
Skellig Michael, Co. Kerry, Ireland (monastery), 56
Skinner, G. W., 15, 16, 163, 164, 177, 200
Skiringssal, 81
slaves/slave trade, 32, 33, 36, 38, 53, 55, 90, 91, 105, 128
Slavic states/towns, 20, 23, 66, 79, 82, 85, 91
Slavic ware, 79, 82, 85, 120, 171
Sliestorp (Haithabu/Schleswig), 78
Smith, Carol, 16, 17, 23, 47, 50, 163, 200
smiths and metalworkers, 118, 119, 126, 127, 144, 180, 183
soapstone vessels, 79, 105, 122, 124, 126, 171
social organisation, 17
Southall, Aidan, 26, 200
Southampton, 10, 69, 98, 111, 112, 165, 168, 178, 181, 202, 203; burh, 166
South Cadbury, Somerset, 33, 166, 168, 171, 178
Spain/Iberia, 33, 37, 38, 55, 67, 90; Moslems, 157
'Spectacles', Co. Limerick, Ireland, 206
spectrographic analysis, 110, 180
Speyer, West Germany, 157
Stamford, Lincolnshire, 168, 177; Stamford ware, 183
state formation, 25-8, 130, 139, 152-60, 174-8, 185-98
Staveren, the Netherlands, 34, 77
Stavelot-Malmédy, abbey of, 131
Stenton, Sir Frank, 9, 86, 166, 190
Steward, Julian, 26
Stockholm, 41
Stolpe, H., 10, 63
Stonehenge, 22
Strasbourg, France, 89, 163, 176
'Strongbow' (Richard, Earl of Pembroke), 194
subsistence strategies, 130-50
substantavists, 14
Sulgrave, Northamptonshire (manor), 140
sunken huts (*grübenhauser*), 41, 51, 61, 62, 80-4, 132-5, 171
Sutton Hoo ship burial, 32, 36, 37, 70, 71, fig. 14, 94, 95, 97, 98, 101, 117, 147; coins, 34, 110
Svein Forkbeard, king of the Danes, 5, 172, 178, 182, 183, 192, 196
Sweden, 5, 10, 11, 41, 43, 51-3, 56, 59, 61-5, 80-6, 89, 95, 98, 100, 118, 120, 121, 124, 126, 141, 144, 145, 172, 173, 183, 193
swords and weaponry, 84, 105, 118, 119, 124

systems-thinking, 5, 152-60, 173, 183-8
Szcecin, Poland, 66

Tacitus, 2, 29, 187
Tamworth, Staffordshire (Saxon mill), 124
Tartaria tablets, 22
Tashkent (emirs of), 157
Tassilo chalice, 118
Tating ware, 59, 60, 80, 85, 117, 120
terp settlements, 4, 29, 40, 43
textiles, 105, 119, 120, 126, 127, 132; silk, 89
Theodoric, king of the Lombards, 30, 32, 37, 122; coins, 86
Thetford, Norfolk, 168, 170
Thetford ware, 208
thing-place, 72, 172, 190
thin-section analysis, 120
Thyric, queen of the west Danes, 192
timber halls and houses, 49, 75, 79, 84, 132-5, 142, 171, 183
tin, 117, 127, 128
Tintagel, Cornwall, 33
Tønsberg, Norway, 98, 173
Topsham, Devon, 33, 67
Torrence, Robin, 200
Tours, France, 48, 163
towns, *see* urbanism
Toynbee, Arnold, 185
trade routes, 11, 29, 31-3, 70-2, 88-125, 181-4, 195
Trelleborg, Denmark, 172
tremissis, 40, 69, 109, 110, 111
Tribal Hidage, 138, 189
Trier, 34, 48, 75, 90, 93, 120, 155, 176; St Maxim, 89
Trigger, Bruce, 12, 26, 163, 170, 176, 184, 199, 200, 208
Trimpe Burger, J. A., 175, 209
Trobriand Islands, 13, 18
Tune boat, 94

Uppland, 55, 210
Uppsala, 210
urbanism/urban institutions/towns, 6, 11, 20-5, 45, 47-50, 152, 158, 163-84, 195, 196
urbanisation, 10, 130, 152, 163, 164
urban economy, 141
Utrecht, 48, 55; bishop of, 77; ship, 96-8, 100

Välsgarde Boat, 94
Van Es, W. A., ix, x, 61, 75, 133, 199-207
Västargarn, Gotland, 53, 64, 81, 203
Vendel period, 36, 37, 84, 86; bead making, 120
Vendel ship, 94
Verdun, France, 91; bishop's palace, 55; monastery, 90; Treaty of, 154-7
Vestfold, Norway, 55, 79, 81, 118, 124; iron ore, 126
Viborg, Denmark, 172, 173
Vierck, Hayo, 118, 134, 189, 200, 206, 210
Vikings, 4, 5, 10, 43, 54, 55, 61, 69, 80, 84, 116, 119, 126, 142, 157-60, 178, 179; cemeteries, 120; Danish states, 192; in Denmark, 182; in Ireland, 194-5; industries, 125; settlements, 81; ships, 95; towns, 171
Viking raids and invasions, 77, 78, 84, 85, 128, 151-60, 168, 172, 173, 179, 189, 194, 208
Vikshögsvären, Sweden, 81, 82
villas, 30, 131, 136, 149
villa economy, 30, 131
villages and rural sites, 61, 62, 88, 125, 126, 131-44, 150, 163, 171, 183, 197

Vita Anskarii, 77, 89, 91
Vorgebirge hills, West Germany, 58, 75, 89, 155, 189; kilns, 36; pottery, 120, 176; coins, 128
Vorbasse, Denmark, 133

Wade, Keith, 70, 72, 142, 202, 203, 204, 207, 208
Walcheren, the Netherlands, 74; island of, 101
Wallingford, Oxfordshire, 171
Wareham, 165, 170, 179
Warendorf, West Germany, 132
Warner, Richard, 116, 201
Waterford, Ireland, 195
Webb, Malcolm, 160, 208
Webley, Derrick, 136, 138, 206
Wergeld, 54
Werner, Joachim, 32, 34, 200, 201; maps, 118
weights and scales, 36, 84, 85, 110, 111, 116, 165; lead, 117
Wessex, 4, 54, 55, 69, 111, 114, 125, 138, 158, 189, 190
Westenschouwen, 74, 89, 118
West Stow, 135
Westwik (Norwich), 73
Wexford, Ireland, 195
Wharram Percy, North Yorkshire, 140
wheel-made pottery, 39, 170, 208
whetstones, 67; *see also* honestones
Whitby: glass, 122; monastery and minster, 144
Whitelock, Dorothy, 163, 203, 208
Wicken Bonhunt, Essex, 142, 147
Wieuward, the Netherlands (coin-hoard), 34

Wight, Isle of, 189, 190; cemeteries, 44
Wihtred, king of Kent, 40, 44, 111, 115
Wijster, the Netherlands, 29, 133
Wilfred, St, 40, 88, 127
William of Normandy, 182
Willibald, St, 69, 90
Willibrord, St, 88
Wilson, D., 62, 199, 202, 205, 206; *see also* Foote, P.
Wilton, Wiltshire, 178
Winchester, Hampshire, 48, 49, 158, 159, 160, 165, 166, 170, 179
wine/wine trade, 33, 38, 59, 105, 127, 128
wine barrels, 68, 75; from Dorestad, 156
Wissant, France, 174
Witton, Norfolk, 135
Wodan, 41
Wollin, Poland, 43, 66
woollens/wool trade, 179, 182
Worcester, 168; bishop of, 69, 90, 128
Worms, West Germany, 88, 157
Wulfhere, king of Mercia, 189
Wuffingas, 37, 70
Wulfstan, 5, 78, 101, 178

Yassi Ada wreck, 94, 95, 129
Yeavering (*Ad Gefrin*), Northumberland, 48
York, 4, 73, 74, 88, 126, 127, 168, 170, 178, 181; Coppergate excavations, 183-4; Viking coins, 208
Yoruba country, 16